A SENSE OF JUSTICE

A SENSE OF JUSTICE

Judge Gilbert S. Merritt and His Times

By Keel Hunt

WEST
MARGIN
PRESS

Library of Congress Cataloging-in-Publication Data is on file.
ISBN: 9781513139142 (hardbound)
ISBN: 9781513141381 (paperback)
ISBN: 9781513141367 (ebook)

Proudly distributed by Ingram Publisher Services

LSI 2023

Published by West Margin Press®

WEST MARGIN PRESS

WestMarginPress.com

WEST MARGIN PRESS
Publishing Director: Jennifer Newens
Marketing Manager: Alice Wertheimer
Project Specialist: Micaela Clark
Editor: Olivia Ngai
Design & Production: Rachel Lopez Metzger
Typesetting: Syd Miles

For all the judges who stand at the gate
in defense of our freedoms and the rule of law

"Liberty lies in the hearts of men and women.
When it dies there, no constitution, no law, no court can save it."
Judge Learned Hand
US Court of Appeals for the Second Circuit
1944

"More than any other institution, the federal judiciary should be credited with initiating the civil rights and civil liberties revolution and with promoting equal treatment for the less fortunate."
Judge Gilbert S. Merritt
The Reporter: The Vanderbilt School of Law
1980

"When all that we have known and done is buried beneath the debris of time, what may be remembered most about us is our legal system. Nothing like it has ever been seen before on this planet, so far as we know. It is distinguished, more than anything else, by its breathtaking generosity to the individual."
Alfred H. Knight
The Life of the Law
1996

CONTENTS

Foreword by John M. Seigenthaler
Introduction by Keel Hunt

Part VI: And The Road Went Ever On

Epilogue

Appendices

FOREWORD

I spent more than 30 years of my life as a journalist, much of it as a national television news anchor and correspondent for NBC News in New York. Throughout my journalism career, the goal was always unbiased and objective reporting. I worked hard with each news story to stick to the facts. Most of the time I think I succeeded. But let me state clearly what this foreword is not. It is not objective or unbiased. My fond recollections of Gil Merritt are personal and emotional. They are connected to my own history and family. They are intertwined with my relationship with my father and his close friendship with Gil. When it comes to Gil, I am overcome by feelings of love and respect for a friend.

For me, memories of Gil are inextricably linked to my father. Gil and John L. Seigenthaler were close friends from my earliest recollections as a child. Even though we weren't related, Gil was family. My father and Gil shared a passion for life, politics, the law, civil rights, free expression and justice. They were fierce competitors on the tennis court and later the golf course. Over their many years of friendship, they shared their challenges and successes. I remember Gil Merritt through that lens. Those memories are wonderful and painful at the same time, now that they both are gone.

As a child and a young adult, I had a front row seat to the life and times of Gil Merritt. This book, written by my friend Keel Hunt, truly captures the Gil Merritt I knew. It's why I'm proud to be a small part of it. Keel began writing the book before Gil's passing. Before reading it, I thought I knew so much about Gil's life. But *A Sense of Justice* reveals so much I didn't know. This book not only explores his remarkable career as a lawyer, U.S. Attorney, and Judge on the U.S. 6th Circuit Court of Appeals, it helps us understand his background, his family, his loves, his passions, and his most difficult challenges. By any measure, Gil's life was an extraordinary one.

Shortly before his death, Gil's son Eli called me and asked if I'd like to spend a little time with Gil. I knew he was very sick. I knew this might be the last time I would see him. When I arrived at his apartment, it was clear his cancer had taken a toll. Gil, tall and physically fit throughout his life, had become thin. It was difficult for him to walk, but his voice was strong. His mind was clear. He was upbeat, alert, and anxious to talk about the past, to talk politics and reminisce about his friendship with my father. That is my last memory. I am grateful to Eli for reaching out to me. It was a last chance to tell Gil how much our family, especially my father, loved him and valued his friendship. It was an emotional moment for me. He told me that he remembered the day I was born—a reminder that Gil had always been a part of my life.

As a child and young adult, I was an observer of many key moments in Gil's personal and professional life. While he had grown up in a privileged and respected family with many advantages, he faced extraordinary challenges. Those challenges might have crushed others, but Gil thrived in spite of them. I have incredible respect for those who are able to succeed in the face of real adversity. In some ways, that best describes Gil.

He faced that adversity at an early age. His father died in a plane crash when Gil was 19 years old. I remember Gil briefly mentioning his father's death several times when I was young. I had never heard the entire story until reading *A Sense of Justice*. This book explains what happened and how this tragic loss shaped Gil's future. My own father lost his father when he was almost the same age as Gil. Shared loss of their fathers is one of many life experiences that bonded their friendship.

The other tragic loss in Gil's life was the death of his amazing wife Louise at age 32. I always felt close to Louise. Our families sometimes vacationed together. My mom, Dolores, and I spent time at Gil and Louise's new house in Franklin, helping her with her with small renovation projects. Louise was one of the most kind and caring people I knew. She took an interest in my young life. She never missed sending me a birthday card or a note celebrating my achievements in school.

Louise was an art lover and art collector. As Keel reveals in the book, she was especially proud of her extensive collection of the famous American artist Ben Shahn, known for his works of social realism. Her attention to design in their Franklin, Tennessee, home just outside Nashville, was worthy of an *Architectural Digest* cover story.

One of my warmest memories of Gil and Louise was dinner on a summer night at the Franklin home with their close friends Herb and May Shayne, Betty and Martin Brown, my parents John and Dolores, and Gil and Louise. I was in my early teens. As an only child, my parents often brought me along to social events like this. I was usually the only young person at the table. These loyal friends, young couples in their prime, celebrated life together. They shared their hopes and dreams, telling stories, discussing the latest headlines. That night I remember the laughter, the joy, and their bright views of the future. I knew, then and now, that it a great privilege to have had a seat at that table of friends.

I was 16 years old when Louise died by suicide at their home in Franklin. As I write about her death now, it is still beyond my comprehension that Louise took her life. It touches a raw nerve that has never healed within me. Their children, Stroud, Eli, and Louise, were so young. This was another tragedy that changed Gil's life forever. Decades later, we've learned more about mental illness and the impact it has on families. Suicide remains one of the leading causes of death in this country. It claims the lives of tens of thousands of Americans each year. I hope the willingness of this family and friends to talk frankly about its impact in this book will be a comfort for others who have suffered the loss of a loved one to suicide.

Once again, in the face of extreme adversity, Gil Merritt rose to the challenge.

But these events in Gil's life are just a small part of the story. This book explores every aspect of his life and career. Keel describes his unique circle of political friends in Nashville and Gil's own political aspirations. He dives into Gil's work as a U.S. Attorney in Nashville and his nomination by President Carter to the U.S. 6th Circuit Court of Appeals, detailing his work on the court, his opposition to the death penalty, his defense of free speech, his controversial decision in the John Demjanjuk case that drew international attention. Keel records the memories of his fellow judges on the 6th Circuit and his many law clerks. He tells the story of Gil's two month stay in Baghdad as a teacher of jurisprudence. The U.S. government dispatched Gil there, with several other federal judges, to help Iraq build a new system of justice following Desert Storm. More than anything, *A Sense of Justice* celebrates Gil's love of the law and his extraordinary dedication to equal justice under it. Keel recounts many phases of Gil's life, including his fifteen years of companionship and love with Martha Ingram. Their romance is a story worthy of reading in its own right. Martha is a well-known businesswoman and philanthropist in Nashville. Over the years, I've fondly referred to her as Nashville's own fairy godmother. When I talked to Martha at dinner recently, she mentioned how excited she was at the forthcoming release of this book.

She wants Nashville to pay tribute to Gil's life and career. "I loved Gil," she said, "and I want others to know about his extraordinary life."

Thanks to Keel's hard work and gift for storytelling, the public now has that opportunity. This book puts a spotlight on the Honorable Judge Gilbert S. Merritt and his remarkable sense of justice. Gil is a model of devotion to family, friends, public service, and democracy that future generations should emulate.

John M. Seigenthaler
October 2022

INTRODUCTION

On a crisp October afternoon in 2020, I was the furthest you can be from downtown Nashville and still be in the same county. I was watching my granddaughter take her pony through its paces out in the rolling far hills of middle Tennessee south of Bellevue. That's when the telephone rang, and I heard the voice of Judge Gil Merritt.

"Can you come see me?" he asked. "I want to talk to you about something." When the caller is a senior judge of the US Sixth Circuit, there is only one answer to that question. So, two mornings later, I was in his chambers in the central city, hearing what was on his mind.

I had never been inside Judge Merritt's chambers before. Glancing up at the high ceilings of his law library, above the old iron spiral staircase, I saw shelf after shelf of countless volumes. In that moment I thought that a Hollywood movie set of an appellate judge's office could not look any grander than this. But these chambers were quite real; this was where Merritt had spent many of his days and done much of his important thinking and writing over forty-plus years on the bench.

It was here now, in this imposing setting, that Merritt broached with me the idea of telling the story of his life and career. It had never been written in its fullness, and he asked if I might be interested in helping him with it. "I only wish I had thought to start it sooner," he told me that day. "I'm thinking someday it could be some value to my children, and maybe my grandchildren."

I had first met Merritt in 1975, when I was a young newspaper reporter in Nashville covering his campaign for Congress, but I had not seen him much since then. As with many of his early acquaintances who were neither lawyers nor other judges, he had been obliged for over four decades (by the canons of judicial ethics) to step away from a more public life when President Jimmy Carter put him on the court in 1977.

Gil and I quickly got down to details. He asked me what a biographical project of this type would involve, how long it might take, what I would need, all the normal questions. He also advised me that he could not participate fully for a few more months, owing to his wrap-up of official duties. He also told me about his health. His cancer appeared to be in remission, but, he added, no one lives forever. Merritt was now eighty-four years old.

We began this project in earnest in January 2021. I soon learned two principal things about Merritt and this work we had set out to do.

First, he would pull no punches. Indeed, as we began our many interview sessions, whether in person or by phone, there was never a question I put to him that he did not answer fully and frankly. As you will see, we covered many memories, the painful as well as the joyful. He did not hold back. In my judgment, he was fully forthcoming.

Second, I soon concluded that while Merritt's story would of course be of interest to his children and grandchildren, it would also be of value to many others. To know his story, in its fullness, is to understand how modern politics of the mid- to late- twentieth century came to be, especially in our region. He and his circle were among the South's earliest Kennedy Democrats in the latter 1950s, and their political strivings, while not always victorious at the polls, did affect the shape of many things, especially in the rise of modern Nashville.

• • •

UNDERSTANDING MERRITT'S LIFE as I did over this past year and a half, became for me a graduate course in the political history of our region. That history is much more than candidates, campaigns, and elections but also the power of friendship and loyalty, the influence of history upon individuals and generations, and how communities of interest have formed and evolved over time in our nation. It is all connected.

I am particularly grateful to Merritt's children and to the friends and colleagues who have also survived him, for their generous investment of time and patience which have helped me tell this most American story.

—KEEL HUNT
May 2022

PART I
BEGINNINGS

ROOTS AND BRANCHES

Two days before Christmas in 1979, Gilbert S. Merritt Jr., judge on the US Court of Appeals for the Sixth Circuit, stepped to a microphone perched on Nashville's Public Square Park, on the high west bank of the ancient Cumberland River where the city began.

By this day, generations of his family had been in Nashville, now a modern city. The Merritts had by no means been the first Nashvillians—as long as eleven thousand years ago this middle part of what is now Tennessee had been a hunting ground for various tribes of Native Americans—and there were more famous names among the white pioneers who had entered this region in their turn. Merritt was, in any case, descended from some of the earliest white families to venture into what Tennessee's first state constitution had called "the Territory of the United States south of the River Ohio." Among those names were the Donelsons, who came by flatboat into the new country, and the Robertsons who journeyed over a thousand miles west overland.

That was why, on this chilly Founders Day morning, city officials had asked Judge Merritt to deliver a suitable speech on the occasion. It would be his task to help an audience of modern Nashvillians know, appreciate, and celebrate all who had come before. For the approximately two thousand modern citizens who attended this event, the air was cold but nothing like the weather had been on that long-ago Christmas morning in 1779 when the founders drove their cattle across the frozen river.

"We gather to remember and celebrate the founding of our town, the formation of our families, the shaping of our character, our history, and our destiny," he began. "We come to remember the ties that bind us together. Two hundred years ago, at Christmastime, our forefathers drove their cattle across a frozen river. They had left steep ridges and narrow valleys of eastern mountains for fertile bottoms and gentle hills. They gathered in a virgin wilderness near this bluff to thank God for his grace and his protection. They asked him to protect and deliver to safety their families who were then on flatboats beginning a long voyage to this place.

"The first settlers were immigrants in a new land. In style and spirit, they were closer to the old millennium than to the new, closer to the Middle Ages than to our post-industrial age. Their nation was not yet formed. Their constitution was not yet written. In the ancient way, they still ground their meal, spun their cloth, and tanned their hides. They still drove their cattle overland and poled their boats down river. They cooked their food over the same open fires their ancestors burned when the millennium began. The combustion engine was unknown. The industrial revolution had not arrived. The modern age had not dawned.

"It is now almost the year 2000. There are great differences between our age and theirs. Yet in the sweep of history, the differences disappear. In order to survive and prosper, in order to preserve their liberties and ensure cooperation among their people, they needed courage, self-discipline, intelligence, willingness to help each other, fair laws to express their highest values and aspirations, responsible leaders to guide and encourage their efforts. Our needs are the same. In our own pursuit of these goals, we can do no better than to celebrate their courage, accept their legacy, and renew our faith in ourselves and the common bonds that bind us together."

It was into this family history that Gilbert S. Merritt Jr. was born on January 17, 1936, at St. Thomas Hospital in Nashville, the only child of Gilbert Stroud Merritt Sr. and Angie Fields Cantrell Merritt. The boy would be called "Buddy" by his family and friends for many years.

He was the eldest of three grandchildren of Maude Catherine Logue and Stockley Merritt. Maude Merritt lived an extraordinarily long life. On January 27, 1980, the day Maude turned one hundred years old, Nashville's Mayor Richard H. Fulton (who shared the same birthdate) came to her Donelson home to celebrate Maude's centenary together with her family and close friends. The mayor brought a proclamation designating it "Maude Logue Merritt Day."

The best surviving memories of Judge Merritt's childhood years are those of his first cousin Rachel Lawrence Merritt McAllister, who lives in Nashville. She and her younger sister, Caroline Donelson Merritt, were Buddy's first cousins, the daughters of John Lawrence Merritt, the fraternal twin of Buddy's father.

"We spent a lot of time together in the early years because we lived on farms in rural Davidson County, which were rather close together," Rachel remembers. "He was always someone I looked up to and loved.

His parents, Gilbert and Angie, always seemed very glamorous to me and were a handsome couple. Our families celebrated Christmas, Thanksgiving, birthdays, and special holidays together.

"One of my early memories is of Christmas breakfasts at Stone Hall, which was Gil's mother's ancestral home. Angie's mother, Mrs. Cantrell, was a little intimidating but always gracious to us. My sister, Caroline, loved the beautiful silver peacocks which were in the center of the table. The first course was always broiled grapefruit with a cherry in the center. Before the meal was served, we three children played together in the music room. Mr. Cantrell was a big-game hunter and there were several bearskin rugs throughout the house, which fascinated Caroline but were a little threatening to me!

"As little children we had telephones... a little early in the age of communication. We loved to call each other. When we were isolated with the normal childhood illnesses, we talked a lot. I always believed he gave me chicken pox over the telephone."

CHAPTER 2

"BUDDY"

From early childhood, Gilbert Stroud Merritt Jr. was known as "Buddy" not only to family members but also to schoolmates and a widening world of friends outside his family circle. The reason was in that last element of his given name—"Junior." There was already one Gilbert in the house at home.

Gilbert Senior was a man of means, prosperous and prominent in the city. His businesses and properties were well-known both within his own eastern end of Davidson County and also in the offices and retail trade of downtown Nashville. Three generations of Merritts were successive owners and officers of Southern Woodenware Company starting with Buddy's maternal grandfather, Dempsey Weaver Cantrell, who was its founder, later Gilbert Sr. and Angie Merritt (Dempsey's daughter), and eventually Buddy, their son. This company was a wholesale supply business serving a diverse retail trade, eventually across the Southeastern United States.

Both branches of the Merritt-Cantrell family tree involved prominent and substantial citizens of Nashville. Dempsey Cantrell was a long-serving deacon of the Donelson Baptist Church and a 32nd degree Mason. He was a chair of the Davidson County Board of Education and a member of the Chamber of Commerce. Later, Gilbert Merritt Sr. was a member of the Belle Meade Country Club (a membership that transferred to his son when Gilbert Sr. died), the Nashville Rotary Club, the Retail Merchandisers' Club, and the Elks Lodge No. 72. He was also a Kentucky Colonel, the honorific bestowed upon special friends by the Governors of the Bluegrass State. In the spring of 1954, the Merritts flew from Lebanon, Tennessee, north to Churchill Downs to attend the Kentucky Derby.

Merritt Sr. owned two Piper Cub airplanes, which he piloted to his business properties in the region. One was a PA-18–135 Deluxe, the other a PA-22 Super Custom. Merritt Sr. also owned two dairy farms, one in Hermitage and the other just south of Murfreesboro in Rutherford

County. (Eventually the family's holdings would also include commercial real estate in Davidson County, including midtown property on Broadway and the Westgate Shopping Center near Belle Meade.) But in the early years, when the future judge was a child and teenager, it was the farms and the wholesale supply business that formed the core of the Merritt family's wealth in the 1950s and afterward.

Buddy's mother, Angie Cantrell Merritt, was likewise active in her civic and church work. She and others in the extended family were involved over many years in the restoration and preservation of The Hermitage, the historic home of President Andrew Jackson. She became the longest-tenured board member of the Ladies Hermitage Association (now called the Andrew Jackson Foundation), serving for forty years. Because of her immediate family's involvement in the dairy business, she chaired the board's farm committee, overseeing the agricultural activities on the Hermitage grounds, for most of those years.

The family contributed regularly to fundraising efforts for the Hermitage museum, and Mrs. Merritt invested many hours of volunteer work on site. Later on, Gil Merritt, while a judge of the Sixth Circuit Court, was a member of the museum's distinguished National Advisory Board.

• • •

OVER MANY VISITS I had with Merritt throughout 2021, his final year, he recalled his childhood and adolescence clearly and fondly. He remembered his growing-up years as having been both privileged yet also conventional for his day and time. He was an only child. As he commented more than once, this meant "I got all the attention—but all the discipline too." Yet he remembered his parents as both strong-minded and loving. They were accomplished, community-minded individuals in their own lives, and devoted parents above all.

By the time Gil Jr. was born—on January 17, 1936—his father had become well-known in Nashville through his businesses, principally in his ownership and active management of the family's suburban dairy farms and of the wholesale supply company.

In Merritt's youth, the family resided in a Donelson suburb and later in the Hermitage community on the eastern end of Davidson County. The Merritt family owned several Nashville-area businesses. As a teenager, at one time or another through his high school years, Buddy worked in each of these enterprises.

He remembered, especially, his time on the dairy farms. One was called Oakwood Farms in Hermitage, and the other in Rutherford County just south of Murfreesboro. Both of these operations were managed for Buddy's father by Cliff Hardin, the father of four children, one of them young Hal Hardin.

There was also work for young Merritt downtown at Southern Woodenware. As that wholesale supply business continued to grow, it occupied three different locations on the east side of Second Avenue. This zone was prominent in Nashville's early history as an important distribution center, first for its strategic location close to the Cumberland River, and later on, near the rail service. Second Avenue was then known as Market Street on the early city maps. Some of the vintage warehouse structures on this east side of Second Avenue still have access off First Avenue directly facing the river landing area where steamboats arrived, for the horse-drawn wagons unloading from the boats.

• • •

At its founding in 1913, Southern Woodenware had only two salespeople. They operated from a small house in downtown Nashville near what was then called Broad Street, the city's main distribution thoroughfare that terminated on the west side of the Cumberland River. As the city's retail activity grew, Southern Woodenware's sales force also expanded across the region.

According to a 1935 company profile, it was "one of the largest and best assorted stocks of Woodenware and paper goods of any house of its kind in the South. In addition to this large and well-selected line of merchandise carried in Nashville, this company is representing a number of mills and factories located in the different sections through the north and east from which it ships large quantities of merchandise direct to its customers."

A good illustration of the breadth of Southern Woodenware's offerings was the full-page print advertisement in the *Nashville Tennessean* on the Sunday after Christmas of 1952. It showcased the extensive array of products that Southern Woodenware then offered to its retail customers. The items ranged from paper goods and housewares to axe handles, paint, school supplies, fishing tackle, and television sets. It was a complicated business, requiring a large and well-coordinated sales team with a working knowledge of hundreds of current product lines, but also good relations with the retail customers at all levels of the organization.

On Second Avenue, the company occupied as many as three different successive locations between 1913 through the late 1950s. The first business address, established by Dempsey Cantrell in 1913, was at 108 Second Avenue just north of the busy corner at Broadway, near the old Silver Dollar Saloon. The second location, from 1916 to 1951, was at Numbers 134–136, which was the former H. G. Lipscomb warehouse (later called Butler's Run by its current owners, Steve and Judy Turner of the founding family of Dollar General Stores). The final location of Southern Woodenware was at Numbers 164–168 in what historians called the Rhea Building. The Merritts would own this structure until 1960, making extensive internal modifications but preserving the historic façade of layered brick and terra cotta, its look a distinctive combination of arched and rectangular windows that overlooked the historic street.

Angie Merritt remembered these early years in an extended interview she gave her grandson Eli in December 1993.

"Gilbert (Senior) built one of the first dairy farms in the county and milked fine, registered Holstein cows. He went to Wisconsin many times to the cattle sales, and if he found what he wanted, he would send his Southern Woodenware trailer truck after them. We also had fine Wilson Allen walking horses and Land Star collies which we bred and sold. 'Bud Wilson' was our fine stallion that took ribbons near and far." A prominent sign, placed near the highway, announced this was the home of "The World Champion Walking Horse Bud Wilson."

"While Gilbert was running the dairy farm, he was also seeing to Southern Woodenware," she recalled. "From an early age Buddy was interested in all the activities on the farm. He was always amongst the happening. He worked at Southern Woodenware when he was older, but even as a child he tagged along with his father."

In his teen years, after school and on weekends, Buddy also worked at the downtown warehouse. The part of this he recalled most vividly in his later years, was one stretch of hard physical labor down in the basement below Second Avenue, when interior improvements were underway. With his tall, athletic physique, Buddy was already a stout young man, but laying the new basement floor was near back-breaking work. Using a shovel and wheelbarrow, the young man helped to prepare the basement level to pour a new concrete floor—hauling out load after load of demolition debris, and bringing in load after load of cement for the mixer.

• • •

SOUTHERN WOODENWARE'S CUSTOMERS extended across the southeast. Reliably supplying them required active daily management with careful attention to a complicated supply-chain—a great number and variety of vendors across a wide territory. All of this would keep Gilbert Sr. especially busy and would take him on frequent trips to New York and Chicago, as well as across the southeastern region of the United States, to keep the enterprise in good operating health. Sometimes Angie and their son would accompany him on these business travels. When commercial airline schedules were inconvenient, the elder Merritt would pilot one of his own planes.

The family business, though privately owned, was collaboratively managed. This involved a regular sharing by the president of business particulars with the entire sales team and office staff. On each Friday, Merritt Sr. would distribute a recurring newsletter that he titled the *Dope Sheet*. Each of these type-written newsletters contained a considerable amount of detail on the status of business: its current assets and liabilities, surplus inventories available for sale, level of borrowing, lines of credit, and other management metrics like weekly sales performance by individual salespeople (which everyone saw). Merritt's rationale was to share these particulars broadly across the organization, giving all his salespeople a clear understanding of the challenges, opportunities, and the imperative to keep everyone selling. From the *Dope Sheet* of April 11, 1952:

> As all of you fellows well know we are attempting to handle a very broad line of merchandise, when you include Fishing Tackle, Furniture, Major Appliances, all the Housewares, drug Sundries, Hardware items and then the Paper and Woodware items. So, you see we have a big job here to do....

> We don't mind laying our cards on the table. In fact, I think it is good business to let all the salesmen, as well as the other folks here at Southern Woodware (sic), know about the inside finances of their Company. A lot of corporations never let the people who get out and work hard and make the business possible, like all of you salesmen, know anything at all about the inside financial background. On the contrary, I think it is good for the business for all the Woodheaded folks to know, and have the inside dope on your company.

"Wooden Headed Boys" and "the Woodheaded folks" were the company's terms of endearment for all the employees, especially the sales team. One company print ad showed the salesmen posing at Nashville's Union Station railroad depot, before boarding a passenger train for Chicago. The Dixie Cup Company, an important supplier, had treated them to this excursion to the Windy City, including an all-day tour of the manufacturing operations, as well as tickets to a Major League Baseball game (St. Louis Browns vs. Chicago White Sox) at Comiskey Park. In the accompanying photo, Merritt Sr. and twenty-six smiling Wooden Heads pause on the boarding platform, each handsomely sporting his standard work outfit: business suit, necktie, and fedora.

The business records suggest this management style worked well. In fact, Southern Woodenware's sales records make clear that this was a steadily growing and financially successful enterprise through the earlier half of the twentieth century. While business volume flattened in the early the years of the Great Depression, by 1942 Southern Woodenware was recording a robust sales volume of $1,117,313. Ten years later, the number had increased to $3.8 million. In 1954, the last fiscal year that Gilbert Sr. was company president and its active boss, net sales had reached $4.5 million.

All this would afford the Merritts a degree of comfort and choice that were beyond the capacity of most families in the city. It would also affect their selection of schools for their only son.

CHAPTER 3

THE CADET'S LIFE

In his earliest years of formal schooling, Merritt attended Donelson Grammar School in the Davidson County public system. This was in the time long before the consolidation of the county system with the Nashville city government, when the school districts were still in separate jurisdictions. The grammar school building still stands (today it is a senior center) on the west side of Donelson Pike near Lebanon Road.

Later, for his middle and high school years, Merritt's parents enrolled him the college preparatory school called Castle Heights Military Academy, in nearby Lebanon, Tennessee. When I asked Merritt years later why Castle Heights was selected, rather than a public high school in Nashville, he said he recalled only that Gilbert Sr. and Angie believed that he would get a superior education there.

Perhaps they were impressed with the notion of military-style discipline, and the school's own reputation in the middle Tennessee region for its rigorous emphasis on academics and athletics. A statement in the school's 1967 yearbook reminded students, parents, alumni and all comers:

> A boy comes to Castle Heights to learn. And those who really want to learn usually do, but not without the desire and work that quality education demands.

Aubrey Harwell, a Nashville attorney and long-time Merritt friend, remembers that Castle Heights was one of several private boarding schools scattered throughout the South at that time. Others in middle Tennessee were Battle Ground Academy in Franklin, Columbia Military Academy, and the Webb School at Bell Buckle. Harwell himself was a student at Webb during this period. He remembers, "A lot of us went to those schools and were boarders, even though we didn't live too far away. There was a certain collegiality among all of us because we had gone through the 'boarding away from home' experience at a very young age—thirteen, fourteen years old when we started. I was aware that Gil had gone to Castle Heights. He had finished high school significantly before I did. I spent two years at Webb School."

"There were two things that were going on societally at that point in time in the South," Harwell continued. "Number one, there were pockets throughout the South, especially in the rural South, where public education was very mediocre. So, parents who had significant assets and wanted to pay for their kids to get a good education were sending them to boarding schools. (At one time, Webb School had more Rhodes Scholars per capita than any US school.) A second driver that was beginning to come into play was the integration issue. There were certain people in the South who were opposed to integration, and they would send their kids away to school. A third category were problem children who needed discipline in a structured environment, and so the parents will send them away to boarding school to straighten them up."

• • •

ROB HOSIER, NOW the administrator of the Castle Heights Alumni Association, told me that 96 percent of the school's graduates went on to college. Many went on to universities within the region, some matriculated at Ivy League schools (including Merritt, at Yale University), and others were selected for the nation's military academies leading to military careers.

Prominent among the alumni of Castle Heights would be future leaders in business, law, education, journalism, entertainment, government, and branches of the US military. That latter category included graduates who became general officers whose careers took them to assignments ranging from the Pentagon itself to service on the nation's foreign battlefields from Europe to Vietnam.

Notable military names on the school's alumni roster include General Wesley Clark, who became the Supreme Allied Commander in Europe, US Air Force General Lance Lord, and Lieutenant General John A. Bradley, who was an Air Force combat pilot and later Chief of Staff to the Chairman of the Joint Chiefs of Staff. Bradley graduated in the Castle Heights Class of 1963. General Bradley's three brothers Leonard, Bobby and Bill also attended CHMA during the years when their father Colonel Leonard Bradley Sr. was headmaster of the school. Their father's office (with an adjacent family apartment) is now the office of Lebanon's mayor.

Over the years, other students at "the Heights" included the entertainers Duane and Gregg Allman, who formed The Allman Brothers

Band; Dan Evins, founder and longtime CEO of the Cracker Barrell Old Country Stores chain; Stan Chauvin of Franklin, Kentucky, who became president of the American Bar Association; the Olympics heavyweight boxing champion Pete Rademacher; US Senator Herbert S. (Hub) Walters; Wyeth Chandler, Mayor of Memphis; Frank Sutherland, editor of the *Tennessean* newspaper in Nashville, and Sam Hatcher, editor of the *Lebanon Democrat* and *Wilson Post* newspapers. (Vice President Al Gore, though not a graduate of Castle Heights, attended summer school there when he was 14, taking business law and typing.)

Castle Heights was founded in 1902. When Merritt arrived in 1946, entering in sixth grade, it was still a boys only prep school. (The first five girls were admitted in 1973.) The Castle Heights campus and its central buildings also still stand, though the school was closed in 1986. Today these facilities are the headquarters of the municipal government of the City of Lebanon.

In its day, Castle Heights was known as a prestigious residential school, with most of the young cadets living in dormitories on the campus. Other students, who were enrolled from Lebanon and Wilson County, as well as the surrounding counties including Nashville, were called "day students" who commuted from their family homes each weekday.

Cadet "Buddy" Merritt began as a young boarding student, but he became a commuting day student within a couple of years. During Merritt's years on the CHMA campus, he would meet other boys who would become his life-long friends. There were 101 members of his 1953 graduating class.

• • •

THE ENTIRETY OF US Highway 70 stretches from North Carolina in the east to Arizona in the west. It rolls across Tennessee—the long way—for 2,381 miles connecting the foothills of Appalachia with the table-flat farmland that runs to the Mississippi River at Memphis. In the middle of this stretch of the old road is the suburb city of Donelson, Tennessee, and two dozen miles further east is the Wilson County seat of Lebanon. Depending on which direction you are driving, the east-bound lane is called "Lebanon Road" and the west-bound is the "Nashville Highway."

Today this route is well-developed with retail and commercial businesses, as well as many residential subdivisions, one after another. But in the middle 1950s, most of what you saw on either side of this highway were dairy farms, grain fields, and seemingly open country as far as the eye could see.

In Buddy Merritt's boyhood, these twenty-five miles could be a lonesome road.

• • •

"WHEN I FINISHED the sixth grade," he recalled years later, "my father and mother thought it would be a good idea if I went to Castle Heights where they felt I would get a better education. And so, I started there to be a boarding student. But I was young and the only child, and I told my mother and father that I was homesick. And my father and mother said, 'Well, son, you can be a day student.' And so, I started catching the Greyhound bus."

Most mornings, in the beginning, Merritt's father or mother would drive him to the Lebanon campus. As the boy grew taller, Gilbert Sr. would give him bus fare to catch the inter-county transit line to Lebanon, which he rode dressed in his snappy military uniform. (His father's businesses required him to drive in the opposite direction, most often into downtown Nashville where Southern Woodenware was headquartered on Second Avenue.)

But occasionally, Merritt told me years later, he would simply pocket the bus fare, hitchhike his way to school and keep the spare cash for his own purposes. This usually worked, owing to the appearance he presented to motorists who could be impressed with his military uniform. Until that one afternoon, when things took a scary turn, and the memory still haunted him years later.

"A lot of the time somebody would give me a ride, and then at the end of the day I'd hitch a ride back home. Until one day there was a guy who was homosexual, who scared me to death. He stopped and I got in the car. But when he reached over and grabbed my private parts, I knew I was in some possible danger. I told him, 'I live right up here, you can just let me out.' Then I called home and they came and got me. Pretty soon, or as soon as I could, I got a student permit driver's license. It would let you drive to school and church, so I started driving a Chevrolet my father got me. That's when I started being a day student and driving up to Castle Heights myself, and that worked out very well."

• • •

ON CAMPUS, THE lives of Castle Heights cadets were anchored in routine, discipline, and high expectations.

For the boarding students, the day would begin at 6:00 a.m. with the rapid bugle notes of Reveille. Some say the wake-up tune could be heard blocks away, as far off-campus as Lebanon's public square downtown.

"This was done by real buglers, not a recording over the PA system, and the bugle would blow at six in the morning," remembers Jack Robinson, who would become a Nashville lawyer and life-long friend of Merritt's. "We'd get up and make up our rooms and have to be in the mess hall by 6:45 for breakfast. Classes would start about eight." At sundown, the day was book-ended in the same fashion, with Taps from the same source.

In between the bugle alerts, there were classes indoors and close-order drills outside. A dress parade occurred every Sunday afternoon at 4:00. In the dining hall, cadets were expected to take their seats in good order, then sit at attention (with arms folded) until hearing the words "At ease." Once each week, usually on Wednesdays, a chapel program would be held in the school auditorium.

Participation in athletics was also expected of cadets at the high school level, and also with marching drills on a couple of weekdays at 2:00 p.m. Back issues of the campus newspaper, as well as *The Adjutant* yearbook, record Merritt as a regular on the tennis, basketball, and golf teams. (On some of these pages, he is identified as "Gilbert S. Merritt" and on others as "Buddy Merritt." In one team photo, he was called "Stroud," his middle name from his father.)

Buddy was a tall, strong young man. In high school, at 6'2" he was a member of the Castle Heights football, basketball, and tennis teams. He also enjoyed baseball. (Into his early 80s, he still had fond memories of playing catch at home with his father. Gil Sr. once proudly said of his son, "He's the most competitive person I've ever known.")

"Everybody was a member of at least some team, either a varsity team or the intramural team," Robinson told me. "That would go on until about 5:30 and then we would go to our rooms and clean up."

Merritt remembers a football injury. "I got my right shoulder injured playing football for the B team, I injured my right shoulder. I had to have a sling on it."

• • •

THERE WERE SCHEDULED social activities, usually each quarter, in Macfadden Gymnasium.

Built in 1937, this gymnasium became the scene of hundreds of commencement formals, Christmas dances, and monthly sock hops. "On Saturday night, it wasn't unusual for us to have movies being shown in the auditorium," Robinson said. "In fact, most times there would be traveling groups that came through, theater groups and things of that nature." A band from Nashville would usually perform for the cadets and their guests. (Merritt and Robinson remember one of the singers was Dolores Watson, the future wife of the Nashville editor John L. Seigenthaler.)

"There would be a dance probably once a quarter," Robinson remembers, "and the Ward-Belmont girls would be invited, or you could invite someone else. It might be somebody from home, but you didn't have to have a date at all. Local Lebanon girls would attend as dates, and this could stir some resentment among other boys in the town, who sometimes resented the Castle Heights men inviting Lebanon girls to the dance. The Lebanon boys would call us goobers." Buddy's cousin, Rachel, would often attend these dances. "I remember," she told me years later, "how handsome Gil was in his uniform."

Buddy's first date was a girl from neither Nashville nor Lebanon. She was Nancy Gore of Carthage, Tennessee, whose home was in the Upper Cumberland hills of Smith County. She was the daughter of US Senator Albert Gore Sr. and Mrs. Pauline Gore, and she was the sister of future Congressman, Senator, and Vice President Al Gore. (Just a few years later, during the Kennedy administration, Nancy would become a founder of the Peace Corps and, later on, the wife of the Greenville, Mississippi, lawyer Frank Hunger.) In time, Nancy's family would become important to Merritt's own political path, especially his appointment in 1966 to the post of United States Attorney for the Middle District of Tennessee.

• • •

THE CASTLE HEIGHTS faculty was a distinguished group of teachers with military backgrounds. Like the cadets they taught, instructors wore uniforms and observed military bearing and decorum. Many of these are recalled in the prolific writings of J.B. Leftwich, who joined the faculty in 1941, in the retrospective of his writings titled View from the Hill: Memories of Castle Heights Military Academy. Leftwich taught mathematics and journalism and advised the student editors and reporters on the staffs of *The Cavalier*, the student newspaper, and the *Adjutant* yearbook. He also wrote regularly for the local *Lebanon Democrat* and was a state correspondent for the *Tennessean* in Nashville.

Castle Heights is also where Buddy learned to fly an airplane. By this time, he had been around civilian flight and private aircraft for years because of his father's work travels. Castle Heights was the only military school in the United States that could boast of a Civil Air Patrol unit, directed by Tom Harris, an English teacher and later a member of the faculty at Cumberland University. Merritt's own flight instructor on the Castle Heights faculty was Sam Burton, who trained him in a two-seater, departing and returning to the small general-aviation facility at Lebanon.

"I learned to fly at Castle Heights," Merritt told me. "It was a little plane, tandem, with the pilot sitting in the front and you had a seat in the back if anybody wanted to be with him. Sam Burton had been a pilot in the Second World War; he flew over 'the Hump' in the Himalayas. He lived in Lebanon and became an instructor. I learned when I was about 17."

Buddy would also fly with his father. (At the Lebanon general-aviation airport, Burton also maintained the two planes that Buddy's father owned.) In later years, Merritt Jr. would travel far and wide, both for his court duties and for personal and family travel. Eventually he would be the pilot on vacation trips with his own young family, and regularly between his home in Nashville and his judicial duties in Cincinnati, Ohio.

But his life-long enjoyment of planes, piloting, and air travel had its origins in his teen years at Castle Heights, and on those afternoons in the air with Mr. Burton. Those would become some of Merritt's most enduring memories from his time at the school. And he would always remember Mr. Burton, fondly, for giving him wings.

• • •

MOST CASTLE HEIGHTS alumni from this period remember the coursework was demanding and the faculty superb, and long after his own graduation, Merritt told me he benefitted from their tutelage and discipline. Each spring the top ten graduates would be featured as first-in-line receiving their diplomas. A special distinction was that the very top cadets, academically, would be recognized as members of *Cum Honore* (with Honors). This was determined by the faculty for meeting four measures of a young man's performance and academic record—Achievement, Scholarship, Leadership, Character—indicating a well-rounded young man. Today, prominent on a display wall at the CHMA Alumni House, Merritt's name is one of only eight from his Class of 1953, which totaled 101.

At the conclusion of commencement ceremonies each spring, the graduating seniors would remove their caps and toss them happily into the air—as do cadets at the US Military Academy at West Point. Many of these young men, as they retrieved their caps and departed the parade grounds with their families, would not see each other again. But, in time, "the Heights" became known for having been the launching pad for careers that would take them high, far, and wide.

In the school history titled *Hail, Castle Heights!* By James A. Crutchfield, published in 2003, the alumnus Dan Andrews (Class of 1945) looked back at his own CHMA years and commented succinctly, "I was educated at Castle Heights—Vanderbilt University gave me my degree."

Ted Lavit, Class of 1957, who composed the foreword to that book, expressed a sentiment that many other graduates of the school surely have identified with over the decades: "Like so many alumni and friends, coming home still captures the imagination of all my youthful yesterdays." Robert A. Reeves of Nashville, member of the Class of 1952, would know Merritt later in Nashville and still remembers him as "Buddy."

Merritt recalled, in the summer of 2021, a long-ago conversation with Arthur Mann, who had been the distinguished academic dean at CHMA. As graduation time grew near, Merritt remembered Mann asking him about his plans and expectations for his next step in life.

> DEAN MANN: Mr. Merritt, where are you going to college? What is your plan?
>
> CADET MERRITT: Well, I guess I'll go to Vanderbilt, where my father went.
>
> MANN: Did you ever think about going up to one of the Ivy League schools? You're a good student, and you can probably get in. Why don't you think about it?

Buddy mentioned this conversation to his father that evening at home. Gilbert Sr. concurred, and soon the two of them were traveling to the Northeast for campus visits to several colleges.

As it turned out, Vanderbilt University would not come into Merritt's life-story just yet, and not at all for college. But it would become important in his life soon enough.

And that is another story.

YALE AND VANDERBILT

As Buddy's high school graduation drew near, a decision on a college was a topic of increasing discussion at the Merritt family dinner table. After the father-son trip to visit schools in the Northeast, the choice eventually came down to three: Amherst College in Massachusetts, Yale in New Haven, Connecticut, and Vanderbilt University in Nashville.

Gilbert Sr. had attended Vanderbilt in his youth. By the time his own son was of age, the father had traveled often on business trips to the Northeast, and he now appreciated the value of a broader perspective than just hometown. This gave a finer focus to the family discussions, and Buddy's preferences were narrowed to Amherst and Yale. The first acceptance actually came from Amherst, but by then Buddy's stronger preference was for Yale. He told me this story:

"I got the admission from Amherst, but at this point I wanted to go to Yale," he recalled. "And, I think without my knowledge, my father called the dean of admissions at Yale—his name was Noyes, I think—and said, 'My son has been admitted to Amherst. He would prefer Yale, but he's got to let Amherst know whether he's going to go to Amherst or not.'

'Well, Mr. Merritt,' Dean Noyes told my father, 'we don't tell people in advance whether they're going to be admitted.' He then said to his secretary, 'Get me the Merritt application.' The secretary went back and got it, and he looked at the file and said, 'Well, you know, Mr. Merritt, we don't give out our admissions in advance, but if your son wants to come to Yale, I suggest that he not tell Amherst that he wants to go there.' And so, my father said to me, 'Son, they're going to admit you to Yale.'"

Buddy Merritt entered the Ivy League college at New Haven in the fall of 1953.

• • •

HIS LIFE WAS DIFFERENT THERE.

Half a century later, on March 13, 2003, at his fiftieth-class reunion,

Judge Merritt gave to his fellow members of the Yale Class of 1957, a speech in which he would recall details of this transition. It had been, he said, a form of culture shock for a young man hailing from a fundamentally different realm of American life.

"For me, coming East for the first time from a dairy farm in Middle Tennessee. Yale was a different culture—more diversity than I had ever experienced," he said. "The lens of my mental life all of a sudden at age 17 zoomed out from the security of life on the farm to an expansive cultural horizon. Cows, milking machines, and silos were replaced by tea at the Elizabethan Club and an all morning long nude physical exam in the grandeur of the Payne-Whitney Gym. But, of course, by today's standards, we were a homogeneous lot of white males—no women, few African Americans, Asians, or Hispanics.

"Not many of you had milked a cow or fertilized a field with manure before coming to Yale," he noted. "I found you deficient in the arts of agriculture. But certainly not in the art of bull."

So a sense of humor helped, even then, and the young man soon adapted to the new environment, culturally and educationally. From that early point, in 1953, Merritt would make more friends that would last a lifetime. He recalled one young man in particular.

"I will never forget my first two weeks in beginning, intensive French. I sat down next to a young man at 8:00 a.m. on September 22, 1953, for our first class in one of the small classrooms over Phelps Gateway looking out over the New Haven green. When we struck up a short conversation before class began that morning, I was relieved. I thought, 'This boy from Texarkana, Arkansas, is just as unsophisticated and unprepared as I am.' That idea did not last long."

That other young man was Richard S. Arnold, of Arkansas. In his own distinguished career, Arnold, would join the US Court of Appeals in the Eighth Circuit, as Merritt would in the Sixth. Another new friend at Yale was a Pennsylvanian, Tom Rohner, Merritt's first roommate. Freshmen were housed on the Old Campus, and Merritt lived at 172 Lawrence Hall. They would face high expectations in their first year of classes, and there would be little social life to speak of until their second year. Sophomore students were then housed in different quarters, called colleges. Merritt was in Davenport College.

His major was English. The coursework and the faculty who taught his classes would give Buddy Merritt a strong grounding in the American language, as well as an appreciation of the classics. Though unbeknownst to him at the time, this training at a formative stage of his life would help prepare him for his career later on in public service, politics, and the law.

• • •

BUDDY ALSO CONTINUED flying lessons in his spare time at Yale, wanting to maintain his skills and to keep his pilot's license active. He corresponded regularly with his father, sending letters with reports on his academic progress. Gilbert Sr. in turn wrote to his son about business growth and developments at Southern Woodenware, what aircraft had been added to the company fleet and occasionally his fatherly advice on which courses of study might benefit Buddy's expected career in the family business.

In one such letter in February 1954, after Buddy had come home for a weekend visit, his father wrote with some advice for the young undergrad:

> Last night after you left, I spent a lot of time going over what— in my opinion—would be an ideal list of studies in the way of 'Liberal Arts Education' as long as you are in school. I made a very careful study of all the subjects available in the Yale catalogue and also the Harvard Business School and have listed this schedule after studying both catalogues carefully. Of course, this is my own personal opinion, which you should only consider and then decide for yourself. In other words, this now represents what I would want myself, if I was in your position and your age.
>
> Since I definitely want you to complete three years of Law at Yale and especially, since I want you to then go on and take two years of special Advanced Business Administration at some outstanding Business School, I have decided that you can get all Economics and Related subjects during the two years you are concentrating on business, which should be at the end of the education—provided the money holds out.
>
> Therefore, I have concentrated entirely on 'Liberal Arts' at Yale after this year. Actually, I think your six subjects this year have been ideal and it's good that you have gotten the first year of basic Economics.

Two weeks later, Buddy wrote to his father—not about his coursework but to report an incident he had experienced in the air. Earlier that day, while flying a rented plane, an aging "J-3 Cub" at about 2,000 feet above New Haven, Buddy's engine stalled and he lost power. He had maintained manual control of the descending plane and managed to land it safely at New Haven Airport, but this news alarmed his father and worried him deeply. He phoned Buddy that evening, and the next day he sent his son a letter back. In the Merritt family archives is an old carbon-copy of the letter that Gilbert Sr. wrote in reply, with an obvious mixture of relief and emotion:

> Frankly, I just about fainted after I read your first page. I know, I turned white, and turned green and then a little purple... I'll bet, you were scared stiff being up over New Haven, Connecticut last Saturday with a completely dead motor in that old J-3 Cub. You were just plain lucky to be up with 2,000 feet altitude, so you could glide into the Airport.
>
> Actually, my breath gets a little short just thinking about your situation. However, let me assure you I especially appreciate your letting me know about it. Of course, this could have happened to me—had I taken the chance on that particular old J-3 Cub.
>
> Your experience proves two or three very, very important things:
> 1. Don't ever fly an old plane—only a late model—nothing older than two or three years old.
> 2. It proves it certainly helps to get that altitude, so in case your motor quits, you have plenty of room to glide in for a landing and also more time to try to revive a dead motor. I noticed yours couldn't be revived.
> 3. It proves it's important to double check every single angle to this plane before going up; gas leakage, in fact—everything.
> 4. There is considerable risk and danger in flying, even a new plane, especially where you don't have at least 300- or 400-hours experience.
>
> Yesterday was real windy here, as I told you last night over the telephone. I am gaining a lot more confidence with the PA-18, in fact, Sam Burton told me Saturday afternoon that I was beginning to handle the PA-18 like a pilot should. I still need more confidence though, and very frankly, I really aim to use all caution possible and I continue to read and get all information possible about flying...

P.S. I am not charging you anything for this advise (sic). At the bottom of your letter, you have a lot of witnesses... your room mates signed your pledge about not flying over Long Island Sound, also jokingly, you agree not to fly an airplane before the year 2,000 B.C.

After the engine quit on you, I don't think this is very funny.

These lines would take on a special significance barely a year later, when Buddy was in his second year of college.

• • •

ON MARCH 9, 1955, the placid world of Buddy's youth and adolescence was shaken by a long-distance telephone call from home. Picking up the receiver, he heard his mother's voice.

Angie Merritt told Buddy that his father had died. As he listened, in shock and profound sadness, she described the circumstances of his father's death that afternoon. It had been violent—a crash of his plane at the farm he owned near Murfreesboro, Tennessee.

The accident had happened at sunset.

Hal Hardin was fourteen years old, a young teen hanging out at the Merritt farm, when he watched the elder Merritt climb into the cockpit of his small single-engine plane and take off solo. This airport is just a quick drive from the Merritt's dairy farm at Hermitage. His destination was the other farm he owned in Rutherford County, just south of the Murfreesboro city limits on Highway 231. It would be a flight of less than thirty minutes. Merritt had flown this quick route many times before this fateful day.

The Rutherford County property included a main house that dates from 1878, in the Southern Colonial style. Nearby is a large barn and equipment shed, and less than a hundred yards to the north of the main residence, across the driveway, is a smaller frame house. It was here that young Hardin's family lived years before this, when the father, Cliff Hardin, was manager of the Hermitage dairy farm. By the day of Merritt's fatal accident, much further west of the main house, a landing-strip had been cleared through the open fields to accommodate his frequent flights to inspect the farm operations on this property. On this afternoon, for the brief duration of the flight, there was no radio transmission from Merritt with the Lebanon tower.

Angie, in her 1993 interview with her grandson Eli, recalled many details of that afternoon. It was clearly a day she would never forget.

On the afternoon of March 9, 1955, as usual I dressed in the afternoon for Gilbert's homecoming, which was usually between 5:00 and 5:30 in the afternoon. But on this afternoon, I had not finished dressing because Gilbert came home 45 minutes to an hour early. While I was still upstairs, I heard him come in and open the door to the hall closet to change into his leather flying jacket. He called to me to say that he was flying to the Murfreesboro farm and was in a hurry. We often flew to the Murfreesboro farm in the afternoons and spent the night. The cook would pack a hot dinner and we would eat up there. But on that day, he didn't want to wait for me because he needed to rush some seed to the Murfreesboro farm so the foreman could get the seed in the ground before the rain came. By the time he had warmed up the plane and was circling Oakwood, I ran out the yard to wave to him. I wanted to say to him, "I'm ready." I know he saw me because he waved at me, but it was too late; he didn't wait to take the time to come back.

I walked around through the flower garden, and in twenty minutes the man called me to the phone. They were calling from the Lebanon airport, saying he had crashed, and they were sending the ambulance from Murfreesboro farm...

As we arrived at the farm, we saw the ambulance pulling out in front of us. The next thing I remember is that I learned Gilbert had died, perhaps when the plane crashed. He was killed instantly.

There had been no witnesses to the crash. The investigation concluded that Gilbert Sr. must have encountered tricky crosswinds on his final approach. That likely threw him sharply sideways in his last moments. The investigators examined the crash site and also the plane, which had been moved into the barn in anticipation of the government inspection. The examination found that the landing gear and one wing were significantly damaged. This suggested to the inspectors that Merritt had been blown sharply off his landing course, sideways into a stand of trees, throwing plane and pilot into a disastrous spin. It appeared the plane had likely come down hard and may have bounced violently once before it slammed to the ground heavily, then flipped over once, and it was over.

Merritt died, according to the death certificate, of a fractured skull and multiple internal injuries.

• • •

BUDDY TRAVELED HOME immediately. Two days after the accident Gilbert Sr. was laid to rest, amid the departed generations of his family, at Mount Olivet Cemetery in Nashville. Dr. Walter R. Courtney, pastor of Nashville's First Presbyterian Church, delivered a moving eulogy. Courtney had known Gilbert Sr. for eleven years and shared a story of his friend's turmoil that Gilbert had only recently shared with him:

> Gilbert believed in the things I stand for but lived with a sense of urgency that drove him past many of the good places of life. He lived as if time were short and there was much to see and do... Four weeks ago, something happened in the life of Gilbert Merritt. For the first time in years, he realized that the rainbows of life could be appreciated for themselves. He saw their fragile but unforgettable beauty as for the first time. They made mere things colorless by comparison.
>
> On March 5, he called his sales force around him and talked to them with unusual seriousness. On March 8, he gathered his office and warehouse staff and spoke to them. On March 9, he died. What did he say to the employees of Southern Woodenware? Here is a synopsis of a two-hour talk, straight from a man's heart:
>
> You all know me and the way I live and do business. You know that I have lived for money and the things that money can buy. I have beaten my brains out trying to find shortcuts to success. I have always driven you people in order to make another dollar. Many of you seldom talk to me; few of you really know me. The fault is not yours, but mine. I have not always been courteous and thoughtful. I just did not take time to give you a chance to know me, and I never took time to really know you. I have been too busy emphasizing business instead of people and living.
>
> You are looking at a man who has been walking down a fool's road. I have now discovered a better road. I have found God.

I have not been happy in recent years. That must sound strange to you, but it is true. I have everything a man could want, but it hasn't made me happy. I now realize that money cannot buy happiness. I always thought it could, but I have been wrong."

Somewhere across the years I lost the main highway of God. Now I have found it. God is the most important friend a man can have, and certainly the most essential one.

On the day he died, Gilbert Merritt Sr., wholesale merchant, owner of many properties, prominent of the town, was forty-six years old.

• • •

AFTER COLLEGE GRADUATION, Buddy's plan was to transfer directly into the Harvard Law School. By this time, he was familiar with the school, and he had a few friends who were now enrolled there. The school accepted his application without delay. But he was not there long. He was not happy.

Years later, over our many conversations in 2021 about his life and family and career, Merritt cited several reasons for deciding to change law schools as abruptly as he did. He mentioned how he missed his father and how the absence of this most constant counselor was still a profound sadness. He also told me how someone had stolen his warm coat (never recovered) in the Harvard dining hall one cold day, souring his attitude about the Cambridge campus early in his first year there. He also mentioned how the absence of his father had affected him and his mother, and eventually the requirements of running Southern Woodenware would figure into his thinking about how much longer he ought to remain in Cambridge.

Most often, he mentioned the name of Dean John Wade of the VU law school, who in a pivotal moment offered to be of assistance. Possibly it was a mixture of all these factors, with a measure of homesickness also. In any case, Gil Merritt—by this time he had shed his childhood nickname—now began his own relationship with the Vanderbilt law school, which was closer to home.

So, transfer he did. Merritt had been a stand-out student in high school and at Yale. Now at Vanderbilt Law he flourished and would find his footing. Over the next three years, he would make many friends who would become important in his life and career for many years afterward, among them US Senator Jim Sasser and Alfred H. Knight. Merritt graduated with honors in 1960, receiving the Founder's Medal as first in his class.

PART II
CONNECTIONS

CHAPTER 5

WHERE JUDGES COME FROM

Before there is any judgeship, no matter how broad or narrow a particular court's jurisdiction, however lofty or low its scope of power, from traffic court to the US Supreme Court, you will usually find a preceding story of politics. For any judge anywhere, the path from preparation to power necessarily began somewhere. In the beginning, you only know who you know.

It is easy to forget this essential detail, given the political independence of courts and of judges in the American system. Whether at a local, state, or national level and before their careers commence, there was first an appointment or a nomination or an election, required on the journey to the bench before the man or woman is addressed as "Your Honor."

Whatever the scope of his or her ambitions may be, and however renowned a judge may eventually become, from the night court magistrate to the justice on the Supreme Court of the United States, the path leading there probably commenced with the patronage of a political friend or the blessing of a local party committee at city hall or the state capitol or in Washington DC.

Histories of courts and judgeships don't always mention this, but it matters who you know. It takes friends to reach the bench.

Even for jurists whose reputations seem historically unsullied by any outside help or influence, the deeper stories show how American courts involved the consideration of friends at the outset:

- **John Jay**, the very first chief justice of the United States, was a close Federalist friend of George Washington, who appointed him to the first Supreme Court in 1789.
- **Roger Taney**, today remembered chiefly for the majority opinion in *Dred Scott v. Sandford* (and its part in leading to the US Civil War), had been politically aligned with President Andrew Jackson. Jackson appointed Taney to be his Attorney General and, in 1836, to a vacancy on the Supreme Court.
- Judge **Learned Hand**'s appointment in 1924 to the US Court of Appeals for the Second Circuit, in New York, can

47

be traced to his friendship with an influential senior attorney in Manhattan. That lawyer was close to President William Howard Taft's Attorney General.

- Chief Justice **Earl Warren**, a Republican, had previously been elected California's Secretary of State and later the 30th governor of that state.

- Justice **Byron White** was chairman of President John F. Kennedy's Colorado campaign in 1960 and afterwards was a member of the "brain trust" at the Justice Department under Attorney General Bobby Kennedy. Two years later, when the next vacancy on the Supreme Court occurred, JFK put White's name in nomination.

- **Sandra Day O'Conner** was the majority leader of Arizona's state senate in the 1960s. When President Ronald Reagan nominated her to the highest court in 1981—making her the first woman to serve there—she was supported by both of Arizona's US Senators, the Democrat Dennis DeConcini and Republican Barry Goldwater.

- Judge **Harry W. Wellford** of Memphis was an early political ally of Senator Howard Baker in Tennessee. Wellford had been Baker's campaign manager in the middle 1960s. In 1970, it was Senator Baker who recommended Wellford to President Nixon for a new US District Court seat in west Tennessee. In 1982 it was President Reagan who (on Baker's recommendation) elevated Wellford to the Sixth Circuit.

In a 1961 article in the *American Bar Association Journal*, Judge Edward J. Devitt of Minnesota captured it well: "Some Judges may become so impressed with their importance that they forget the practical facts of their judicial birth."

"It is a fact," he continued, that most federal judges are appointed through the influence or approval of United States senators or other political officials, and many state judges are elected under party labels. This is not to detract from their qualifications, especially in recent years when the absence of objections from the American Bar Association is almost a prerequisite to federal appointment. In practical effect, judicial appointments, federal and state, must now be acceptable to the organized Bar. So long as the United States Senate has the constitutionally granted authority to advise and consent in respect to judicial appointments, it is unlikely that some politics will not be involved in most of them. But as long as we get qualified Democrats during a Democratic administration and qualified Republicans during a Republican administration, we are doing about as well as can be expected. The truth remains, however, that 'most judges' reach office through politics, and that, I emphasize, is not a sinful thing at all."

It was true in Merritt's case. By the time his moment came in the fall of 1977, his "planets had aligned" in a comparable fashion. He was not only prepared by training and scholarship but also well connected.

By then Merritt had a circle of prominent and politically connected friends in Nashville, both within and outside the municipal government, as well as at the state level and in the nation's capital. The Nashvillians in this circle were men who knew him and his abilities, as well as his record as an activist for the Democratic Party. They thought well of his preparation through college and law school at Vanderbilt, though it was different from any of their own.

• • •

MERRITT'S OWN CIRCLE likely began with his friendship with John Jay Hooker, Jr., an engaging and charismatic young man. Hooker also had benefitted from connections that had much to do with his family and his law school chums at Vanderbilt, particularly his classmates who had taken their JD degrees in his class of 1957. He was the younger of two sons of the prominent trial attorney John Hooker Sr. and his wife Darthula, and young John Jay's path through the law school introduced him to friends who would also become famous as their respective careers matured.

Among Hooker's law-school classmates through the middle 1950s were the United States Attorney (and future Watergate prosecutor) James Neal; the combative labor and civil rights attorney George Barrett; the federal District Court judge Thomas Higgins; Tom Shriver, later to be the thrice-elected district attorney general for Davidson County, and Bill Henry of Memphis, whom President Kennedy would appoint to chair the Federal Communications Commission. In a colorful 2002 profile of this class, entitled "They Might Be Giants: How the Vanderbilt Law School class of '57 shaped a city," Nashville journalist Matt Pulle described this cohort of rising lawyers and their eventual influence downtown.

Members of that particular VU Law class, the reporter observed, "may well be the most impressive and influential group the university ever sent packing into the real world." Pulle continued:

Neal, Barrett, and Hooker and, to a lesser extent, Higgins and Shriver, were the ultimate insiders. They mixed politics and the law with ease and skill. It started back in the '60s when Henry, Hooker, and Neal became aligned with President Kennedy and his brother Bobby—a boon to all three of their nascent careers. Around the same time, Barrett helped elect Richard Fulton to Congress, when Barrett represented the young politician in an outrageous voting scandal. Fulton later became mayor, hiring Barrett for nearly a million dollars' worth of city legal work.

• • •

"THEY WERE THE giants of that generation," the Nashville attorney Brad MacLean told me, in 2021. (For many years, MacLean and Merritt co-taught a course on the death penalty at the VU law school.) "They were friends. They knew each other, and they drew upon each other. They supported each other. It's hard for me to imagine a John Seigenthaler without a George Barrett. It's also hard to understand any of these people without a Gil Merritt."

"What really upsets me now is that, as these giants leave us, I don't see others taking up that role as pillars," MacLean added. "Charlie Warfield, who was one of the founders of Metropolitan Government in Nashville, died in February of last year. John Seigenthaler died not many years ago. We are losing this generation. As I look around now, and the lawyers I see in their 40s and 50s, they don't know who these people were."

• • •

INTO THAT HEADY mix also came a young man named John Lawrence Seigenthaler, the oldest of nine children of a working-class German-Catholic family on the city's near north side. Seigenthaler was a graduate of Father Ryan High School and attended Peabody College. He did not head to law school but instead joined the staff of the Nashville *Tennessean*, the local morning newspaper where his uncle Walter Seigenthaler was the circulation manager.

Having grown up in Nashville, he knew the city well and he soon became a favorite of the Evans family, the owners and publishers of the *Tennessean*. In fact, Silliman Evans Sr., originally from Texas, had been a political ally of FDR himself and, partly because of it, had acquired the morning newspaper out of federal bankruptcy in the 1930s. Evans then made it the newspaper's editorial mission to support the Democratic Party, its candidates, and Roosevelt's national recovery program. Evans embraced the broad social and economic aims of the Roosevelt administration's New Deal, notably the Tennessee Valley Authority and its promise of electrifying and lifting the rural South.

One of Seigenthaler's early achievements as a young investigative journalist was his reporting on abuses within organized labor, with a particular focus on the Teamsters Local 327 in Nashville. This soon came to the attention of Robert F. Kennedy, then a Senate staff lawyer for the McClellan committee investigating organized labor nationally, and the Teamsters President Jimmy Hoffa in particular.

Jim Squires, another young the *Tennessean* reporter during this period (and later the editor-in-chief of the *Orlando Sentinel* and *Chicago Tribune*), told me he believed it was Hooker who first mentioned to RFK the investigative work that young Seigenthaler had done in Nashville, centering on the Teamsters Local 327. But Seigenthaler's own recollection, according to his private notes from this period, was that his first meeting with Bobby Kennedy in 1957 was arranged by two other men, the Pulitzer Prize-winning reporter Clark Mollenhoff and also Kennedy's brother-in-law Sargent Shriver. But that initial visit did not go well, according to the private notes, and he mentioned his disappointment to Mollenhoff. "That evening over dinner, I discussed this with his friend, Clark Mollenhoff, who was the Washington correspondent for the *Des Moines Register and Tribune*. Mollenhoff had helped, along with Sarge Shriver, to get my appointment with Kennedy. Mollenhoff had phoned Kennedy to suggest that it would be worth his time to talk with me." Mollenhoff then made a second effort, and the next meeting was more productive. "It wasn't until a second meeting in DC that they hit it off," his son John Michael Seigenthaler recalled.

What most interested RFK at this point was Seigenthaler's recent reporting for the *Tennessean* that led to the ouster of a Chattanooga judge, Raulston Schoolfield, for accepting a bribe from the Teamsters union to fix a case. In any event, this early encounter and conversation lead to Seigenthaler's lifelong friendship thereafter with the Kennedy family.

When Senator John F. Kennedy of Massachusetts was elected President in 1960. Bobby became his Attorney General, and Seigenthaler was soon appointed administrative assistant (essentially the AG's chief of staff) at the Department of Justice.

CHAPTER 6

THE CIRCLE OF FRIENDS

In the late spring of 1960, Merritt received his law degree at Vanderbilt. He enjoyed his time at the law school and the friendships he developed there. Many of these would last a lifetime.

He also revered the dean, Dr. John Webster Wade, a scholar and author of significant textbooks on the law of torts. Wade would become an important mentor to the young man and eventually a life-long friend, too. It was Wade who invited Merritt to join the Vanderbilt law school faculty with the title of assistant dean and instructor. During that following academic year it was also Wade who advised him to think about continuing his legal education with a more advanced degree in the law, knowing he would need it if he became seriously interested in a more permanent role on the Vanderbilt faculty. Merritt therefore applied to the Harvard Law School, where he had begun his legal studies soon after his college graduation, before transferring (with Wade's help) back to Vanderbilt. In 1962, Merritt added the Master of Laws degree to his growing resume.

Then he returned to Nashville. By this time, he believed that the next step would be a career in the practice of law, not in academia, that likely lay before him. Merritt would nonetheless maintain a life-long affiliation with Vanderbilt and its law faculty and students, and especially with Wade, who was the dean from 1952 until 1972. In 1995, when Wade died at 83, the young federal appeals judge who had been his protégé from the 1960s on, wrote a memorial tribute to his old mentor. The piece, which was published in the *Tennessean* newspaper as well as the *Vanderbilt Law Review*, and it read in part:

> Outside my family, he is the person who has had the most in-
> fluence on my life as a lawyer and a judge, my philosophy, my
> sense of justice, and my way of thinking about the law. He was
> the master. Doubtless many other lawyers and judges who sat
> at his feet feel the same way. During his long, sixty-year era of

accomplishment in the law, he had a commanding influence on the lives of thousands of students and teachers and on the law in general.

• • •

MERRITT'S FIRST LAW FIRM AFFILIATION was in the downtown offices of Boult Hunt Cummings and Conners; the senior partner there, Reber Boult, had been Merritt's father's lawyer and an officer in the family business, Southern Woodenware. Merritt also developed new friends at city hall. It was during this period, meanwhile, that civic leaders in Nashville were attempting by referendum to introduce a new consolidated city-county government encompassing Davidson County.

An initial referendum in 1959 had failed, but a second attempt succeeded in 1962. The sitting county executive, C. Beverly Briley, had campaigned for consolidation under the new charter, and he was subsequently elected the first mayor of the Metropolitan Government of Nashville & Davidson County. Very early in the Briley administration, Merritt was appointed associate director of the Department of Law. He was only 27.

As with Briley himself, many of the key figures in Merritt's early circle are gone now, making it difficult to know precisely how those in what became his personal circle of friends first encountered one another, who met whom and when, and in what sequence the extended circle initially formed. (Seigenthaler, the *Tennessean* editor, died in 2014, Hooker two years later.)

It is likely that Seigenthaler himself, who returned to the newspaper from Washington in 1962 after his formal role in the Kennedy administration ended, became the principal convener of these close friends and associates, with regular encouragement from Hooker. The synergy likely accelerated once Seigenthaler was elevated to editor-in-chief of the *Tennessean* (by Evans's surviving heir, Amon Carter Evans). Tam Gordon, a staff reporter at the afternoon *Nashville Banner* who later worked for Seigenthaler when he ran the First Amendment Center at Vanderbilt, knew well the scope of this influential circle. In our 2021 interview, she recalled that "Seigenthaler was at the very center of it."

Over the following decades, an assortment of other savvy political friends came into this circle who believed they could assert and sustain the elements of a re-born progressive movement within Nashville and across the South. The region was heading into a period of political tumult—owing to growing demands for civil rights, and political conflicts over the war in Vietnam—that would present both challenges and opportunities for ambitious young players.

It was said that the Kennedys themselves, looking well beyond the mid-term elections in 1962 and the President's re-election in 1964, probably envisioned the opportunity for an emerging progressive Democratic base across the South. (Hooker's own campaign for governor of Tennessee in 1966, though it failed, possibly began as a manifestation of this hope. It was followed by national news media, including network correspondents Roger Mudd and Sander Vanocur largely thinking that Hooker himself might become a candidate for president later on.) In any event, the main progressive-minded players who gravitated to Seigenthaler's orbit in Tennessee's capital city at this early point, and eventually to Merritt's own circle of intimates, were these:

William R. Willis, law partner of Hooker and his brother Henry Hooker. Their firm—Hooker, Hooker & Willis—was situated on Union Street in downtown Nashville in the zone of the city's most prominent banks, government offices, and watering holes. (In the preceding century, Union Street had also been the address of Andrew Jackson's law practice.) Very soon Hooker, Hooker & Willis became the lawyers for the Nashville *Tennessean*.

Their firm, with Willis and Knight taking the lead, represented the *Tennessean* in a high-profile libel case in 1975 by James Hooper of Columbus, Mississippi. President Ford had nominated Hooper to a seat on the three-member board of directors of the Tennessee Valley Authority. When the *Tennessean* published a seven-part investigative series about Hooper's business record, Hooper's political support evaporated in the US Senate—with Tennessee Senator Bill Brock opposing his confirmation—and the nomination was withdrawn. Hooper then sued the newspaper and its senior reporter Nat Caldwell for libel. A summary judgment by US District Court L. Clure Morton (a Nixon appointee recommended by Senator Baker) finally dismissed the suit.

Alfred H. Knight was later a senior partner in the re-named firm Willis & Knight (and a key litigant in the Hooper case against the *Tennessean*). Merritt told me years later that Al Knight had been his best friend from law school. When Gil and Louise married in 1964, Al was the groom's best man. He also became godfather to the Merritt's first-born child, Stroud. After President Lyndon Johnson appointed Merritt to be the new US Attorney for middle Tennessee, Merritt hired Knight to be his Number 2. The two men would remain close until Knight's death at 74 in 2011. Over his career, Knight was widely respected among lawyers and many judges as perhaps the superior legal writer of his generation.

Marian Harrison, later a Judge of the US Bankruptcy Court in Nashville, was a young lawyer at the same law firm at the beginning of her own legal career. She remembers Merritt, in the early years, as a frequent visitor to their law offices at 214 Union Street.

George Barrett, a tenacious labor lawyer and civil rights advocate, had been a close friend of Seigenthaler's since childhood. As a young man, Barrett had joined Estes Kefauver's campaign for US Senate; in 1976 he was Jim Sasser's Senate campaign manager. (Barrett's wife Eloise, who died in 2013, had been a good friend of Gil's wife Louise. Later on, the Barrett's daughter Mary would babysit the Sasser children.)

Barrett would become best-known for bringing a landmark lawsuit— *Geier vs. Blanton*—challenging Tennessee's racial dual system of higher education. For this case, which would extend through most of Barrett's life, he had been well prepared, deeply grounded in issues of the civil rights movement. In 1960, he defended college students arrested for trying to eat at Nashville's segregated lunch counters. And a year later, he helped to overturn the re-election of Nashville congressman J. Carlton Loser because of fraudulent ballots. Barrett went on to represent Democratic officials accusing Republicans of trying to intimidate black voters in the 2002 general election by challenging their identifications and signatures. In a 2013 commencement speech to his alma mater, Spring Hill College in Mobile, Barrett described how his career had been shaped:

> I went to law school to become, in the words of Justice Brandeis, a social engineer, and as such, my practice as a lawyer has been marked by advocating for the rights of the disadvantaged. Whether they be working people, or poor people, or nonwhite people, or just people without a voice, I have advocated for them against the powerful and the unjust.

Barrett also represented the Highlander Center at New Market, Tennessee, where Rosa Parks and others were trained in community organizing, when it sued the Tennessee Legislature to halt its investigation of the center for possible links to communism. "'I'll sue anybody but the Pope," the Catholic Barrett once famously told a reporter. When he died, the former Vice President Al Gore said Barrett had been "a beacon of progressive politics for three generations of Tennesseans."

Mary Barrett Brewer remembers how her father encouraged his three daughters to choose their own career paths. She also remembered his closeness to Merritt. "George, like Gil, thought people should do what they wanted, regardless of their gender or their skin color. He had the first integrated law firm in the south. He helped to integrate the Vanderbilt Law School. My sisters and I were reared in a union-favorable family. I've been a public-service lawyer for a long time. It's quite a rewarding job. I can put my head down on my pillow every night knowing I've done something good, when you've been reared in a home like that.

"It was a time when people could disagree and still talk," she added. "They got close to each other, and they could work with each other as human beings. Now people don't have any interaction; it's not better. People tried to get along. They talked to each other. Gil Merritt came from that era when people talked, tried to negotiate, and make things work."

Frank A. Woods was first a young law clerk in the Hooker-Willis law firm who became a successful business entrepreneur, banker, and early political backer of Hooker's. In 1964, Woods was state co-director of Young Citizens for Lyndon Johnson. Two years later, when Hooker ran for governor, Woods was his statewide co-coordinator (Woods' younger brother, **Larry Woods**, together with Charles Bone, also became prominent in the growing circle of friends in the 1966 campaign.)

Frank, in his own subsequent business career, would become a CEO and owner of the Shop at Home Network and was involved in the launch of CMT, the Country Music Television network, and also the Americana Television Network. His advice was regularly sought by statewide Democratic Party candidates, including Tennessee's Governor Ned McWherter, as well as Senator Jim Sasser. He was also an influential supporter and adviser to President Carter.

Frank and his wife **Jayne Ann Woods**, also a lawyer, were a glamorous power couple in Democratic politics. They had met in college, and in 1964 Jayne Ann was crowned "Miss Nashville" and was first runner-up for "Miss Tennessee." In 1975, she was appointed by Gov. Ray Blanton to be the Commissioner of the Tennessee Department of Revenue in his administration. She was a prominent volunteer in Carter's 1976 campaign for President in Tennessee. The Woods' fashionable home was on Glen Leven Drive in southern Davidson County, near the Tennessee Governor's residence.

In May 1981, ahead of Sasser's 1982 Senate re-election campaign, Frank and Jayne Ann were among the top-line hosts of a large fundraising event for Sasser at a downtown Nashville hotel. The evening was billed as a "roast" of Sasser by six of his US Senate colleagues from across the country; attendees remember the roasters included Senators Bill Bradley of New Jersey, Frank Church of Idaho, Howell Heflin of Alabama, Fritz Hollings of South Carolina, David Pryor of Arkansas, and Sam Nunn of Georgia—all Democrats and members of key Senate committees. Earlier that evening, Frank and Jayne Ann hosted a high-dollar pre-event reception in their Glen Leven home. The evening altogether raised $290,000 for Sasser—at the time a single-day fundraising record for a Tennessee political campaign.

Anna Durham Windrow, who was a young staffer for Sasser at this time, remembers Merritt had a special relationship with her boss. "Anything about Gil Merritt that came up in our office, Sasser was involved. The relationship he had with Merritt, we all knew that was a sacred one. Sasser felt Gil was a brilliant man with a tremendous moral compass. I remember Sasser honoring that relationship with Gil Merritt in a way that was private but strong—and we all acted accordingly."

Hal Hardin, a lawyer with his own early connections to the *Tennessean* newspaper, was a son of a tenant farmer and his wife in Hermitage, Tennessee. (The Hardins worked on the Merritt dairy farms). Years later, during the time of Silliman Evans's ownership of the morning newspaper, the publisher owned a 33-ton yacht called *The Tennessean Lady*. Hardin was its captain and chief pilot, dashing in his crisp white uniform.

The way Hardin first met the Woods brothers was, oddly enough, while working in a commercial pea cannery in Walla Walla, Washington, when all three were in their late teens. Over the next decade, they would become fast friends in Nashville and find themselves within the Hooker-Seigenthaler political orbit. In the early 1970s, these men, with other young Democrats across the state, organized "The Tennessee 100" with a vision of taking over the Tennessee Democratic Party and they were successful.

Lafayette ("Fate") Thomas, another of Seigenthaler's chums from childhood, became a prominent political operative in the city and manager of many get-out-the-vote local campaigns. Later on, some would call him a kingmaker, as he gave organizational backing, including election-day help, to candidates from mayor to governor.

Thomas would be elected sheriff of Davidson County in 1973, served three terms, and became a leader in the National Sheriffs Association. During his years as sheriff, Thomas was a colorful, flamboyant personality on the Nashville political scene. He hosted a large annual gathering, called the "Sure Shot Rabbit Hunters Supper" at the Nashville Fairgrounds, for political friends. It was not so much about the barbecued rabbit that was served but the chance to meet and be met. This event drew political players from a wide spectrum of politics, often crossing partisan lines. Thomas would welcome Republicans (like Senator Howard Baker and Governor Lamar Alexander) as well as Democrats in Congress and the Tennessee General Assembly, and all manner of precinct captains and other friends of the Democratic regime. From this mix of local leaders and their supporters, the event was a must-attend for anyone hoping for any elective office in Nashville. From this mix of ambitious personalities and exuberant camaraderie came a shared belief in the possibilities of life and politics.

In 1990, Thomas' colorful career ended abruptly. He was convicted in federal court on charges of using his government office for private gain. (Willis was Thomas's lawyer.)

• • •

EACH MEMBER OF THE CIRCLE had an enviable personal resume and was accomplished in his own right, but of course each was different from the others. Only Hooker and Merritt came from family wealth. Seigenthaler grew up in a working-class family, and Hardin was the son of tenant farmers. Yet, between these and the others, the circle seemed over time to yield an extraordinary synergy that benefited them all in various ways. Not all these young men in Merritt's early circle would necessarily have announced themselves as "Kennedy Democrats" at this point. Seigenthaler himself could afford to be politically independent in that way, owing to his crusading newspaper's progressive reputation, and Hooker was innately flamboyant, but the others at least were obliged to work for their livelihoods in what continued to be a generally conservative business environment. Yet to one extent or another, they all were shaped during this formative period of the early Sixties by the political energies, emotions, and notions of opportunity that accompanied JFK's vision of a New Frontier. In this way, they also shaped each other. Hardin meanwhile joined the US Peace Corps, serving in South America, organizing communities in the jungles of Colombia. Returning to Tennessee, he became an activist for Democratic candidates. In the 1966 campaign for governor, Hardin was Hooker's personal aide and driver, and Hardin's star rose among party leaders. In 1974, though he had not supported Blanton in his 1974 race for governor, he was Governor Blanton's first judicial appointee, serving as a Circuit Court judge and, later, as the presiding judge of the trial courts. In 1977 President Carter appointed Hardin the US Attorney in Nashville.

This circle, especially in combination with the investigative staff resources that Seigenthaler now directed at the morning broadsheet, very soon became a factor in local and state elections—and especially so in that first election of Nashville's young Congressman Richard Fulton in 1962. Barrett was visibly and forcefully engaged in challenging the official returns from the inner city's corrupt Second Ward, where early returns favored the incumbent Democrat J. Carlton Loser. Seigenthaler meanwhile had assigned a half-dozen news reporters to interview voters door-to-door. The re-count favored Fulton, who went on to serve seven terms in the US House. (In 1975, Fulton would become mayor of Nashville and serve there for a dozen more years.)

This sort of stirring made for colorful and competitive politics over the next three decades, in Tennessee's capital city, with the liberal *Tennessean* and the more conservative afternoon *Nashville Banner* frequently squaring off on their pages, sometimes on the front page.

That much soon became well-known and even controversial locally. Less visible were the inner workings of Merritt's widening circle of friends and their gathering influence. Politically, theirs was a reform generation of progressives who in Tennessee had grown frustrated and weary of the leap-frog tradition of alternating administrations of the Governors Frank Clement and Buford Ellington, with their fungible cabinets that would keep the state government safely under a conservative domination.

Jim Free, a Columbia native who became the youngest chief legislative clerk in America under Tennessee House Speaker Ned McWherter, was a generation younger than Merritt and his circle, but he knew most of these men. In my 2021 interview with him about Merritt, Free called them "Gil's Posse—What a bright, fun, accomplished group of men!" Free would become Carter's 1976 campaign manager in Tennessee (McWherter was Carter's state chairman), and he joined Carter's White House staff as an important congressional liaison following the January inauguration.

Four surviving contemporaries who knew them all were the attorneys Aubrey Harwell (who went on to form a law firm with Jim Neal in 1971); Charles W. Bone, who hailed from Sumner County as had Neal and Willis; Larry Woods, Frank's younger brother who became a Democratic Party debate coach and activist in his own right; and the long-serving state representative Steve Cobb of Nashville.

"It was a strong symbiotic kind of relationship," Harwell told me. "John Seigenthaler was the editor of the most powerful newspaper in the state. John Hooker was a brilliant man, yes, but his father was one of the most well-respected and honored lawyers in the state. Jim Neal prosecuted Hoffa, and was close to the Kennedys, as was John Hooker, as was Seigenthaler. And so that group was really, really tight. Frank Woods was significantly younger than the rest of them—he was a year or two older than I was—but Frank was part of the Hooker inner circle.

"Gil was a part of it. And every one of these individuals had a sphere of influence, John Jay had his brother Henry, and he had Willis. Al Knight was Willis's law partner, and he also was close to Seigenthaler because Willis was lead counsel for the *Tennessean* in the glory days. This group touched every significant base in town, and collectively the sphere of influence of these individuals was huge. It included the major players, the banks, insurance companies based here and their executives, but they also had something unique that others in Nashville didn't have. They had a national connection that was incredible because Seigenthaler was on Kennedy's staff. Neal was Special Deputy to Kennedy."

Bone told me his introduction to the circle came in 1966 "where I got to be in the room, the youngest person there, with all these guys including Seigenthaler and Bill Henry. All of them had lively discussion together, with a lot of room for dissension and debate. You can't have that many lawyers in one room and not have lots of strong opinions." Larry Woods remembers it this way:

"Seigenthaler picked who he wanted to be in the circle. There were also several interlocking circles, like a Venn diagram. John had one circle of political friends in Nashville, another circle of newspaper people, there was the Kennedy circle—Bobby, Ethel—in Washington, and he had a circle of cultural people who had helped in the arts in Nashville, and so on."

"Thinking of the times I was in the room with those people, in political and social meetings, most of them would speak to the politics of a given situation," Woods added. "But Gil Merritt's contribution, on the other hand, was always a little quieter, more intellectual. He would usually address only the public policy aspect of things. He understood politics and how important it was, but his contribution was moreso the role government had, and what policy could do for the community. It was not 'What can politics do for me?' but 'What's good for the community?' That was first, second, or third for him. Therefore, I've always felt his later career as a judge was ideal for him in many ways. He had the position and status to think through and reflect on the direction we were moving—how fast or slow—and what that meant for everybody, not just for 'me and my friends.'"

Cobb, like Merritt, had gone to an Ivy League college in the East and then returned to Vanderbilt for his legal training and law degree. In 1974 he was elected to the first of six terms in the Tennessee General Assembly. Thoughtful, affable, and willing to work across the aisle with Republican members, Cobb became a durable and influential political figure in his own right. He had the *Tennessean*'s editorial endorsement in each of his legislative election campaigns.

In our 2021 interview, Cobb located himself within that extended Venn diagram that Woods had described to me earlier: "The way I thought of that group," Cobb recalled, "was that I was really not a part of it, but that they accepted me. I felt I had access to them, but I was doing more my own thing."

• • •

L. John Haile was a young Vanderbilt grad when he began his journalism career in the *Tennessean* newsroom. He covered the Tennessee legislature and also worked as city editor for one year. (He would later relocate to Florida where he became the top editor of the *Orlando Sentinel*.) Haile remembers both the heady energy of the *Tennessean* newsroom in his day, and Merritt's involvement in Seigenthaler's tight political circle.

"Gil was in the office a lot," he told me. "He was part of that group that was making political decisions. Gil's interests seemed to lay more so on the public-service side. He didn't have to worry about money—he'd married into the Hooker family. I thought, maybe, he wanted to be a judge someday. Barrett wanted to raise hell about civil rights and so forth. John Jay was in the thick of it and probably thought he was the focus of all, but I don't know that he was. Nobody did anything without John Seigenthaler's approval."

He also spoke of Fulton, the congressman and later mayor who died in 2018. "Dick Fulton really wasn't part of that inner circle. They all supported Dick, of course, and he was a big player in the city. But he wasn't part of them. He was more a product of what they did than part of the inner circle."

The journalist Bruce Dobie was another who observed Merritt and his extended circle over several decades as a reporter for the *Nashville Banner* and later as editor/publisher of the alternative weekly *Nashville Scene*. In our 2021 interview, Dobie told me he had been struck by the political and social contrasts between the Merritt's personal family background and suburban upbringing with his newfound network as a young lawyer downtown.

"Gil Merritt was 'to the manor born,' right? I mean, even though he was from Donelson, he was born wealthy. And he goes to Castle Heights and all that, and so you would've thought he would've fallen in with Pat Wilson (industrialist) and Nelson Andrews and Bobby Mathews (developers) and Ken Roberts and Denny Bottorff (bankers) and all that, but he doesn't. He falls in with the Irish-Catholics, and with Fulton, who was raised in East Nashville. Seigenthaler and Barrett, Irish-Catholic, and those East Nashville boys—he falls in with them."

Dobie continued, "So, it really had to come from, I guess, a fervent belief in the issues of the day—civil rights and voting rights, Medicare, Social Security, all that. Here was a man who was truly liberal down to his core. Socially, he's a member of the Belle Meade Country Club, and later on, he plays golf at the Golf Club of Tennessee, had a house out there. He dated Martha Ingram (arts patron and wealthy businesswoman). But, by the same token, here's a guy whose politics were not the politics of his social milieu.

"He was an interesting cat," Dobie added. "He was a brave guy, obviously."

• • •

RAYMOND THOMASSON WAS a teenager and a grocery clerk in 1966 when he encountered Hooker's wife, the former Tish Fort. He remembers her as an engaging but essentially shy young woman, and how they would chat briefly as he carried her shopping bags to her car.

That's when she invited him to a political organizing meeting at the Hooker home, on Brookfield Avenue in Belle Meade, and he went. This led to Raymond's involvement in what emerged as Hooker's first campaign for governor. Four years later, now involved in Hooker's second run for the office, Thomasson had become close to Fate Thomas and would join him in his many political involvements that followed Hooker's 1970 campaign. In our 2021 interview, Thomasson recalled the workings of the Seigenthaler-Hooker circle, how its influence gathered into the 1970s and beyond, and how that energy eventually extended to encompass the politics of many Nashville activists.

"The 'circle of friends' is a good way to think about it," Thomasson told me. "Many who were in the leadership of the city—or who wanted to be—were touched by it. You were either in that circle, or of it at some point in time."

CHAPTER 7

A New Government

In the middle of the twentieth century, Nashville made US municipal history when local leaders successfully merged the old city and county governments into one entity in 1962. It had been a long, rancorous task, but advocates for consolidation were convinced the new structure would be better suited to the demands of future urban growth.

It took them two local referenda, in fact, to accomplish this controversial task of government re-organization. An initial vote in 1959 on the recommendation of a charter commission was defeated at the polls, but the new charter in a slightly different form was finally adopted three years later. The new countywide Metropolitan Government of Nashville and Davidson County was the first of its kind in the United States. A new Metro mayor, C. Beverly Briley (who had previously been the county executive), together with a large legislative body, were sworn in the following April, and the hard administrative work began to combine duplicative departments of education, public health, police, public works, and other municipal services across a large jurisdiction.

By this time, Merritt had finished work on his advanced law degree at Harvard, and he was introduced to leaders in the new Briley administration. Some felt Merritt was especially young for such a role, but apparently it was his recent preparation in the law of local government charters that impressed Briley, himself a lawyer. The young man was soon hired as the associate director of the inaugural Department of Law, reporting to the Director of Law Neill S. Brown.

This was already a heady time for city governments in Tennessee, particular in the largest cities, for another reason. The Supreme Court of the United States, in its landmark *Baker v. Carr* reapportionment decision in 1962, was setting in motion an historic re-distribution of legislative power across the nation. Municipal leaders in Nashville and Memphis had brought this original lawsuit, beginning in Nashville's chancery court, to challenge the fact that Tennessee's legislature had not redistricted itself in half a century. That neglect, combined with historic shifts in population from rural to urban centers, meant that rural interests had an unfair portion of power and influence in the Tennessee General Assembly.

In 1962, the Supreme Court compelled Tennessee's legislature to redraw its district lines more fairly based on actual US Census counts—reflecting more recent shifts in population distribution—and a subsequent ruling required the same regular updating of congressional district maps. Merritt had not been directly involved in the original case (it commenced in 1958) but subsequent court filings bore his name as an attorney for Nashville's legal department.

• • •

NASHVILLE'S CONSOLIDATION OF city and county governments had created a large entity in two respects.

It established a single geographic jurisdiction covering 526 square miles, making Tennessee's capital the seventh largest city in the US, according to the US Census Bureau. (The city of Atlanta officially encompasses only 134 square miles and has fewer people within its city limits, but Atlanta's larger effective population covers several counties.) Also, the new legislative body serving Nashville was now unusually large. The Metropolitan Charter Commission, which recommended the new municipal structure, essentially blended the old city council with the county commission into a huge law-making body of forty members; this gave Nashville the third-largest city legislative body in America. Today still, only New York City and Chicago have larger city councils than Nashville.

Combining the two legislative bodies was a political compromise, of course, and it immediately sparked opposition from important African-American leaders who had been elected previously from inside the old city limits. They predicted there would be a diminution of black representation, but sixty years later the proportion of minority council members in the Nashville's Metro Council has continued to grow.

• • •

CREATION OF NASHVILLE'S consolidated Metro Government, in which Merritt was an early official, required a period of adjustment and time for the elimination of program duplication among the many departments and other agencies. This transition was complex—requiring streamlining that touched the administration of schools, public works, health, hospitals, and law enforcement, among other departments—but generally it was successful and efficiently managed.

Briley and his staff got high marks for managing through the new government's early years. Over the following years, Briley's team and other Nashville leaders were often consulted by the officials of other US cities about how this unusual feat had been accomplished and how it was going. Briley was later re-elected to two more terms, the maximum for Nashville mayors at that time. In 1969, he was elected president of the US National League of Cities.

• • •

MERRITT WAS ONLY twenty-seven years old when he took on the role of a senior counselor in Nashville's new government.

In surviving correspondence and records of interviews, there is only scant mention of anyone questioning his youth and experience. Some senior leaders in the new Council questioned how a man this young could be sufficiently prepared for such new responsibilities, at a time when both news media and other cities were looking on. But Merritt enjoyed the confidence of Brown, his boss in the Law Department, and of Briley, who was the chief executive. It appears, overall, that Merritt's legal training credentials and his scholarship in municipal law was sufficient to convince the important leaders of the new government.

His comparative youth would be questioned later on, in some cases at decisive moments of opportunity, but not at Nashville's City Hall.

CHAPTER 8

THE YOUNG US ATTORNEY

When anyone would ask Merritt how he became the United States Attorney in Nashville, at the extraordinarily young age of 30, he would relish telling the story: how he had asked Senator Albert Gore Sr. for his support, and what the senator said in reply.

The year was 1966. By this time Merritt had become a friend of the Gore family, having dated daughter Nancy during high school. Albert Gore had been in Congress since 1945 and was now in his third Senate term. He is remembered today for taking bold stands—from advocating for civil rights to his opposition to the war in Vietnam—but also for his sense of accountability to his constituents and their views. He had a high sensitivity to their opinions, especially when it came to himself and his career in the Congress.

Merritt went to see Gore about that US Attorney position. The senator's first response, Merritt remembered, was, "Aren't you awfully young?" By the end of this brief visit, the young man's spirits had fallen. He felt discouraged, but that was not to be the end of the story. That evening, at the dinner table, Senator Gore told his wife Pauline about Merritt's visit.

ALBERT: Buddy Merritt came to see me today. He wants to be the U.S. Attorney.
PAULINE: What did you tell him?
ALBERT: That I thought he's a little young.
PAULINE: Well, how old is he?
ALBERT: He's twenty-eight or thirty.
PAULINE: Now, Albert, what were you doing when you were that age. What were you doing at 28?
ALBERT: I was superintendent of the Smith County Schools.
PAULINE: Albert, I imagine he knows about as much about being a US Attorney at his age as you knew about being a school superintendent.

Senator Gore proceeded to make the appointment.

Sasser remembers that Mrs. Gore "was a very strong supporter of Gil for the job, and I put in my two-cents worth. I thought Gil would be a great US Attorney. Then Senator Gore appointed him, but I do recall that Senator Gore had some reservations about his youth."

• • •

WHEN MERRITT'S CONFIRMATION as the new US Attorney finally came, he was sworn in by two federal district court judges whom he much admired, William Miller and Frank Gray, in Nashville. His pretty wife Louise stood beside him as he took the oath of office. Merritt's first hire in the new office was Al Knight, one of his close confidants from the Hooker, Hooker and Willis firm, to be his top-most deputy. They had met in law school and, by this time, had been close friends for several years.

Very soon, Merritt began to bring a new level of diversity to the federal prosecutor's office in Nashville. He hired Carlton Petway Sr. to be a new assistant US attorney. A graduate of Tennessee State University and the University of Tennessee law school, Petway thus became the first African-American to serve as an assistant US Attorney in the middle Tennessee district. In 1971, he would be elected to the Metropolitan Council of Nashville and Davidson County.

Petway, who died in 1991, is remembered decades later by many in the Nashville legal community. "There was not a better trial attorney in Nashville than Carlton," the lawyer Walter T. Searcy III told me. "Carlton Petway was methodical, well-prepared, and that's what trial law is all about," Searcy noted. "He had a law firm with Julian Blackshear and Carlton Lewis, currently a Juvenile Court magistrate and faculty member of the Nashville School of Law. Mr. Lewis, later a partner in Petway's law firm, remembers Petway as an accomplished attorney, teacher, and mentor of young lawyers in Nashville. "Mr. Petway was really a 'father figure' to many young African American lawyers," he told me.

Merritt also hired the first woman to be an assistant US attorney in Nashville. Martha Craig (Cissy) Daughtrey, a native of Covington, Kentucky and a young Vanderbilt alumna, who would become a trailblazer for generations of young women lawyers and judges. Working on Merritt's new team was her first job after law school, at a time when more traditional law firms in Nashville had not yet crossed the gender line in their hiring of young law school graduates.

• • •

DAUGHTREY'S OWN CAREER would eventually make her iconic for a generation of young women of the Tennessee Bar. The start of it, however, was more humbling.

In the early years, she had trouble connecting with a Nashville law firm. She had been aiming for a spot at one of the larger law firms in Nashville—a tough goal for a young woman in the middle 1960s. The big firms were not hiring women into such roles. She credits Kenneth L. Roberts, another Vanderbilt trained lawyer, who was then working at Commerce Union Bank downtown, for providing her first job in the city.

"His was the third bank that I tried to get hired in," she remembers. "And I have to say, he hired me to do something I really wasn't interested in doing." The position was in the legal department, but the tasks were largely clerical—registering stock certificates—and nothing at all to do with legal theory, legislation, litigation, or courtrooms. It was, she told me, drudgery.

Through her husband, the *Tennessean* reporter Larry Daughtrey, who then spoke to Seigenthaler about her, this landed her an interview with Merritt. "I don't remember exactly how I got in to interview with Gil Merritt," she told me, "but I'm pretty sure it must have been through Larry's contact, through John, who was a very close friend of Gil's. They played tennis together and all of that. And Gil was in a pinch. I'm not saying he didn't hire me for my talents, but he was in a pinch.

"They had sent an FBI agent out to check on me and my background," she remembers. "This was 1968. Traditionally it's the youngest agent in the office, and the least experienced, who go out on these checks. This young man talked to Frank Woods and said, 'Well, Mr. Woods, do you know of any subversive organizations that she belongs to?' Frank thought for a minute and said, 'Well, she was very active in that group, the VSS.' The agent wrote all this down in his little book. Frank was referring the Vanderbilt Student Senate."

"Anyway, some of this stuff got back to Larry. When he found out they were asking about our love life, he got his back up and called Gil and said, 'If you don't call that FBI agent off, I'm going to get my rifle and go shoot him in the back.' I don't know whether Gil took him seriously or not, but he called the FBI, the senior agent in charge and said, 'Could you put somebody else on this assignment? It's just not working out.' And that was that."

By then, the political waters in Washington were changing colors. Lyndon Johnson had abruptly announced he would not run for re-election. In November, Vice President Hubert Humphrey could not muster his own voting majority and lost the general election to Richard Nixon, the former governor of California. Democratic jobholders everywhere could see their federal patronage days were numbered.

"It was the late summer or early fall of 1968, and there was a big election coming. And in those days, it wasn't just the US Attorney that left (there were only eight slots in that whole office at the time) and when the administration changed (this time from Democrat to Republican) everybody left. "Carlton had left and Al Knight was already gone, and Gil was just having trouble keeping things going."

"There must have been somebody else in there that was handling the criminal cases because, you know, women didn't serve on juries back in those days much, and so I think Gil was a little nervous about putting me in front of a jury hearing a criminal case. So, he sent me all the civil stuff, which was pretty interesting to deal with—tort claim actions, and a lot of different things that I really enjoyed. But what happened, of course, was the Democrats lost that election, and Gil was out by the following spring. Charles Hill Anderson came in, and he famously said to somebody, 'They may be ready for women ADAs in other districts, but not in this middle district of Tennessee,' and that got back to me, of course. He was ready to call me in and tell me he no longer needed my services. By then there were a lot of young men who would have been interested in being hired when I was, but they were nervous about the outcome of the election. Now they'd all come in—Fred Thompson was in the office next door to me—I could name all the young Republican male lawyers who came in at that point."

Daughtrey was briefly assigned to handle criminal cases on appeal in Cincinnati. "They figured, you know, I couldn't do much damage to them up in Cincinnati. When I came back, Anderson was gone somewhere, out of the office, and I put a resignation letter on his desk, cleared out my office, and I was gone."

Joining Merritt's team as an Assistant US Attorney commenced a long series of "first woman…" hires and appointments for Daughtrey that would denote her distinguished career over fifty-plus years at the bar and bench. In the early days, it was all aided not only by her training and preparation but also by her own circle of friends, colleagues, and new peers. During her relatively brief time on Merritt's staff, she met other senior hands in the Nashville legal community. One of these was Thomas Shriver, the county district attorney.

With the Johnson-to-Nixon transition in Washington well underway, on one Shriver's visits to the federal building, he offered Daughtrey a job at the Davidson County Courthouse as an assistant district attorney. "I'm really shorthanded," she recalls Shriver saying. "I've got three vacancies. Would you like to move over to my office?"

"I jumped at it, of course," she told me, "and so that's where I was for a few years until I went to Vanderbilt, to the faculty." She was working at the law school when a vacancy occurred on the Tennessee Court of Criminal Appeals. Many friends and colleagues encouraged her to seek this new opportunity. Bill Willis, the *Tennessean* attorney, was at this point a member of the state's Judicial Selection Committee (Governor Ray Blanton was also a Willis client) and Willis promoted Daughtrey as a strong candidate for the appellate court vacancy. "Of course, Bill and Gil and Seig were all friends, and that's how my name got passed along. Bill Willis was solidly behind my candidacy, and of course none of those people had ever seen a woman judge either."

In 1990, Daughtrey was appointed to the Tennessee Supreme Court by Governor Ned McWherter. She served there until 1993, when President Clinton nominated her to a new seat on the Sixth US Circuit. There, she would serve alongside Merritt until he fully retired, in the summer of 2021. Daughtrey took her own senior status on January 1, 2009.

"Gil was the one that gave me a chance, I mean a real chance," she says, with gratitude. "And so he is the hero in my memoir."

• • •

THE YEAR BEFORE his appointment by President Johnson to be the new United States Attorney in Nashville, Merritt was well known around town. Among other things, he had taken a high-profile role on the local issue of whether the Nashville Bar Association should be racially integrated.

He was still an official of the Metropolitan Government—the associate director of the Department of Law in Mayor Briley's administration. The integration question had divided the NBA membership since 1962. The NBA numbered nearly six hundred lawyers at this time. Black lawyers usually affiliated with the smaller J.C. Napier Bar Association (later re-named the Napier-Looby Bar Association) which then counted seventeen attorney members.

In a debate at Vanderbilt's law school in October 1965, Merritt forcefully supported the integration side. His opponent in that forum was the lawyer Jack Kershaw, a member of the White Citizens Council.

"How," Merritt asked, "can we hold up the symbol of our profession—a blindfolded lady with a pair of scales—and say to the world that we stand for 'equal justice for all,' and then tell a fellow lawyer that we will not allow him in our professional organization because he is black, because his skin is not white like ours." He blamed the current exclusion on the "uncon- cern, callous indifference, and inertia" of some NBA members and officers. "You ask the officials of the association about it, and they don't want to talk about it. They want to forget it."

Two months later, the argument continued at the Nashville Bar's an- nual membership meeting. In the new year, NBA members were asked to vote on the question, and the formal decision was made to integrate.

Gilbert Merritt Jr. was descended from the Donelson family, who were among Nashville's earliest settlers. Here, his paternal grandparents Maude Logue Merritt and Stockley Donelson Merritt on their wedding day October 11, 1905. Photo courtesy of Rachel Merritt McAllister.

Gilbert S. Merritt Sr., father of the future judge, was owner of several businesses in the Nashville area, including a prominent wholesale supply company, and two dairy farms. Photo courtesy of Judge Merritt.

Merritt's maternal grandfather, Dempsey Weaver Cantrell, founder of Southern Woodenware Co. Photo courtesy of the Merritt family.

Buddy Merritt, age 5, with his father, Gilbert S. Merritt Sr. Photo courtesy of Judge Merritt.

Gilbert Merritt Sr. and Angie Merritt stand beside his Tri-Pacer airplane at the municipal airport in Lebanon, Tennessee. Photo courtesy of Hal Hardin.

Young Buddy Merritt formed some life-long friendships while a student at Castle Heights Military Academy in Lebanon, Tennessee. Photo courtesy of CHMA Alumni Association.

"Stone Hall," a Merritt family home over many years, sits atop a hill overlooking the Stones River in Hermitage, Tennessee. Photo by Keel Hunt.

The log cabin called "Eversong" still stands on the Stone Hall estate. In earlier times, it was a favorite haunt of the Merritt children. Photo by Keel Hunt.

Cliff Hardin, shown here at age 24, was the manager of the Merritt family's dairy farms and the father of five children. Photo courtesy of Hal Hardin.

Hal Hardin, son of Cliff, worked on the Merritt farms in his youth. He received his law degree from Vanderbilt University. He became a state court judge in 1975 and two years later the US Attorney for the Middle Tennessee District, appointed by President Carter in 1977.
Photo courtesy of Hal Hardin.

This was the central administration building at Castle Heights Military Academy while Merritt was a student there. After the school closed in 1986, this structure was converted to municipal offices for the City of Lebanon, Tennessee. Photo by Keel Hunt.

Gil Merritt became an avid tennis player in high school. He enjoyed playing with friends and colleagues throughout his life. Photo courtesy of CHMA Alumni Association.

Merritt, upper right, with three classmates. Military uniforms were the order of the day for students at Castle Heights. Photo courtesy of CHMA Alumni Association.

The highest individual honor for a graduating Castle Heights senior was to be selected for Cum Honore (with honors). Merritt was one of only eight in his graduating class to be chosen. Photo by Keel Hunt.

From the office letterhead of Southern Woodenware Company. This Merritt family business was headquartered for many years on Nashville's historic Second Avenue, originally called Market Street. Photo courtesy of Judge Merritt.

Merritt and his mother Angie (seated) at the wedding rehearsal dinner for his first-cousin Rachel Lawrence Merritt and her fiancé Joseph McAllister on June 30, 1961.
Photo courtesy of Rachel Merritt McAllister.

Moments after their wedding in 1964, Louise and Gil Merritt depart Christ Episcopal Church in downtown Nashville. In the background, to the right, is the Estes Kefauver Federal Building. Photo from the Nashville Banner *Archives, Special Collections Division, Nashville Public Library.*

A new generation of Merritt children pose with their parents and great-grand-mothers. From left, Louise Clark Fort holds great-grandson Eli; Louise Fort Merritt holds her daughter Louise Clark Merritt; Gil Merritt's grandmother Maude Merritt; and Gil Merritt holds his eldest son Stroud. The Tennessean *photo by Bill Preston.*

PART III
THE MAP OF THE WORLD

CHAPTER 9

LOUISE

How Gil Merritt and Louise Fort found each other, back in the late 1950s, is a bit of a roundabout story.

Years before Gil met Louise, he dated her sister Tish Fort. Then, in 1959 when Tish married John Jay Hooker, he became something of an intermediary, as he would be in so many stories of Tennessee and its politics over the second half of the twentieth century. In any case, Louise's sister Tish told me this story...

"I had been seeing John Jay and Gil, at the same time," she said. "In the summer of 1958, I had been to a two-year college and had finished that, and I had applied to go to the University of Texas and was accepted. But after I met John Jay and we got serious, I canceled those plans. John Jay and I married in 1959.

"When Louise came home for the holidays at Christmas, John Jay and I were having some company over to meet the Governor of Kentucky (A.B. "Happy" Chandler was then in his second term, 1955–59). John Jay wanted Gil to come because Gil was a Democrat and he was his friend and was bright, and that's when I said, 'Well, I think we ought to get Louise and Gil. I think I'll ask my sister Louise to come.'"

And so they did.

• • •

LOUISE WAS THE youngest of four daughters—Aggie, Julia, Tish, and Louise—of one of the city's most prominent families. Their grandfather, Rufus E. Fort Sr., a medical doctor, had been one of the co-founders of the big National Life and Accident Insurance Company, one of Nashville's leading employers for many years and its executives among the city's most influential business leaders. In addition to its vast regional insurance trade, National Life owned WSM-AM radio and its weekly Grand Ole Opry radio program. Louise's father, Rufus Jr., also became an executive of National Life.

Louise was a graduate of Parmer Elementary School and Harpeth Hall School in southwest Nashville. In 1961, she graduated from Briarcliff College, and later from Columbia University, where her studies in art history and international affairs interested her the most.

She and Gil made a striking young couple, and soon they were discussing marriage. But when Gil first proposed to her, he told me, Louise urged him to take time to speak with her doctor, the Nashville psychiatrist Otto Billig. "She wanted me to have the full picture, about her personality, her emotional side, and the issues she had had." Gil did this and learned from her doctor that she had experienced occasional mood swings. Billig told him that Louise had been diagnosed with a form of "manic-depressive disorder" (using the medical terminology of the time, currently called bipolar disorder). It was a mild case, Billig said, and he had prescribed medication. Soon, the couple discussed all of this together, and they agreed to proceed with their wedding plans.

They married on July 10, 1964, at Christ Church Episcopal, in downtown Nashville. Louise was attended by her sisters, and Gil's best man was Al Knight, his friend since law school. (Directly across Broadway from Christ Church stands Nashville's federal courthouse building, where Knight would later join Merritt in the United States Attorney's office.)

The *Tennessean* item that reported the afternoon wedding on its society pages noted that the couple would honeymoon at Sea Island, Georgia, and would then return to Hermitage to live. But it would not be Hermitage. Merritt told me later that while there had been some talk within his family (chiefly pushed by his mother Angie) of setting up housekeeping in Hermitage, Louise had confided she would prefer to live in Nashville proper.

Instead, and with the help of John Jay's mother, Darthula Hooker, they secured an apartment upstairs from hers in the Belle Meade Apartments building, at the corner of Harding Place and Belle Meade Boulevard. Later they moved into a single-family home nearby on Honeywood Avenue and, in 1971, they relocated their young family to Franklin, Tennessee.

• • •

IN FRANKLIN, A half-hour drive south from Nashville, Louise and Gil bought a historic home on Fair Street, at the corner of Seventh Avenue North. Historians call it the Harris-McEwen House. The oldest part of the structure at 612 Fair Street dates to 1830.

This had been the home of Cary Harris, a local newspaper publisher who later was the Commissioner of Indian Affairs under President Andrew Jackson. John B. McEwen, a lawyer and businessman, was a mayor of Franklin during the Civil War, when the house served as a Confederate hospital. After the war, in 1867, McEwen extensively renovated the house in the Italianate style with a slate roof, arched windows, and a two-story rear section.

The style and scale of this extraordinary antebellum structure had caught the Merritts' attention when it came on the market. Its renovation potential had appealed to Louise's talents for interior design, and the couple proceeded make it their own through multiple improvements, though careful to keep it in harmony with its legacy appearance. The changes would also make it a more suitable home for the needs of a young family. (Their son Stroud, daughter Louise Clark, and second son Eli had come along by this time.) Their updates to the house included the additions of a pool and tennis court, as well as a conversion of the detached smokehouse structure into a private study. Soon, they would enjoy tennis and pool-time with family and friends, and Gil would shortly begin to host a regular tennis time for his Nashville friends on Sunday mornings.

The Merritt children were still very young at this point, and so there was minimal entertaining in these first months on Fair Street, though neighbors describe the young couple as welcoming hosts. Friends who knew them then describe Louise as "charming," "lovely" and so "easy to talk to." The Merritts would go out to dinner occasionally, or they would have neighbors in, but the family also enjoyed the relative quiet of the historic Franklin community, in contrast to the social whirl of the Belle Meade parties in Nashville. Even so, neighbors remember Louise as a "gracious" hostess in her own new Franklin home.

"Louise and Gil were not real social," Tish told me. "Of course, John Jay and I had grown up in a different environment than Gil had grown up in, in the sense that our parents knew each other, we belonged to the same clubs and that kind of thing. And I don't think that appealed to Louise at all. I think that's why they moved to Franklin.

"When her children and mine were little and about to go into birthday parties, I remember Louise talking about how it was really just a 'fashion parade' about which little girl had on the prettiest petite dress, and the prettiest bonnet, that kind of thing. I think Louise just didn't want any part of that. And I think there'd also been conversations about Gil running for mayor, and I think Louise had made her point that she didn't want any part of that, either."

• • •

THEIR LIFE TOGETHER on Fair Street, however, was more to Louise's liking and for Gil even a welcome respite from his more public life in Nashville. The smaller scale of Franklin seemed to suit them both. The house was only a short walk from the Franklin town center. St. Paul's Episcopal Church, which the family attended, was only a block away from their front door. On Fair Street, their lives proceeded at a more agreeable pace.

"Louise told me how she and Gil would read to each other," Tish continued, "and how they would sometimes lie on the floor in that wonderful library there at home in Franklin, and just 'report' to each other on their days. They enjoyed reading poetry together and talking about travel. I remember that Louise and Gil had a map of the world. They had a four-poster bed, and they attached a map of the world to the under-side of the canopy. In other words, they would lie in bed and look up at that map and talk about where they were going or where they had been. They would talk about travel and life.

"Louise became very interested in the artist Ben Shahn, and she got Gil so interested that they went to New Jersey. They had called and arranged an interview, to go out to his home and visit with Shahn, and I think they purchased one of his portfolios. They worked on their gardens together. I envied that. I wanted that in a personal relationship with a husband, and Louise and Gil had it for a number of years."

Louise and Gil especially loved traveling, and she would also take trips with her sister Tish when that was possible. When it wasn't, they would correspond about sights they each had seen. From a letter Louise wrote to Tish from London, on November 8, 1970:

> This afternoon we spent a lovely day in Regents Park at the most wonderful London Zoo. Chi Chi, a grand woo panda bear, is the only one in captivity save a male in the Moscow Zoo. She is enchantingly funny and cuddly— when we saw her, she was rolled up tight in the corner feigning hibernation. Next time we might get to see her roly-poly walk...
>
> Last night we went to see *A Bequest to the Nation* about Lord Nelson and Lady Hamilton—a good, sometimes very funny (Zoe Caldwell as Lady Hamilton) play of the week before Trafalgar. Tomorrow night we are to see *Abelard and Heloise* which is supposed to be a real grabber. Tuesday we go to Edinburgh...

That letter was written only days after Hooker had lost his second race for governor of Tennessee, defeated by the Republican Winfield Dunn of Memphis, the first Republican that Tennessee had elected in half a century. But Louise's words were not about politics but a loving message of commiseration for her sister:

> I hope you and John Jay are well. I hope you all are at Gatlinburg at this time and are able for the moment to have a partial catharsis. Come to some place like London or Mozambique where you know no one, and be anonymous for a few days. It has always been soothing to me to be able to be anonymous for a short while—not forever, mind you, but to be at scratch and to be able to start from there if you like. Gil and I think of you both and of the dreams you share for a full life filled with accomplishment—it is never easy, I am sure, to give up even temporarily those dreams which are precious to you. I only hope at this hour of despair that you both individually and together will remember that not only did others share in your dreams, but you shared in the dreams of others and that such rarified moments are a trust to the heart and to the spirit. I am sorry for the state of Tennessee that it will lack in the next four years and perhaps forever the brilliance of John Jay's leadership as governor and of yours as First Lady...

• • •

JUST AS GIL always looked forward to the Sunday tennis matches at home with his buddies, so did Louise with her friends who would join her for doubles on the new court at the Franklin house. His Sunday regulars included John Seigenthaler, Henry Walker, David Pollack, Herb Shayne, George Paine, and John Sergent. Hers were May Shayne, Betty Brown, and a few others.

It was on another Sunday morning at the Fair Street house, in 1973, that the devastation happened—the Sunday morning when Louise was lost.

On this weekend no tennis matches had been scheduled with the regulars for several reasons. Louise would be returning on Friday from a few days in New York City with her sister-in-law Alice Kirby Hooker Buchtel. Called "Teenie" by friends and family, she was the flamboyant older sister of Henry and John Jay Hooker. (Teenie died in 2004.) In

Manhattan, the two women had likely indulged Louise's love of contemporary art with visits to galleries, and probably some shopping at stores in the city.

On this particular weekend, the Merritt's daughter Louise Clark, then seven, was staying with her grandmother Angie at Stone Hall out in Hermitage. She remembers sleeping in the "Eversong" cabin that had thrilled all three of the Merritt children as youngsters, with its bunk beds and woodsy, adventurous feel. Her brothers Stroud, eight, and Eli, six, had remained at home in Franklin with their dad on this weekend. Louise's usual Sunday morning routine was to slip quietly out the door and walk to the early service at St. Paul's Episcopal Church, a block south from her front door. It was therefore not unusual for Gil to arise, look in on the boys, but not see his wife for the first couple of waking hours.

Then the telephone rang. Gil answered in the bedroom. It was Tish, calling to say she had hoped to catch up with her sister to hear all about the New York trip. Gil replied that Louise seemed not to be at home just then; possibly she was still at church, he said. He promised Tish he would let Louise know to return the call.

Then he went downstairs, and he made his way into the kitchen. There he found not Louise but a single yellow envelope, sitting on the countertop addressed simply to "Gil." Inside was a note in brown ink, in Louise's distinctive script, filling two pages of her sunflower-yellow note paper, the kind that folds into its own envelope. He read this message quickly. This is what Louise had written:

Dearest, dearest Gil—
This is a Valediction Forbidding Mourning, for in our eight years together we have had separately and together more beauty and truth, more laughter and tears, more love and dignity than are outwardly granted to others in a lifetime of todays.

Give yourself to our children—give them of your strength, your unrelenting kindness and justice, your devotion to good and to warm goodness, your deep center of rugged sensitivity and your bright exalting intellect whose superstructure is of the extraordinary rather than the ordinary. Give to them of the center of your soul—the soft and the hard. But remember to give and to take from them, for they have much joy as they were borne out of our love.

And give yourself to a woman who will love you more gently than I. She could love you no more, no better, but more gently.

Til death us do part,
Louise

I wish to write Stroud, Clark, and Elijah separately but the night is almost over and there is not enough paper in the world for me to recount to them the separate and collective joys they bring to me and the unexplainable sorrow in my heart.

• • •

HE RUSHED OUT to the Smoke House.

The renovation project had transformed a separate rear structure that they continued to call the Smoke House into a kind of quiet retreat space, the thick walls of the small building buffering any street noise from the outside. The remodeled room held a brass-framed day bed, where Louise would often spend private moments alone, reading and resting.

As Gil entered this room now, Louise lay motionless on the day bed. A 22-caliber rifle lay beside her.

Probably in shock, he then phoned Rufus Fort, his father-in-law. Rufus in turn called Tish, telling her that Louise was dead. Tish remembers her father saying Gil had told him it appeared Louise had taken her own life. (Investigators found a single wound to the chest and declared the death a suicide.) No one else had heard the shot.

Louise was only thirty-two years old.

• • •

NEXT GIL PHONED the Franklin police, and then his mother in Hermitage, asking her to bring his daughter home. He needed to gather the children and break this terrible news. At this moment, the daughter Louise (she had been given her mother's name, Louise Clark, though in her early years through high school she went by her middle name "Clark") was still at Stone Hall. Her brothers, who had remained at home in Franklin, were still asleep in their beds upstairs in the main house.

Angie and young Louise then drove to Franklin, mainly in silence, as the daughter remembers. Once there, Louise remembers walking from her grandmother's car up the steps to the front door, wondering why so many people were standing in her yard on a Sunday. Years later, one of the adults who had been standing in the front yard on that morning told her they remembered hearing the girl's screams from inside as she learned the terrible news.

• • •

IN THE SHATTERED days following, a funeral service for Louise was held at St. Paul's Episcopal Church, the small parish sanctuary on Franklin's West Main Street. St. Paul's had become their family's home church, and Louise especially relished the peace of this sanctuary, of the sermons she heard, and of the scripture lessons she learned and often copied into her notebook.

Jeanie Nelson, who in the early 1970s had been a young associate at the Gullett, Steele, Sanford, Robinson, & Merritt law firm, was one of many family friends who attended. She recalls the deep sadness of seeing the three small Merritt children as they walked back up the aisle to exit the church after the service concluded.

"Of course, that church was packed," Nelson told me. "The world felt in shock. I don't know that I had ever experienced so close up, a suicide, that had hit this circle, the law firm circle, the family circle."

Louise was buried at Mt. Olivet Cemetery, among the preceding generations of Merritts and Forts.

• • •

WITHIN A VERY few days, Gil Merritt reached out to John Seigenthaler with a special request. John told me more of this story in 2014.

"After she was buried, Gil said, 'John, I just can't believe that Louise would do this without leaving me another note of some kind, telling me more.' He asked me if I'd go back to the house with him and help him look for another letter." The two men soon met at the Fair Street home, and they began an anguished search. John remembered this as a sad, emotional exploration through the house, but a successful one.

Gil himself told me later: "Louise had been under the care of a psychiatrist. She had been depressed for about six months. But I couldn't understand that she didn't leave me any notes. It was strange, and not like her. I talked to the psychiatrist. He said if there were any other notes they'd be in a particular book she'd told him about, where she had done some drawings and painting. I knew exactly where it was, in the library. John was with me. I went to the library, opened the book, and there they were. Two letters. They tried to explain—in the words of a very, very depressed person—why she was doing what she was doing. I'm sure John read the letters."

All three notes, including the original that Gil had discovered in the kitchen on Sunday morning, were kept years afterward in a small clay pot from the kitchen. These were later moved to a shelf in the family library. Over the next few years, young Louise remembers, she would occasionally ask her father to take the notes out and read them aloud to her and her brothers. She told me she found this intimate family exercise to be personally therapeutic. Her younger brother Eli shared a similar memory. Later on, throughout their teen years, both worked through the shock and grief. Louise and Eli later became psychiatrists.

Louise remembers that she kept her mother's notes nearby at hand for several years. And then, she didn't. "The funny thing is," she told me, "I had those notes for the longest time. And just in the last couple of years, I realized, I don't need to keep them anymore."

• • •

In the days following Louise's death, Gil remembered how his friend Seigenthaler had continued to be a particularly helpful presence.

"John came down to Franklin and we played tennis almost every day," Gil told me years later. "It was therapeutic for me, and John understood that. He was a great friend, and a very thoughtful friend. That kind of loyalty—I look back on it with great thankfulness. It helped me get through a very difficult period."

The young United States Attorney was now the single parent of three pre-teens. Rachel McAllister, his first cousin, remembers that difficult period. "Gil now had the formidable job of raising three children alone, with the committed help of his mother. The children, and later his grandchildren, were always a source of great pride." He was always quick to acknowledge the support he had from many people during those difficult days, especially his mother Angie. She quickly became a steady presence and source of practical help, especially with the young children.

Judge Ruth Kinnard was another.

Ruth McDowell Kinnard was a neighbor and from a long-time

Franklin family. An Alabama native, she had known Merritt since his time as US Attorney, when she became his law clerk in 1967. Later she was appointed to a judgeship of the US Bankruptcy Court for middle Tennessee—the first woman to be elevated to the federal bench in Tennessee. Ruth was also a leader in Franklin's historic preservation movement.

After her death, in 2001, Ruth's daughter Judith Kinnard Cabot published *Remembering Ruthie*, a book of remembrances of her mother by family and friends. In it, Judge Gil Merritt wrote this:

"She became the good friend of my wife, Louise Fort Merritt, when we moved to Franklin in 1970 and became her neighbor. Thereafter, she became a mentor for my children—Stroud, Louise Clark, and Eli—as they were growing up in Franklin. She taught their Sunday School classes at St. Paul's and had a major impact on our lives for many years. When my wife died in 1973, Ruth went to Disneyland with us after the funeral where we began the process of adjustment and healing that gradually takes place in the face of such a life-shattering event. All of us turned to her many times over the next twenty-five years."

• • •

SUSAN SIMONS, LIKE Louise another daughter of Nashville's business elite, had known Louise Fort in college. (Her father, Ben Willingham Sr. was president of Genesco Inc. and later of Burlington Industries.) After school, these two young women re-connected back in Nashville and resumed their close friendship. Susan mentioned a comment Louise had made once about the Fair Street house—that she thought it might be "haunted." There was, in any case, already no shortage of history at 612 Fair Street.

Judith Kinnard Cabot, Judge Kinnard's daughter, had been another close friend of Louise in Franklin, during the Merritts' years on Fair Street. Judy was three years younger than Louise and reminisced from her own time in high school admiring Louise's good looks and easy grace as a fashionable young woman. This is how Judy remembers Louise:

> She was a glamorous creature to admire. I really got to know her when she and Gil moved to Franklin and created a universe of bold colors, vitality, and celebrity panache as friends from all over flocked to their home. In the back city garden were a

swimming pool and a tennis court where good-hearted competition flourished. Her deep laugh could often be heard floating over the ether creating a feeling of lighthearted joy.

On Sunday mornings they would walk across the street to St. Paul's Episcopal Church and occupy one of the front pews. She would sit back, one arm flung across the back of the bench, to turn toward the priest with obvious relish in the sermon.

She often wore a glorious colored scarf tied as a headband with her long thick chestnut hair flowing down her back. The rest of us, hair corralled usually in a bun, sat primly as expected.

I admired her so much, her style, her taste, that I chose her china, *Vieux Chine*, as my own. And we bought for our home in Massachusetts a huge restaurant Garland stove as she had. Every day her gift of a whimsical Italian pottery pig stares me in the eye, his back bristling with wooden spoons.

I remember well the calendars she made each year of her children's paintings and sent to friends. Kids' art kept, even memorialized, not in a scrap book, but in a useful object beautifully designed to share. She took one of the large bedrooms, the right front corner, and turned it into a private space for herself with hanging racks of exotic clothes and her private treasures. It may have been there that she wrote her journal entries. They had esoteric titles giving off intimations of deep philosophical exploration. Quotes she loved on all aspects of life filled them with thoughtful comments of her own.

She was someone curious enough to be interested and disciplined enough to make the entries.

I think she loved the house, which like most large, older homes, provided charm with the need for lots of maintenance. It was a palette, a backdrop for a life for her family and also for sharing. She offered to have a wedding reception when I married in the house as my grandparents, the Claiborne Kinnards had done. And she promised that like they did, she would strew orange blossoms everywhere.

By the time of our marriage, in 1975, she was gone.

CHAPTER 10

THE TWO-MAN RACE THAT WASN'T

In 1975, Nashvillians voted in the third municipal election under the consolidated city-county "Metro Government" charter in Nashville and Davidson County. The charter limited the mayor to three consecutive terms, meaning Mayor Briley could not succeed himself again.

The popular Congressman Richard H. Fulton, a Democrat from East Nashville who had now served a dozen years in the US House, ran for the open mayoral seat and won. So, Fulton was obliged to resign his congressional post. (He would go on to serve his own maximum three terms at City Hall.) This made necessary an unusual off-year scramble for Nashville's District 5 seat in Congress.

Several well-known political figures in the city—young and old, from traditional to progressive—quickly jumped into the race: Clifford Allen, the county's elected tax assessor and a Briley nemesis; state Rep. Mike Murphy; the District Attorney Tom Shriver, and Merritt, the United States Attorney in this district. All the four were Democrats, and each man brought to the race his own base of political support, some of them more seasoned and substantial than others. The primary contest through the summer months of 1975 was aggressive if brief.

Allen, at 63, had been a state senator years earlier (1949–51) and he would be supported by many of the city's old-line establishment influencers, including the conservative editorial page of the *Nashville Banner* newspaper. Murphy, 32, was already serving in the Tennessee General Assembly and was a popular young Democrat from the west side of town. Shriver, a former legislator, was now the elected District Attorney for the county with a number of current and former assistants in his corner; Hal Hardin was his campaign manager.

Merritt, 39, had not been elected to any public office (though he was now the top federal prosecutor for middle Tennessee, by presidential appointment). Of course, he would have the enthusiastic backing of the *Tennessean* front office, including Seigenthaler and the publisher Amon C. Evans. Merritt thought he could count on some Republican support; the attorney Lew Conner chaired a group called "Republicans for Merritt."

• • •

SEIGENTHALER WAS, IN effect, Merritt's campaign manager.

He was already an ultimate hands-on editor, closely supervising editorial decisions at the newspaper office at 1100 Broadway. Accordingly, his newsroom was always close to the action in most local and state political races, including giving advice to some favored candidates and their campaigns. (Notable in this record was the 1962 congressional election in the 5th District when the morning newspaper had played such a decisive role, with the *Tennessean* reporters exposing corruption in the city's 2nd Ward. While the votes were still being counted into the early morning hours at the Election Commission office ten blocks away, Fulton had privately napped on the publisher's sofa just off the main newsroom before awakening to the news that he had won.) Now, thirteen years later, with Merritt in the race to determine who would succeed Fulton, the *Tennessean* newsroom staff (and especially Seigenthaler) were not bashful about taking sides in another activist role.

"It was definitely a 'newsroom' campaign," Tom Ingram remembers candidly, recalling that political summer when he was a young reporter there. (In 1974, Ingram left the *Tennessean* staff to be a top campaign aide to Republican Lamar Alexander's unsuccessful campaign for governor that year. Alexander would run and win four years later, with Ingram as his campaign manager.) "There were several of those 'newsroom campaigns' in that day," Ingram remembers. 'Wayne Whitt (the veteran City Hall reporter who was sometimes referred to as "the 41st Councilmember" for his behind-the-scenes influence) was usually the campaign manager, but Seigenthaler was definitely in charge when Merritt ran for Congress."

Roy M. Neel, who would become Vice President Al Gore's chief of staff two decades later, was at this point a young Vanderbilt grad. He had majored in English and art history. He had been a sportswriter at the *Nashville Banner* and was finishing a book on the first 75 years of Vanderbilt basketball. He remembers Merritt calling him, asking about political polling. Neel took on this consulting assignment and soon reported back with his recommendations for Merritt's campaign messaging.

Frank Sutherland, then a young *Tennessean* reporter (who would succeed Seigenthaler as editor of the *Tennessean* fourteen years later), was one on the news staff who covered Merritt's congressional campaign. He remembers one illustrative example of how Merritt would take Seigenthaler's advice and promptly act on it. Very late in the primary campaign period, Merritt had found little traction against the more veteran politicians in the race. Sutherland recalled that Seigenthaler convened a quick strategy session in his editor's office, where he announced an idea that had come to him for the next day's news coverage.

"Gil," he said, "let's try something different tomorrow morning," the editor said. "You call a press conference down at the courthouse. We'll cover it." At this time, the lobby of the Davidson County Courthouse and City Hall was very near to Mr. Allen's tax assessor's office on the first floor. "And you say, 'This campaign has turned into 'a two-man race between Clifford Allen and me!' That's the quote."

Public opinion polling was not nearly as sophisticated then as now, and particularly so in elections at the municipal level: Where the voters stood on any day before Election Day was frankly anybody's guess. In any case, Merritt proceeded to do and say as the Seigenthaler prescribed. But Seigenthaler's catchy soundbite did not turn out to be true for Merritt. On primary night, in early August, it was Allen who came in first in the actual voting. Murphy was in second place. Merritt finished fourth.

That night, after the votes were counted and the winner announced, Mike Murphy told reporters: "Well, Mr. Merritt was right. But the 'two-man race' turned out to be Mr. Allen and me."

• • •

IN MERRITT'S CAMPAIGN, there had been one significant organizational problem. The US Attorney had never actually moved into the Fifth District. He had been born in Davidson County and had lived there until he left for college, all true enough, but throughout the summer he maintained his voting residence on Fair Street in Franklin, on the politically wrong side of the Williamson County line for someone wanting to be the congressman from Nashville.

His opponents, of course, missed no opportunities to refer to Merritt's residency in their own public appearances. Allen frequently would refer to "my opponent, Mr. Merritt, who lives in the next county..." Murphy also seemed to enjoy referring to "Our friend from the other district."

When I asked Merritt years later about his decision to stay put in the other county, the single father of three answered me candidly. In the two preceding years, his home and family had been through a staggering level of upheaval. Sutherland, who covered Merritt's 1975 campaign and observed him on a daily basis that summer, speculated that "Gil's heart wasn't in it."

But if his heart wasn't in it, why did Merritt run at all in 1975?

Forty-seven years later, with so many of his contemporaries and confidants now dead, we cannot know what part the circle of friends played in his decision to attempt such a prominent elective office. Was he reluctant? Did he decline at first, then change his mind? To what extent did those in his political circle or others persuade him to run? Was he eager in the beginning, then his enthusiasm cooled?

On the one hand, a campaign for Congress did align with Merritt's sense of his own career path and his professed idealism about public service. It would have resonated with the progressive politics of his closest friends, certainly of his brother-in-law John Jay Hooker, who by this time had run three statewide campaigns. Merritt had long admired the political figures he knew in his twenties and early thirties—from Albert Gore Sr. to the two Kennedys. Merritt had met Senator Robert Kennedy, an electrifying candidate for president, in the middle of April in 1968 just weeks before his assassination.

Kennedy had come to Nashville to speak at Vanderbilt's IMPACT Symposium, and later that evening to a more intimate gathering in Seigenthaler's home that Merritt attended.

"What we need in the United States is not division," Kennedy said early that evening at Memorial Gymnasium. "What we need in the United States is not hatred; what we need in the United States is not violence and lawlessness, but is love and wisdom, and compassion toward one another, and a feeling of justice toward those who still suffer within our country, whether they be white or whether they be black."

Kennedy's driver that evening was a young volunteer named Charles W. Bone, then a law student. Bone remembers sitting on the floor at Seigenthaler's home: "I sat on the floor and listened to the two close friends (Kennedy and Seigenthaler) discuss their shared vision of the world becoming a place where all of us could find a way to live together in peace." It was on this night that Merritt met Senator Kennedy and shook his hand. RFK, after his return to Washington, followed up with a personal letter to Merritt that remained in the judge's office files ever after.

Dear Gil:

I was pleased to have the opportunity to meet and talk with you at John Seigenthaler's home during my recent visit to Nashville. In a political campaign there is too little time for such discussions of problems, and so the opportunity afforded by this meeting was especially worthwhile.

I hope that our paths will cross again during future visits to Tennessee. Meanwhile, if there is any matter which you feel should be brought to my attention, I would be more than grateful if you would do so.

With warm regards,

Sincerely,

Robert F. Kennedy

But there would be no more visits to Tennessee for Bobby Kennedy. Seven weeks later, on June 6, he was murdered in Los Angeles.

Merritt's first professional passion was the law—by applying it, interpreting it, and not by making law as legislators do—and it would soon become his life's work. Louise had died only two years before the special congressional election of 1975, and he was now the single parent of three young pre-teens. In his loss of Louise—that singular and abiding grief of his life—his memories of her, of her death, and of his concern for the welfare of his young children—all this may have overwhelmed any notion of abruptly relocating them—even if only a few miles up the Nashville highway—to yet another new home.

"It was just easier," Merritt told me in 2021, "to stay there and not uproot my family."

CHAPTER 11

THE NOMINATION

By the time Merritt's own moment came, in the spring of 1977, he was well prepared and also well connected.

Democrats were newly ascendant now in Washington in the political upheaval of the immediate post-Watergate period. Not only had President Nixon resigned his office, an unprecedented event in the late summer of 1974, but a month later the new Republican President Gerald Ford had pardoned his predecessor. Not only did Ford's efforts at re-election now seem doomed, but news of the Nixon pardon threatened many other Republican campaigns across the nation, and Jimmy Carter's challenge to Ford now soared in all the turmoil. In any case, the young scholar-lawyer Gil Merritt now had important friends in Washington, too.

One of these was Jim Sasser, the Nashville lawyer and now the new junior US Senator from Tennessee. The other—Carter of Georgia—was now the 39th President of the United States. With friends like these, Merritt was in a new and rarified position in the region's political taxonomy, and he had accomplished this in the old-fashioned way: for the Carter and Sasser election campaigns, Merritt had helped them both raise money.

• • •

MERRITT AND SASSER had known each other for nearly twenty years by this time. They were roughly the same age, born in the same year (Merritt in January 1936, Sasser eight months later), and after college they both had taken their legal training at the Vanderbilt law school. However, for several years thereafter, they had little occasion to interreact as young lawyers in Nashville. But each had his own political kinship to the Gore family.

Sasser's father had been close to Albert Gore Sr., chiefly through his work over many years as a field representative for the US Department of Agriculture and particularly as the State Conservationist with the US Soil Conservation Service. Over time, those roles helped the younger Sasser establish an invaluable network of political connections across Tennessee.

He told me he had not known Merritt well at Vanderbilt, and wasn't close to Seigenthaler in these early years, but there were other early friends in common. He met Al Knight at Vanderbilt law school. And Jim's wife Mary had been a college roommate of Nancy Gore's.

When Gore Sr. ran for re-election in 1970, Sasser became his Nashville campaign manager. After Gore lost that race, to the Republican Bill Brock of Chattanooga, Sasser returned to his private law practice. In 1973, he was elected chairman of the Tennessee Democratic Party, serving until 1976, when he ran against Brock himself, taking back Gore's old Senate seat for the Democrats.

"I was always politically interested and interested in public policy and in government very much, but I was not really active politically much," he said. "I became active in the (1970) Gore campaign because they asked me to—first, Nancy, and I said no, and then Pauline (Senator Gore's wife), and I said no again. Then Senator Gore called me, and I just couldn't say no to him. I got active, and we didn't have any money and no organization there in Davidson County. I had to raise the money and everything else. We did some things that had not been done there before. We put in telephone banks and had a computer set-up where we could go down the street and know who's where and knock on doors. Anyway, we carried Davidson County by a large margin, and that was sort of a star in the crown of the Gore campaign, which had sagged in other areas in middle Tennessee. After that, I was very disappointed at Gore's defeat because I thought he was absolutely right on things like the Vietnam War. I thought he was right on the civil rights issues."

After Sasser became the state party chairman, he and Merritt got to know each other better. "I'd go up to see Gil in his law office, and we would have lunch together occasionally. We were not the closest of friends, but we were good friends and enjoyed each other's company. Then when I ran in '76, the first thing I had to do was beat John Hooker in the primary. The *Tennessean* and John Seigenthaler, of course, supported Hooker through the primary. Then after I won the primary, that's when I had to face Brock. I had seen what Brock had done to Gore in 1970 with negative ads, so I went to Gil and asked him to become the counsel for the campaign and alerted him what was going to happen at the end that I was sure that we'd get a final 10 days barrage just like Gore got—negative television and negative radio. I wanted Gil to see if he could keep some of those things off the air because I thought they were slanderous and untrue."

"When the barrage started, Gil went into action, and I think he wrote some pretty stern letters to some of the television stations, maybe threatening to sue, but just calling attention to the inaccuracies and the slander in the ads and calling them libelous. Some of the television stations wouldn't run all of them, and some of the newspapers wouldn't run all of the newspaper ads that he read there at the end, but most of them did. He was helpful in getting some of them down."

• • •

MERRITT TOLD ME it was Rosalynn Carter, who had been the First Lady of Georgia, who phoned him one day, asking him to join her husband's campaign for President.

He figured this call had come about on the recommendation of either Jim Free, the long-time protégé of Tennessee Governor Ned McWherter, or from McWherter himself. Free was already centrally involved in Carter's Tennessee campaign at this point, and he was in close coordination with the Carter campaign fundraising in Tennessee.

In short order, Merritt was named the Carter campaign finance chair for Tennessee. With Jim Free, and in close coordination with McWherter, Merritt introduced Carter to donors at campaign events across the state. Free recalled how Tennessee became a favorite campaign stop for Carter, geographically near to Georgia and considering the placement of its five principal television markets, all of them with significant viewership in neighboring states. At one such event in Nashville, Merritt presented Carter with a coonskin cap— the iconic campaign symbol of the late Senator Estes Kefauver. On the podium, Carter swiftly put the cap on his head and flashed the toothy Carter smile to the loud delight of the crowd in the room.

In the November election, Carter carried Tennessee in a landslide over Ford, with fifty-six percent of its vote. In the Senate race, more than 1.4 million ballots were cast statewide, with Sasser winning better than fifty-two percent of them.

• • •

VERY SOON AFTER his Senate election, Sasser remembers he began hearing about the various vacancies in government for which the President would look to the state's Democratic senator for recommendations on who to appoint or nominate: US Attorney, US Marshal, Farmers Home Administration, and so forth.

"Gil's name was mentioned—I can't remember how it came up—and I thought at first we were maybe thinking about a district federal judgeship for him. Anyway, maybe it was John Seigenthaler who suggested that Gil would be better on the Court of Appeals, and I agreed with that. I thought that Gil would be an excellent judge by way of his education, by way of his background, and, to quote Shakespeare, I thought he could temper justice with mercy. Although he came from a distinguished background, he was not an elitist, and he had, I found, a common touch and had a sense of compassion about him. I thought he would make an excellent federal judge on the Court of Appeals, or in the district, or even on the Supreme Court at some point."

Sasser's strategy for sorting out the federal appointments he might recommend was to establish a "judicial review commission" in the state to review prospects for court vacancies. Sasser asked John Wade, his old Vanderbilt law school dean, to chair this new panel. They would interview prospects and then narrow them down to a list of three names, for the senator's consideration. He would then forward one name to the White House— and it would be not only a great time-saver but also a considerable political buffer for the new junior senator.

"Dean Wade was a wonderful man," Sasser said. "We all admired him and respected him enormously. He was a man of high ethics and very wise. He was a great chairman of the judicial commission." Merritt, in due course, was one of three lawyers on the short list that Wade forwarded to Senator Sasser.

"I proposed Gil," Sasser noted, "and I ran into some opposition from Griffin Bell, who was the new Attorney General. Griffin was from Atlanta and had been one of the early supporters of Carter, going back to his governor's days. We had a little tussle there. I think maybe I went to see the President about that, and he chose Gil. I think Griffin Bell thought Gil was too young and hadn't had enough seasoning to be on the Court of Appeals. Griffin may have had his own candidate."

• • •

SOON AFTER THE holidays following Carter's election, Jim Free had a new office address: 1600 Pennsylvania Avenue. He had been important to Carter's southern campaign, and in due course he was one of several trusted political advisers who now had desks in the East Wing of the White House.

"So we win the election and President Carter appoints me Special Assistant to the President for Congressional Liaison, doing the President's bidding on his policies on Capitol Hill. So I'm sitting in my office in the East Wing of the White House, and I get a phone call from Susan Clough." She was President Carter's executive assistant.

"Susan said, 'Jim, the President wants to see you, in the Oval Office,' and she added, 'Right now.' I take off through that beautiful marble hallway there on the ground floor of the White House and into the West Wing, and go into the outer office, where Susan sits, and she said, 'They're waiting on you. In there.'

"So I go into the Oval Office and there is the president, Hamilton Jordan (the President's Chief of Staff), and the Attorney General Griffin Bell, and his assistant Terry Adamson, a Justice Department lawyer. All seated on the sofas, except for the President.

> CARTER: Jim, you worked in the campaign with Gil Merritt and know him pretty well.
> FREE: Yes sir, I do, pretty well. He's a good man.
> CARTER: What do you think of Gil Merritt?
> FREE: Well, sir, he's a lawyer of excellent reputation back home. His involvement and his assistance in the campaign were just absolutely critical, in my opinion, in the early days of the campaign, with Scoop Jackson and George Wallace and all of these other folks who would obviously get a percentage of votes in Tennessee. But the main thing is, back home, he's looked upon as a well-recognized jurist.

"The room got real quiet, and I was taking deep breaths, wondering 'Oh, God, what's the next question going to be? But the President just said, 'Jim, thank you very much. This is very helpful.'

"And then I left."

• • •

THE SENATE'S CONFIRMATION of Carter's Merritt nomination was, by today's standards, a quick one.

This was just weeks after President Carter had made his formal nomination— lightning-fast in contrast to the twenty-first century protracted practice of highly partisan delay and angry Judiciary Committee hearings. Merritt's relatively swift confirmation, aside from his own superior qualifications, was also chiefly due to the stature of Tennessee's Senate delegation at that time (Howard H. Baker Jr. was the Republican Leader in the upper chamber at this time) as well as a more general nod to the new post-Watergate Democratic president.

Merritt's consideration by the Judiciary Committee was brief and uneventful. There had been only a few questions that needed answering. In my 2021 interviews with Merritt and Sasser, both recalled that there were questions (from the committee's Republican side) about Merritt's political fundraising for Sasser's 1976 campaign. (Merritt acknowledged submitting three $1,000 donations in the name of his own young children.) They also anticipated questions about his handling of a case while in the US Attorney's office involving the former *Tennessean* reporter Wendell Rawls, now a correspondent for the *New York Times*. (Those questions never came, though Rawls was present in the committee's hearing room in case they did.). Otherwise, with guidance from the White House and some unofficial targeted advocacy by Seigenthaler and others in his old circle of friends, the nominee from Nashville moved through the process with no difficulty.

• • •

ON OCTOBER 29, on the Senate floor, Merritt was approved on a voice vote, but first both Baker and Sasser spoke at length.

> BAKER: I am extremely pleased to express my unqualified support for the nomination of Mr. Gilbert S. Merritt, of Nashville, Tennessee, to be US circuit judge for the Sixth Judicial Circuit of the US Court of Appeals. I know and have the highest respect for Gil Merritt as a person and I am familiar with his many noteworthy accomplishments… Gilbert Merritt has the rare blend of experience, ability, and judicial temperament to excel on the Federal bench, as he has excelled in so many previous endeavors. This capable citizen of Tennessee is, in my opinion, uniquely qualified to fill the vacancy on the Sixth Circuit Court of Appeals created by the passing of another Tennessean and highly respected jurist, the late Judge William E. Miller. I enthusiastically support the nomination of Gil Merritt and unequivocally commend him to my colleagues as an individual most worthy of their confirmation. He will prove a further complement to the already distinguished bench of the Sixth Judicial Circuit.

SASSER: Mr. Merritt is an extraordinarily able and competent attorney. His distinguished career in the bar is qualification enough to fill this position. He has demonstrated compassion and sensitivity for the problems of this difficult age. Additionally, he has exhibited the wisdom to assist in resolving these great questions. Time and again, he has shown fairness and equity in his legal practice. He has accepted unpopular cases and has done more than his share of pro bono work. He knows well the abilities and shortcomings of the judiciary...

Sasser went on to summarize Merritt's schooling and legal scholarship, and how they had been law school classmates at Vanderbilt. He concluded with a final comment on Merritt's family heritage that was not quite factual, and the new appellate judge would chide the senator about it later.

SASSER: My colleagues will be interested in knowing, also, that Mr. Merritt is a direct descendant of another great Tennessean, Andrew Jackson.

This statement, though harmless, was not true. The nation's seventh President had been childless. Jackson had no direct descendants. Merritt and his family well knew the Jackson story, and he told me he enjoyed ribbing Sasser later, saying, "Jim, you have called me a bastard before the Senate of the United States!"

• • •

MERRITT'S SWEARING-IN CAME on November 18. It was a happy family affair at the Kefauver Federal Building, on Broadway in Nashville. The Merritt children were there, along with other members of his extended kin. The oath was administered by Chief Judge Harry Phillips of the Sixth Circuit.

"The day he was sworn in to the Sixth Circuit judgeship, all the family was present," Merritt's cousin Rachel remembers. "Our grandmother 'Mammy' Merritt was 81 at the time—seemed much older to us—and was driven into town. They were a bit late and the proceedings had begun. She came in her black dress, hat, and gloves up the steps as fast as she was able—screaming, 'Wait for me, wait for me!' It was a bit of levity on a solemn occasion."

CHAPTER 12

NEW VENUES & OLD GOATS

B y the mid-point of the twentieth century, Nashville was a bustling
town and already a city of many contrasts.

Tennessee's capital had become a successful regional hub for many
types of businesses, owing principally to its location near the geographical center of the North American continent, its concentration of colleges
and universities, and transportation links to other regions. Three interstate highways would soon crisscross here, commercial air service was
accelerating, and the ancient Cumberland River was carrying a growing
volume of products to America's heartland and beyond. Census figures
also confirmed the growth in human terms.

Nashville was also a segregated city—with separate and unequal
neighborhoods, workplaces, and schools, and great gulfs in the economic
circumstances of families across the county. The inequality was mani-
fested in the dual systems of elementary and secondary education and
so much else that shaped disparate lifestyles across Davidson County
and its growing suburbs. Substandard housing, especially near the state
capitol grounds, contrasted sharply with the easier habitats in the capital
city's suburbs to the east and west.

Segregation divided the professions, as well as schools and social structures. In 1965, Merritt himself was directly involved—on the pro-inte-
gration side—in the ultimately successful effort to desegregate the white-
only Nashville Bar Association, during his tenure as associate director of
the Metropolitan Government's Department of Law. African American
lawyers had joined the much-smaller Napier-Looby Bar Association,
though its officers and members largely favored integration of the NBA.
Most lawyers in prominent firms kept silent as this issue drew more attention. Seigenthaler's newspaper gave this dispute within the legal profession a full measure of coverage with news and opinion pieces.

In 1965, as the issue was coming to a head, Merritt joined in a debate
held at the Vanderbilt Law School, among other venues. He spoke in
emphatic terms as an advocate for racial integration.

• • •

ANOTHER QUIETER WAY in which Nashville's professional elite organized themselves through the twentieth century was in private dinner and luncheon clubs. These would in most cases meet either monthly or bi-weekly in members' homes. These settings across the city became a distinctively Nashville tradition for both intellectual and racial understanding.

The common practice in these groups was for members to take turns hosting a meal, and for another member to be assigned either to introduce a guest speaker or present an original research paper on a timely topic in a subject of his own choosing (but outside the realm of his day-job). These were prominent men of the city, generally lawyers, doctors, professors, and college presidents. Women were mostly excluded from these discussion groups until the first decades of the twentieth century.

Joseph L. (Jack) May, whose prominent family founded and operated the venerable May Hosiery Mills in Nashville, wrote about this social phenomenon in his 2008 book titled *A Confetti of Papers*.

> Nashville may be unique in this respect: It seems to me that it has an unlikely number of men's intellectual societies of surprising longevity. The Old Oak Club was founded in 1888, and the Shamus Club was founded in 1927. There are other groups: Zodiac, Coffee House, Round Table, Old Goats, and The Gang of Six, to name those that quickly come to mind. Are there parallels in Jacksonville, or Louisville, or any-other-damn-ville? Somehow it does not seem likely.

May told me that he believed a lot of the energy and interest in forming initially and then maintaining these clubs has been the significant concentration in Nashville of so many colleges and universities. Over the years, the succeeding chancellors of Vanderbilt University in their turn and the presidents of Lipscomb, Fisk, and Belmont universities were usually on the membership rosters of one or more of the dinner clubs. Membership has usually been fixed at a maximum number, partly to keep logistics and cost of meals manageable. When a vacancy occurs, because a current member retired or died, a new member would be introduced.

Most of the organizations arose from professional or ethnic communities. **The Shamus Club**, for instance, drew from business leaders and educators from the city's Jewish community. Members of the **Agora**

Assembly included distinguished physicians, lawyers, and professors in the city's African American community. Many of these gentlemen were associated with either Fisk or Meharry Medical College.

The Round Table dates its founding to February 28, 1884. Leaders of the group published a 118-page commemorative membership directory in 1984, taking note of their centennial year. On the title page, it described their purpose as *"A Dining Club of Gentlemen Which Meets Monthly in the City of Nashville, Tennessee."*

The **Agora Assembly**, according to the historian Linda T. Wynn, was established on November 3, 1922. Its stated purpose was to stand as "Watchman on the Wall" with respect to the economic, educational, and political environment of Nashville's African American community. Members included John W. Work II, the founding director of the Fisk Jubilee Singers; Jasper T. Phillips; T. Clay Moore; William N. Sanders; Doctors James B. Singleton Sr. and James B. Singleton Jr. (the Singletons were both dentists); Dr. Thomas Talley, Fisk professor of chemistry and a collector of African-American folk songs; Fisk Dean Alrutheus A. Taylor; the physician and pastor Dr. A. M. Townsend; and Donley H. Turpin, former Dean of Meharry's School of Dentistry.

Over the decades, the lecture topics discussed in these forums ranged widely. Members brought sometimes elaborate, scholarly presentations on the significance of recent scientific discoveries, issues of federal government policy affecting communities—from race relations in America broadly to growth and development in Nashville—and occasionally a presentation of music.

Merritt was a long-time member of the **Old Goats Club** and a regular participant into his later years. The Old Goats was founded in the 1950s by the Vanderbilt Chancellor Harvie Branscomb and businessman Cecil Wray. Later on, the Old Goats membership included Jack May, the author Ridley Wills, Vanderbilt professors Erwin Hargrove and Dean Mark Wait, the historian Walter Durham, the Nashville District Attorney Torry Johnson, Todd Jones, Taylor Wray, Bob McGaw, and the lawyer Bob Walker.

PART IV
COLLEAGUES AT THE COURT

CHAPTER 13

THE SIXTH CIRCUIT

Federal appellate courts were not established in the US Constitution, but by the Congress in 1891. The delegates to the constitutional convention at Philadelphia had disagreed on whether to ordain any inferior courts after establishing the one Supreme Court of the United States. The delegates' choice in the end was to leave that work to the people's elected representatives.

The nation's founding charter thus provided only that, "The judicial power of the United States, shall be vested in one Supreme Court, and in such inferior courts as the Congress may from time to time ordain and establish."

Other tribunals in the federal system came about pursuant to the "First Judiciary Act of 1789" which created a Circuit Court and thirteen District Courts. The district courts were provided with some staff support, but the first Circuit Court was not. Early panels of three judges—two Supreme Court justices plus one district court judge—commenced their circuit-riding duties and must have soon learned hard lessons about the geography of the young country.

Currently in the US system, there are thirteen federal appeals courts. Nationwide there are a total of 94 federal trial courts, organized regionally into a dozen geographical regions, or circuits. Each of these regions has its own Court of Appeals for disputes in cases arising from its region. Also, a "US Court of Appeals for the Federal Circuit" has jurisdiction for reviewing certain kinds of disputes (such as appeals in patent-infringement cases) from anywhere across the nation.

As the US population grew, Congress would periodically realign the early groupings of states to form the official circuit designations. At the outset, in 1801, the Sixth Circuit included two districts in Tennessee, one in Kentucky, and two "territories" that eventually became the modern states of Ohio, Indiana, and Michigan. When statehood came to Ohio (in 1803) and Michigan (in 1837), and the re-sorting of states among the circuits proceeded, the modern Sixth Circuit eventually emerged with Kentucky, Michigan, Ohio, and Tennessee within its jurisdiction.

Justice Ruth Bader Ginsburg, very early in her legal career, had clerked for Judge Richard S. Arnold in the Eighth Circuit. (Arnold and Merritt had met in college at Yale, where they became lifelong friends.) After Arnold's death in 2004, Ginsburg wrote the introduction to his 2009 biography, in which she described the important position of the Court of Appeals (this "other court") in the federal system.

"We study the United States Supreme Court because it has the final word on the very few cases it hears each year," she wrote. "But for ordinary people, and for nearly all civil disputes and criminal prosecutions that end up in the federal court system, another court is far more important. That court—the United States Court of Appeals—consists of nearly two hundred judges spread geographically throughout the United States. While the Supreme Court decides around one hundred cases each year, the judges of the court of appeals decide thousands. The percentage of cases in the federal courts that make it all the way to the Supreme Court is minuscule—less than 1 percent."

• • •

THE FIRST SESSION of the appeals court for the Sixth Circuit was held at Cincinnati on June 16, 1891.

Among other organizational decisions, the court adopted thirty-four rules of procedure and admitted forty-eight attorneys to practice before them. Over the following year, the court's caseload expanded, and so did the number of judges. One of the new members was William Howard Taft of Cincinnati, later the 27th President of the United States (1909–13) and Chief Justice of the Supreme Court (1921–30).

The first woman circuit judge in the US also served here: Judge Florence Ellinwood Allen of Ohio, nominated by President Franklin D. Roosevelt in 1934. She served until her retirement in 1959. Early in the New Deal period, Judge Allen and two district court judges heard the appeal in *Tennessee Electric Power Co. v. Tennessee Valley Authority* in 1937. This was the private utility industry's bold assault on FDR's push for public power, challenging the constitutionality of the TVA Act of 1933. The case would determine the fate of the TVA. The trial, held in Chattanooga, took seven weeks.

Judge Allen wrote the opinion upholding the constitutionality of the TVA, and the Supreme Court affirmed. The agency proceeded with its historic mission to lift the middle South out of the mud, control flooding, and introduce cheap power and a revival of hope to rural Americans across seven states.

• • •

WHEN MERRITT JOINED the Sixth Circuit, in November 1977, replacing the late Judge William E. Miller of Nashville, it was a time when the volume of litigation across America had begun to swell in all the circuit jurisdictions. This was certainly true of the Sixth Circuit, said John Hehman who was the Clerk of the Court in the Sixth Circuit when Merritt took his new seat there.

"It was a nine-judge court back then," Hehman recalls. "They were all males. There was one African American judge there, Wade McCree. It was a very gentlemanly court; Harry Phillips, from Nashville, was the chief judge. Of course, all these other judges were older men. Back then the appointment of a federal judge, it seems to me, was oftentimes somebody in their late 50s or very early 60s who was a prominent lawyer. This was to be the capstone of their career. Judge Merritt, of course, was much younger, so he was distinctive in that regard. I recall that because he was bright, personable, and he was familiar with federal litigation. He had been around judges lots of times."

Colleagues of Merritt's on the court and its staff remember him as cordial, cooperative, and a quick study. This would contribute not only to good relations among the judges but also in his essential interactions with staff members in the routine workings of the court. "Annually, the circuit also had a conference in which the judges, district judges, and the Court of Appeals judges would all assemble at a location and the conference would be attended by invited lawyers, lawyers who were invited by the judges. I think every judge could invite maybe one, maybe sometimes two people. So, Merritt was very familiar with the judges and they with him, as well. But I think because he was very personable and respectful, and he sort of hit the ground running because he was familiar with federal litigation. Judge Merritt quickly fit in."

Hehman remembers Merritt was an early participant in streamlining the court's work. "The caseload was increasing in the '70s. In the appellate court, there are three judges that sit on every case, and I think there was around four hundred cases per panel. That meant that every judge was sitting on about four hundred cases annually. Of course, when you think about a new case coming in, you've got briefs from the parties.

You've got to do some research. You've got perhaps oral arguments. Somebody's got to write a decision. They sit in panels of three, so you've got to collaborate with and persuade your colleagues or be persuaded by them. So, there's a lot behind the scenes going on.

Hehman continued, "The caseload was growing. They no longer could have oral argument in every case. We created some procedures to look more carefully at the cases when they came in. The staff would look at them and say, 'Well, this maybe qualifies for a summary disposition.' We had a separate summary disposition calendar. It was still three judges on each panel. If one judge felt that the case needed to be argued, or a lawyer appointed, there were no questions that it would be done. Judge Merritt was the chair of that committee that looked at alternative ways of combining these calendars and reducing the oral argument sessions."

When Merritt became chief judge of the Sixth Circuit, he was also appointed to the Executive Committee of the Judicial Conference of the United States. Hehman noted that this appointment was by William Rehnquist, the Chief Justice of the United States, and this moved Merritt into the top leadership rank among the entire federal judiciary.

"My understanding from people at the court was that Merritt also was very good about reaching out to staff, picking up a phone, talking to them when he was in Cincinnati. He would always get the senior staff together for a meeting. He would participate in that and wanted to see what their issues and concerns were, and to see how he could help in that."

Hehman was succeeded in the 1980s by Len Green as Clerk of the Court. It was on Green's watch that Merritt was designated Chief Judge of the Sixth Circuit in 1989. (The chief judge serves a seven-year term. Whenever a vacancy occurs, the next in line is the most senior active judge who had not yet reached the age of sixty-four.) At the time Merritt became chief, the court's staff in Cincinnati included several young technicians who were skilled in computer science.

"Judge Merritt had the full seven years of his term as our chief judge and that was the time we had so much development," Green told me. "I'm sure he'd have been the first to tell you himself that he was not on 'the leading edge of technology,' but he was more than willing to allow those who were knowledgeable to see what they could develop, and ultimately that benefited everybody."

Merritt quickly became known in the Cincinnati office for his ease in asking the court's staff for advice on technical matters relating to the administrative flow of information. In his early years, this became helpful as the volume of cases continued to mount.

• • •

MERRITT'S FIRST JUDICIAL offices in Nashville were on the seventh floor of the Estes Kefauver Federal Building, on Broadway in the central city. The spot is on a natural rise in elevation eight blocks west of the Cumberland River, and two blocks east of the Union Station rail hub. The Kefauver Building was then the headquarters of the US District Courts for the Middle District of Tennessee, as well as numerous other federal district offices including the US Attorney and FBI. But even as Merritt was being confirmed in Washington, renovations were beginning at the old Customs House on the corner across Eighth Avenue east of the Kefauver Building, and it would soon become the official home of Merritt's offices and of other Nashville-based judges of the Sixth Circuit.

The Customs House had long been a fixture of Nashville's historic architecture, partly because of its prominent location on Broadway. This striking example of Victorian Gothic architecture also had a notable political pedigree. President Rutherford B. Hayes had originally caused the Customs House to be built at this location, and its genesis was both economic and political as part of his bridge-building efforts with secessionist Tennessee in the period following the Civil War. This stemmed from Hayes's back-room pledge in the contentious 1876 election to pour money into the South for Reconstruction in order to gather the Electoral College votes he needed from the southern delegates who had committed to the Democrat Samuel Tilden. In any case, as a sign of his administration's commitment to sectional reconciliation, Hayes came to Nashville in the first year of his presidency and laid the cornerstone for the city's impressive new Customs House.

• • •

OVER THE FOLLOWING century, this building would have many uses. It became administrative offices of various federal government agencies, including draft boards of the US Selective Service. Eventually the structure required extensive renovation, and the federal government withdrew from its ownership. Having no justifiable need to invest further in its upkeep, the US General Services Administration conveyed the Customs

House to Nashville's municipal government for a token annual rent of one dollar.

The local metropolitan government, during the Fulton administration, issued a request for proposals to identify a suitable developer. An entity calling itself Customs House Associates Ltd., involving the architecture firm Gresham Smith, won the job and entered a long-term lease with the city. By the early 1980s, new tenants included various offices of the federal courts and a law firm. I spoke recently with Gary L. Everton, who had been a young Gresham staff architect at the time, about the splendid civic jewel that re-emerged in 1981 from underneath long decades of coal soot and interior decay.

"We did the overall historic renovation of the Customs House in 1979–80 and then did the tenant build out for the Bankruptcy Courts and the Sixth Circuit chambers in 1980 or 81," Everton recalled. "I remember that it was a running joke with the developers about how ironic it was that the federal government didn't have any use for the building in the early 70's so they sold it to Metro Nashville for one dollar and then the very first paying tenant to move back into the renovated building was the Federal Government! Actually, giving the building to Metro and then Metro putting out an RFP for a developer to renovate it was probably the only thing that saved it from demolition had the GSA kept it. The developer having a long-term lease was able to capture the 20% tax credits for the historic rehab, when either of the government entities would have never been able to find the funding to do it."

The judicial offices at the Customs House today are impressive, with a dramatic nod to Nashville's past. Merritt's own offices on the third floor featured high ceilings and tall windows, including an impressive working law library. These rooms overlook the busy Broadway thoroughfare below and, across the broad street, the corresponding stone façade of Hume-Fogg High School.

CHAPTER 14

SARA

The people who have known Judge Merritt's labyrinthine chambers the best over the years—his children, other judges, at least two generations of young law clerks, the administrative personnel, solicitous lawyers—all of them knew Sara Pettit. For 44 years, she was Merritt's trusted confidential assistant, administrative manager, major-domo of his outer office, and scheduler and keeper of the routines and rules of the judge's shop.

Before you would see Judge Merritt in his offices at the US Customs House, whatever your purpose, it was Sara who would see you first. This gracious Southern woman was there with him over the decades, from the very beginning of his long judgeship in November 1977 to his retirement on June 1 of 2021.

They had met before all this began, as far back as the days of his law partnership at the Gullett Sanford firm in downtown Nashville. After Merritt had departed his office, in 2021 she also quarter-backed the wind-down of things for him at his chambers in both of the stately courthouses in Nashville and Cincinnati.

Sara was uniquely qualified.

She was the only child of Ray and Louise Pettit, who lived in Murfreesboro. There, Sara became a musician, learning to play the piano and alto saxophone, and she joined the high school marching band and concert orchestra. After high school she enrolled at Middle Tennessee State University, where she majored in business education and minored in music.

Sara told me it was at MTSU that she also took a course in business law that "really resonated with me." Considering her options for post-graduate studies, Sara enrolled at the Nashville School of Law, then located downtown near the Tennessee state capitol. On the first night of the first term, her first class was in criminal law, where the instructor was Nashville's District Attorney, Tom Shriver. Another course, on constitutional law, was taught by the Nashville attorney Clay Bailey. "I never dreamed," she observed years later, "how important that course would be in my career."

With her law degree in hand, Sara's first job was as an investigator in a Nashville law firm that represented insurance companies. Then she heard about an opening at another firm in the city, Gullett, Steele, Sanford, Robinson, & Merritt, where Gil Merritt had become a partner (when his appointment ended as the US Attorney for Middle Tennessee). At this point, she had not met Merritt, but she applied for the job. The interview went well. Merritt offered her the job, and she took it. She soon learned of his friendship with the Democrats Jim Sasser, running for US Senate, and also with Jimmy Carter, running for President.

"Judge Merritt mentioned that he might be interested in a federal judgeship someday, if it all turned out," she remembers. "He was so much younger than the other judges, but Judge Harry Phillips was Chief Judge of the Sixth Circuit at this point, and he was from Nashville and originally from Judge Merritt's law firm, so you know that was a good connection. I thought I'd give it a year and see how it went."

By the middle of the first week in November 1976, both Carter and Sasser had won.

• • •

IF YOU TALK with any of Merritt's one-hundred-plus law clerks who served for a year or more in his chambers over parts of five decades, they uniformly will tell you of Sara Pettit with near-reverence and great respect.

Ralph Davis was one the earliest of Merritt's law clerks (1986–87). He remembers it was Sara who contacted him after he applied for a clerkship, replying that the judge wanted to speak with him.

"Sara is a fantastic woman," Davis told me, "and I know Judge Merritt would credit a lot of his success to her tenacity and organization. I hope she feels as good about her career with the judge, as I hope the judge feels about his own, because she's an extended public servant who deserves a lot of recognition for the contribution she made to the court, and to his chambers, and to all of us who've passed through there. The clerks come and go, and Judge Merritt was always clear about this. He was very clear that you should never make him choose between the happiness of a clerk and Sara's happiness, because Sara was going to be there long after you were gone. Which was, honestly, a very important lesson for a young man to learn. And I learned it mostly the easy way… once in a while, the hard way. But I think the world of Sara. She's a treasure."

Virtually every man or woman who clerked in Merritt's chambers, assisting him with research, memoranda, and other prep for appellate court sessions gave a consistent assessment of how the office worked. Even

Leonard Green, who was the Clerk of the Court for the Sixth Circuit for many years, told me, "Sara is a national treasure, as far as I'm concerned."

John Hehman, who was the Clerk of the Court for the Sixth Circuit in the early years of Merritt's judicial service, added, "Judge Merritt was really ably assisted by Sara Pettit. I think you probably have picked this up from others, but Sara is a particularly well-organized person. She's devoted to Judge Merritt. She's very detail-oriented, but she also understands the big picture. She's very respectful, but she's also very respected. She reached out to others when she came on the court in a very personable kind of way. People took to her and people liked her very much."

• • •

IN THE LAST week of July 2021, Sara traveled to Cincinnati once more. She was on a final official duty to the headquarters of the Sixth Circuit, at the Potter Stewart United States Courthouse. Her mission this time was to pack up the last of Merritt's papers for sorting, shipping, and storing. Much of this material would be archived in the court's library. The judge's personal papers would be sent to Nashville.

This would be a bittersweet day. By now, Sara had become the longest-serving administrative manager in the US Sixth Circuit. On this visit, she noticed on her desk that someone had thoughtfully placed an arrangement of white roses, with four bunches of blue hydrangea blooms (blue being her favorite color). And a special reception was held for her and another long-serving court staffer who was nearing retirement, in the court's *en banc* conference room.

The Kentuckian Boyce F. Martin Jr. (1935–2016) had followed Merritt as the circuit's chief, and the current chief was Judge R. Guy Cole of Ohio. To this July reception, Cole came with special words for Sara. He spoke neither from a script nor even notes, but from the heart.

"Sara is just beloved by the whole court family," Judge Cole told me, "so they actually gave her a laptop to stay in touch with everybody. What I am trying to convey is that... I came on the court in January of '96 and Gil was just beginning his last year of being our Chief Judge. It's a seven-year term, so he had served at least six years by this time.

"I remember, in that first six months, being in touch with Chief Judge Merritt and he told me, in a very nice, respectful way, that Sara is in charge of all things involving his chambers—and really, he said, of Chief Judge Merritt's life. And I did find that to be the case. And to this day, her dedication and devotion in the most professional of ways to Gil, was just unmatched. I think she devoted almost all of her professional life to Gil. He was just so active nationally as a judge, but she was the point person. Gil clearly just relied heavily on her for all the detail things—the logistics, the organization of chambers. The clerks knew that they were clerking for Gil, but they knew that the first line of management really was Sara. She got a law degree, but her commitment to Gil was just all-encompassing.

"Without ever breaching decorum, she was the face of Chief Judge Merritt's chambers. She was the person that anyone reaching out to those chambers dealt with initially. She would go above and beyond whatever the immediate request was to get things done. She would make whatever calls needed to be made. Her level of organization was just incredible. I have this image of her as encyclopedic knowledge of every aspect of Judge Merritt's chambers' operation. It's just what any chief judge especially needs, or any judge, anyone who was in that sort of a managerial relationship where you've just got one person handling so many aspects of your professional and personal life.

"She was just so well-liked and respected by the entire court staff at Cincinnati. Whenever Judge Merritt would come to Cincinnati he would try to reach out to different people because we're only there for a week, every seven weeks or so. She just played a big part, I know, in making people feel valued and appreciated, and people who work for the court knew they could go to her with any kind of question.

"I would also say she was discreet," he continued. "She did not breach confidences. A chief judge has a lot of matters that involve confidences, and Sara has had that level of professionalism long before the age of social media and over-sharing of information. When you talked to Sara, you just knew that she was handling whatever the information that you're presenting to her in the most professional and appropriate manner.

"She's just an institution," Judge Cole added. "She's one of a kind with the court and, as wonderful and dedicated as many are, I don't know if there will ever be another person like Sara."

• • •

SARA, LOOKING BACK over the years of her service, told me recently that she believed the work she did for Judge Merritt had value—to him, to his colleagues on the court, and to the cause of justice.

"I have been blessed to have a meaningful career. It has been a privilege to work with Judge Merritt to uphold the rule of law and see that equal justice is done for everyone. I am thankful to have had this opportunity."

CHAPTER 15

THE JUDGES

When Judge Waverly D. Crenshaw Jr. was a child, his family lived in a poor inner-city section of Nashville, in the neighborhood that surrounded the Napier and Sudekem public housing projects, on the city's near southside.

Today, Crenshaw is the chief judge of the US District Courts for middle Tennessee. He is quick to credit many people for inspiring him to attend college and also study the law—his own family and also community leaders like the city councilmen Bob Lillard and Z. Alexander Looby. He also regards Judge Merritt, together with the late Judge John Nixon (another Sasser sponsor and Carter nominee) as having been among his most revered role-models.

"I was Judge Nixon's fourth law clerk," Crenshaw told me. "That was early on in his judicial career, and he and Judge Merritt were close friends. I think Merritt had been helpful and supportive when Judge Nixon was going through his own nomination and confirmation process. They were both from that Southern progressive tradition, like Bill Leech (Tennessee's state attorney general, 1978-84) and others, in terms of the issues that the south was still dealing with, with race. Judge Nixon had been in the civil rights department of the Department of Justice, and Judge Merritt had been US Attorney in Nashville.

"I admired them both, as a young black lawyer who grew up in Nashville," he continued. "They were kind of the shining beam of hope that race relations and racial issues were being taken seriously in the larger community. And that gave a young black boy from south Nashville a lot of hope about what the future would hold—and was certainly instrumental in my belief that the legal profession was a way to address some of the outstanding issues that still remained in our community. We were still going through school desegregation. We were battling with busing. A man named Casey Jenkins was running on a very conservative race-based campaign for mayor, opposing school busing for racial balance, and he almost won. But here I was, in Nashville, working for Judge Nixon as a district judge and frequently seeing Judge Merritt. And that made quite an impact on me in terms of wanting to stay in Nashville and to have a career here."

• • •

JUDGE CISSY DAUGHTREY was an associate justice on the Tennessee Supreme Court when President Clinton elevated her to the Sixth Circuit bench in 1993. Throughout this time, the appeals court's routine remained essentially unchanged. The judges worked principally through three-judge panels, considering the cases assigned to them by the chief judge; the work being administratively coordinated through the central staff of the circuit. They would convene in Cincinnati, working over a three-week period in courtrooms at the Potter Stewart US Courthouse, deliberating in panels and occasionally sitting *en banc* for full court hearings when necessary.

For many years, Merritt would fly himself to Cincinnati and back, piloting his own private aircraft. Once there, the judges, their clerks, and other staff would find lodging at various hotels downtown, usually within walking distance of the courthouse. (Merritt preferred to sleep on a cot he kept in his office. In the mornings, he would shower in a gym facility downstairs.) The entire court would customarily remain in Cincinnati for three weeks. Judges typically would invite their spouses to join them and would meet for dinners in small groups. Because of the heavy workload of cases, they did not usually go home on the weekends.

"I think a lot of the judges became really, really close friends," Daughtrey told me. "They were up there with their wives and each other. That kind of collegiality simply doesn't exist anymore… it's just not the same place at all."

• • •

IN HIS CHILDHOOD, Judge Eric L. Clay attended racially segregated public schools in Durham, North Carolina. He attended college at the University of North Carolina at Chapel Hill, where he was Phi Beta Kappa, headed several student organizations, and he excelled in academics. After his college graduation in 1969, he went north to Yale Law School and afterward worked as a law clerk for the Sixth Circuit Judge Damon Keith in Detroit. After his clerkship, Clay went into private practice in Detroit, joining a new law firm.

Clay was appointed to the bench by President Clinton in 1995, but confirmation did not come until nearly two years later. "As the nomination and confirmation process went along, we got into 1996, and it was getting a little close to the next presidential election. The Republicans, who controlled the Senate at the time, didn't want to call my name up for a floor vote. They obviously were trying to hold the seat open so that they could give it to a Republican in case Clinton might lose the election. Of course, he prevailed. I was renominated and finally confirmed in '97. And Judge Merritt, at that time, was serving as Chief Judge."

They had met before. Clay had been a delegate to the Sixth Circuit's annual judicial conference several times over the years. These are exclusive regional events with distinguished speakers and attendees, usually including the Supreme Court justice for the circuit, as well as all district court and bankruptcy court judges therein, and selected leaders from the private sector. Consequently, the conferences were held at some very nice resort venues—on the level of the Greenbrier Resort at White Sulphur Springs, in West Virginia, and the Grove Park Inn at Asheville, North Carolina—and in other hotel conference centers both within and outside the circuit boundaries. During Merritt's seven years as Chief Judge (1990–1996) these annual conferences were held in Hilton Head, South Carolina; Traverse City, Michigan; Columbus, Ohio; the Grove Park Inn; and Mackinac Island, Michigan.

• • •

The workload for appellate judges also has its own rhythm.

"The Sixth Circuit gets about 5,000 appeals per year, which is an enormous number of appeals," Judge Clay noted. "So, we've got sixteen active judges, which would be all the judges from the four states. And then, on top of that, we've got senior judges, judges that used to be active but have taken senior status. So, we have to take care of all those appeals. Fortunately, we do have resources to assist. I think most of the active judges have four law clerks in their chambers. And then, in addition, to help screen some of these cases, and work up on some of these cases, we have a staff attorney's office to help with some of that work. And then, we also have a motions attorney's office, because, on appeal, lawyers are filing motions. And then, of course, there are staff and supporting entities to assist the judges in the work. But however you look at it, there's a lot of appeals. And the importance of the court of appeals, as a matter of fact, is that most appeals stop at this level."

He said he was impressed over the years with both Merritt's work ethic and his willingness to consider arguments.

"The great thing about Judge Merritt," Clay told me, "is that he was open to actually listening to the arguments presented by the parties, by the litigants that bring up matters before the court. Some judges have an ideological orientation, or a fixed position on various legal issues, that has consequences for the way they view cases and dispose of arguments presented to the court. Over time, that could amount to a fairly rigid perspective on recurring legal issues, or the work that these judges perform over half of the court. Judge Merritt was different from that because I think he's unusually open and open-minded to considering arguments and trying to look at a case in all its aspects, and actually looking at the record of the case. Judge Merritt has been unusually flexible and open-minded, and really trying to get to the truth of the matter."

Clay told me about his own introduction to the Sixth Circuit and the large volume of cases that descended upon him, at his private law firm office, soon after he was confirmed for the court (he was not yet in his new chambers) and how Merritt quickly came to his aid.

"There are only a couple of weeks to get ready to participate in oral argument as a member of the panel of the court. And I mentioned, sort of as an aside, that this was, of course, in the days before we had all this electronic information technology. Now, of course, all of this information comes to us via digital devices, but back then everything was in the form of paper brief. I was rushing to try to prepare for this court session. And I go down to Cincinnati, and I am on a panel with Judge Merritt. I don't know if he did this to alleviate some of the pressure on me, or this is what he routinely would have done. Judge Merritt took upon himself to describe from the bench the factual basis for each case, what the legal issues were in all of the cases, one after the other. And there were something like half a dozen cases that he ruled upon or disposed upon in that fashion, one case after the other. And it was just a brilliant performance. I had never seen anything like that. It was just an impressive statement of the court's position and ruling, orally from the bench. And obviously, he was doing most of this just from memory. And I think the entire courtroom was just terribly impressed to see such a performance. You don't see that level of discourse and ability coming straight from the bench, because some of these cases were quite involved. It was just an incredible performance. So, that really was my first introduction, as a judge, to sort of the quality of judging that Judge Merritt was capable of."

• • •

JUDGE R. GUY COLE OF COLUMBUS, OHIO, joined the circuit in 1996, some two decades after Merritt. He grew up in an African American community near Birmingham, Alabama. The name of the neighborhood was Smithfield, but it became known as "Dynamite Hill" because of bombings that targeted the homes of civil rights activists and others. (Dr. King would sometimes stay in the home of Mr. and Mrs. John Drew, neighbors of the Coles two doors down the street.)

In 1962, Cole's family moved to New Haven, Connecticut, because of the systemic racial discrimination in Birmingham and largely because one of his two brothers was seriously hearing impaired. The Birmingham school system did not have any services, or did not make any services available to him, especially in the segregated school system. "Really it was at the insistence of my mother, not so much my father, who really, I think, would have preferred to stay in Birmingham, in his hometown, that we moved up to New Haven. It was the next year, 1963, when Cynthia Wesley, who lived next door to me, died in the church bombing. We were childhood friends, along with Carol Robertson, one of the other girls in that group of four. That was kind of my Birmingham experience. After that, I went to school in the northeast, and ended up out here in Ohio to work for a law firm, Vorys, Sater, Seymour & Pease." One of Merritt's early law clerks, John Kulewicz, is a partner there now.

Cole left the firm briefly, for a turn as judge of the US Bankruptcy Court, then rejoined the firm "with the intention of staying until I retired." He was forty-one years old. Within six months, he got a phone call from Judge Nathaniel Jones of the Sixth Circuit, saying he was thinking about taking senior status and that he hoped Cole would be open to an appointment to the circuit bench.

"Several months later," he remembers, "I'm working at my desk in the law firm, and I get a call from the receptionist that there are two judges who are in the lobby who'd like to see me."

COLE: Do you know who they are?
SECRETARY: One identified himself as Judge Nathaniel Jones.
COLE: Okay, I'll hurry right down.

When Cole got off the elevator, he saw Judge Jones, and he instantly recognized the man next to him. "I think that's the first time I'd met Judge Merritt. I was totally surprised. Gil was the chief judge of the circuit at that point. They asked if we could find a place to talk, and I found an empty conference room, and we went in and talked. Essentially Nate had enlisted Gil to travel up to Columbus from Cincinnati—a two-hour drive—to help convince me to be a candidate for Judge Jones's position.

"Gil was never one to be shy in those situations, or a wallflower, or to sit back and not say much. I do recall him participating actively in the discussion, to the effect that he had past contact with the Clinton administration, and knew the President, thought that the President would view my candidacy favorably. I don't think he had talked to President Clinton at that point. I don't know if he ever did."

In any event Cole agreed, gratefully. Clinton nominated him in June 1995. He was confirmed by the Senate in late December and sworn in by Judge Jones on January 2. In 2014, Cole himself rose to the position of chief judge of the Sixth Circuit.

• • •

IN NOVEMBER 2017, on the occasion of Merritt's 40th anniversary on the court, Judge Cole wrote him a letter reflecting on what judges do and the importance of the Nashvillian's example.

> It seems like yesterday that I joined the court in 1996 during your tenure as Chief Judge. I recall the esteem in which your fellow judges held you for your selfless dedication to the Court and the public it serves. That commitment to the public good has been a common thread throughout your career. You honorably served your community as city attorney, as United States Attorney in Nashville, and as a member of the faculty of Vanderbilt Law School.
>
> As I perform my responsibilities as Chief Judge, I am often inspired by your leadership as Chief Judge. You always placed the Court above the interests of any one judge or group of judges. You adhered to constitutional principles, the rule of law, and ethical considerations over any ideological or philosophical position advanced by any judge or judges.
>
> So, on the celebration of your 40th anniversary on the

Court, I applaud your staunch commitment to the Constitution, your leadership of the Court as Chief Judge, and your devotion to your native city of Nashville.

• • •

JUDGE JANE BRANSTETTER Stranch joined the court in 2010, nominated by President Barack Obama. She was one of Merritt's younger colleagues on the court, but her family had possibly the longest professional relationship with Gil Merritt.

"She was the daughter of one of our greatest lawyers," Merritt observed, paying respects to the late Cecil Branstetter, Jane's father. "Mr. Cecil" was a prominent Nashville attorney with a long career in labor law. He was also as a member of Nashville's original Metropolitan Charter Commission. She noted that the two men had much in common, principally a "hopefulness about the future."

"Gil was born to lead," she told me. "It is in his nature. And a court is fortunate to have someone with those capacities. We haven't always had that. You've got to have somebody who has a practical understanding of how to run a meeting, how to move issues forward, how to reach consensus. And those are skills, but they're also a little bit akin to who you are and your nature.

"Gil's nature was perfectly suited to lead, and he was a very good leader. He understood relationships, he understood authority. He was not apologetic about his positions. He was good. He understood how large entities are structured. He understood how you get things done. It doesn't do you any good to have a good idea, if you have no understanding of the system that's necessary to either accept it or then implement it. I think his nature was such and his upbringing was such and his comfort with himself was such that he was able to lead. He went to Castle Heights. I'm not a fan of military academies, just to be honest. But they inculcate an understanding of order and rank and relationships within ranks and how organizations operate. So that in some ways, I think, became second nature to him that then enabled him to accomplish things. And it also enabled him to know how to function within a system. Don't get me wrong, you've got to have people who challenge a system, you got to have people who attack a system, but you also have to have people who defend it. If we are only one or the other, we all lose.

"I think Gil was politically oriented enough to know that change was needed and to be willing, what is it they say? How I'm trying to think of the question, how do you love people? How do you take care of people? It's that you want the best for them, and you're willing to be used to get it. I think Gil was on a different road. I think he had both the background and the history and the self-confidence to make that difference. We are fortunate when we have a leader like that. We've seen of late, frankly, what happens when you have a leader that does not have that vision. It's very, very dangerous. Or any vision, except for self. And for us to accept that is an attack on democracy. It's an attack on the rule of law. It's an attack on the justice system. I just think Gil was a fine man. He had a little bit of the Renaissance person in him: broad interests, broad ideas, broad goals. I think we are becoming narrower as a society. The more you narrow, either the group you run with or the ideas you lose, the fewer options you have. Gil was a guy that did not have to be narrow. He could live with the tension between all those ideas and chart a path that was a way to go forward. I think he had both government and community at heart."

• • •

MERRITT WAS RESPECTFUL of the court's traditions and protocols but was never a stickler personally about honorifics.

William P. Morelli, the long-time general counsel at Ingram Industries, remembers an early chat with Merritt at a social function hosted by Martha Ingram. At the time, she was chairman of the board of directors of the privately held company, based in Nashville, and Morelli served as secretary to the board as well as executive vice president of the corporation.

Morelli recalled this brief exchange:

MERRITT: Hello, Bill. I've heard some very good things about you and your work at Ingram.
MORELLI: It's a pleasure to meet you, Your Honor.
MERRITT: Please, call me Gil!
MORELLI: Judge Merritt, there is no way I can bring myself to call you Gil. Your experience and stature and my ingrained training to treat judges with respect—just won't let me do it!

But Merritt insisted. Years later, Morelli told me that his hesitation in that moment wasn't due to a junior attorney's awe of an appellate jurist. "I had over twenty-five years of practice by then."

• • •

NEAR THE END of February 2021, Merritt received a thoughtful letter from Judge Jeffrey Sutton of Columbus, Ohio. In three months, Sutton would succeed Judge Cole as the next chief judge of the Sixth Circuit, the position Merritt himself had held from 1989 until 1996.

In contrast to Merritt, the Kennedy Democrat and Carter nominee, Sutton had been nominated to the court in 2003 by a Republican, President George W. Bush. After receiving his law degree at Ohio State, Sutton had been a young law clerk at the Supreme Court, working first for Justice Scalia and later for Justice Lewis F. Powell. In 2021, Sutton's elevation to chief of the Sixth Circuit was acclaimed by The Federalist Society.

Though they hailed from different political traditions, Sutton's letter to Merritt now captured the regard of one scholarly jurist for another—and of the personal esteem that can transcend politics and ideology and undergird the capacity for working together successfully.

February 25, 2021
Dear Gil,
It is difficult to believe that the inevitable for us all has come for you: a retirement from the Sixth Circuit.

From my first day on the Court, in truth even before that, to today, you have been a wonderful colleague—and now a dear friend. No one on the court was more respected than you were when I arrived. It therefore meant a lot to me when you reached out to me during my difficult confirmation process and encouraged me to hang in there. Once I joined the Court, you became a valued mentor and an indispensable source of insight about the Court and its customs (many of which you helped to create).

When I think of the Court, it is difficult not to think of you. While I missed your tenure as Chief Judge, everyone speaks of it with such high praise. Now that it is almost time for me to become Chief Judge, I know that I will think often of what you would have done during my tenure as Chief. I may not be able to pull off your innate fairness and gentlemanliness, but I certainly am going to try. Already, I frequently invoke your name and ideas when they relate to this or that case or this or that issue.

Here are some things I am going to miss about you as a colleague. Each December, it was a pleasant surprise to get your tasty Christmas gifts. While I am not sure how often I thanked you for them, they were always much appreciated by me, Peggy, and our ravenous children. I will miss being on a panel with you, particularly during oral argument. No one thought harder about a case during argument than you did. Sometimes, indeed, I even thought I could hear your brain working. You were a fierce proponent of oral arguments, and you knew how to get the most out of them. I am going to miss one of your greatest qualities: You never let difficult legal disputes get in the way of relationships. What a wonderful and powerful example. I am going to miss lunches and dinners with you. Some of my favorite experiences on the Court over the last eighteen years have amounted to nothing more than a meal or a drink with you.

That is a lot to miss—too much in fact. While I may not be seeing you in Cincinnati in the near term, I plan on finding a way of getting to Nashville to see you, perhaps in connection with a visit to Vanderbilt or to see my friends Willy Stern and Jack May.

Thank you for your valued friendship and immense service to our shared calling and Court.

Fondly,
Jeff

Chapter 16

The Law Clerks

Over the better part of six decades (1977–2021) Merritt employed an astonishing 117 young men and women to serve as law clerks in his Nashville chambers.

This type of opportunity usually begins with an interview with the judge, sometime between their second and third year of three-year law school experience, and the actual clerkship begins after graduation with the law degree in hand. A clerk's year of service is often called informally "the fourth year of law school" but this is serious on-the-job training, where classrooms and lecture halls are replaced by courtrooms. Typically, the job entails lots of long hours on legal research on real cases affecting human lives.

Clerking for an appellate court judge, whether at the circuit or Supreme Court levels, is an especially elite experience. On the official websites of the law firms they eventually join, young attorneys will often proudly invoke the name the jurist he or she served as a clerk.

A good many of Merritt's young clerks came to his attention through law school referrals or the judicial clerkship vehicles (such as the OSCAR service) that are common to law schools and available online. But a judge will also reach out more directly to a young law student whom he knows, often through family connections or from informal referrals from law schools. This was all true of Merritt in staffing his chambers. His first hire, in 1977, was **Henry Walker**, son of Hugh Walker, a longtime editor at the *Tennessean* newspaper. The last clerk, serving from just after Labor Day 2019 to Merritt's retirement in the spring of 2021, was **F. Dalton Thompson**, grandson of the late US Senator from Tennessee, his namesake Fred D. Thompson.

After their clerkship year, these new lawyers who served in Merritt's office went on to professional posts across the nation and, in some cases, around the world. They became associates in law firms large and small, or professors at elite law schools, or leaders in business, or in government at high-level policy positions. For instance…

- **Nancy-Ann Min DeParle** joined the administration of Tennessee Governor Ned McWherter, as Commissioner of the Department of Human Services, creating the innovative TennCare program that replaced traditional Medicaid, and then joined the administration of President Barack Obama and became an architect of Obamacare.
- **Vijay Tata**, born in India and a Yale grad, became chief counsel in the administration of The World Bank.
- **Lee Breckenridge, Maria O'Brien**, and **Glenn Reynolds** were three who went on to distinguished professorships on the law school faculties of Northeastern University, Boston University, and the University of Tennessee, respectively.

• • •

WHEN YOU ASK any of the former law clerks about their time in Merritt's chambers, they are quick to describe the place as a professional but collaborative, collegial work environment. Uniformly, they commended Merritt's work habits, intellectual rigor, and also his openness to their opinions and other observations about the casework at hand.

Breckenridge remembers Merritt's "special ability to dispense with the trappings of hierarchy in order to engage in far-ranging conversations about the meaning and purpose of legal requirements. He asked our views, challenged our recommendations, and steered us into new lines of inquiry and research. We felt included in the debates and motivated by Judge Merritt's own civic mindedness and commitment to achieving fair outcomes."

"What a modern man he was in some ways," DeParle told me. "He was raising those three kids on his own, and when he came in and he met with us the first week he said, 'Hey, so I want you to know, I'm working from home. So, I'll be in the office a few days a week during these hours, probably in the morning, because the kids are in school. But then I'll be there, and I'm always reachable by phone.'"

She and others described the day-to-day internal process of research and writing, in close collaboration with Merritt. "There were cases where I wrote every single word on the page, and yet I didn't write the opinion, and that's hard to explain," she said. "He would sit with you and talk to you about what he wanted to say. He would tell you, 'Okay, here's what I'm thinking about this case. This is what I believe the law says.'

He would sort of direct you and then you would go and try to draft it. Then it would come back—sometimes heavily, heavily edited—and you'd rewrite it.

"Maybe, at the end, I could honestly say of a given opinion, 'Well, I typed each one of those words.' But that was all—he wrote the opinion. It was his mind, his thinking. I was like a scribe for him."

• • •

Reynolds, who principally teaches constitutional law and administrative law at the University of Tennessee, spoke with me at length about how he found in Merritt not so much a boss as a teacher and mentor.

"I really just learned a lot from him. And that's what I mean when I say he was very much a teacher in that role, which is what you want when you're a law clerk; that's what you really want from your judge. And some judges are that way. And some judges treat you like the hired help. Some judges treat you like you're best friends; they go out drinking with you all the time. And Judge Merritt was more the teacher than either the buddy or the autocrat, and in the long term that's what was great."

• • •

O'Brien, who had been at Yale Law School and had lived mainly in the Northeast US, told me her clerkship with Merritt in Nashville was her first time to live in the South for an extended period. "I thought I would use this time as an opportunity to be in a part of the country that I was not terribly familiar with. It was a wonderful year for me, not only professionally but I loved Nashville when I was there. I don't know if I was Judge Merritt's first black law clerk, but I found Nashville to be friendly and open. Every time I would get lost, somebody would help. Today, Nashville seems frankly a more prosperous place now, more places to shop, new things in the arts.

"I don't think I ever saw Judge Merritt angry, even once. What I appreciated about him was that he was always very honest with us clerks, very candid, always gracious. He hosted dinner at his house. We would talk about the death penalty, women's rights. He was always eager to hear what we thought, as people who were barely twenty-five years old. We talked about the First Amendment, questions relating to freedom of the press, and religious organizations. For us, it was a chance to interact with someone who was very intelligent and who had worked on these issues. By today's standards, he was super-collegial. He would always listen to others politely. In some of the oral arguments, we knew he disagreed, but he would never cut a lawyer off. He treated them with respect in public. I think that kind of behavior is sorely lacking today. He set a standard that I try to emulate."

• • •

RALPH DAVIS, WHO has had a long career in business rather than litigation, said his time as Merritt's clerk "remains the most important year in my professional life, and he's the single most important person in my professional life. He's been a real North Star for me in a lot of respects, professionally.

"He always took an uncommon interest in the futures of the clerks that he had through the office. It's not, 'I'm trying to groom a cult of personality around me,' but much more so, 'I'm interested in who you are, what makes you tick, and what you're trying to do and how I can help with that.' And so that, again, it's just one of the things that when you talk to people about clerking for Judge Merritt, they would tell you upfront, was just different, and I would say is a major reason why I told you what I told you about the experience. I would gladly repeat it today if I could. It was an amazing year for that, among many reasons, but certainly that high on the list."

• • •

MICHAEL J. GERHARDT remembers how he shared an interest in politics with Merritt. During his clerkship year, he remembers making contact with Al Gore's staff, with the judge's help, and afterward joined Gore's first campaign for the US Senate.

"I really had a very strong interest in keeping my feet in the real world," he said. "I didn't have an interest in becoming an Ivy Tower scholar who had no real attachment to the real world. I was more concerned about how law can make a difference. So, Judge Merritt and I would talk about my interest in stuff like that, and he made suggestions for different paths I might consider. I recognized very quickly that the end of our clerkship was going to coincide with the Senate race in Tennessee, and so Judge Merritt mentioned trying to connect with Al Gore's campaign. I met with the Gore people and made arrangements, after clerking for Judge Merritt, to then work for Al Gore's first Senate campaign."

• • •

AMY RAO MOHAN especially remembers her work with Merritt on the *O'Neal v. Bagley* appeal, from a 2013 death penalty conviction, during the final months of her 2012–13 clerkship.

James O'Neal had been convicted in an Ohio court of murdering his wife. In 1993 he was sentenced to death. His conviction at the trial court was affirmed by other Ohio state courts including the Ohio Supreme Court. One of his final appeals to the Sixth Circuit Court of Appeals, was heard in 2013 by a three-judge panel that included Merritt, Judge David McKeague, and Judge Guy Cole.

In law school at the University of Tennessee, Mohan did her best to avoid classes involving criminal law and the death penalty. Also, before she became a lawyer, she had studied broadcast journalism at Northwestern University's Medill School of Journalism and she worked as a reporter for the CBS affiliate station in Nashville from 2004 to 2009, and she had served as an official media witness at the 2006 execution of convicted murderer Sedley Alley. "In my career in news, I had spent a lot of time covering crime and so forth, and I was determined to only practice civil law. I didn't want to deal with anything criminal, and I never took any of those classes in law school. But when I got to my clerkship with Judge Merritt," she told me, "I started thinking about the Alley execution, and my feelings about that type of work changed."

"I really enjoyed working on death penalty cases with Judge Merritt," she said. "He was so thorough and passionate about the death penalty cases. One thing he always would tell us was, 'The law has a heart, too.' And that you can't just look at the words of a statute, but as he would put it—that the law has a heart, as well."

In the O'Neal case, she continued, "It was a man who had what we thought was a very severe intellectual disability. I felt like I became engrossed in that case and almost obsessed with it. When we got to the oral arguments, Judge Merritt and I had really been hopeful that he would have convinced the other two judges on the panel to overturn the death sentence due to the intellectual disability. But it was clear during the argument that we had not. After the three judges deliberated, Judge Merritt called his clerks and we all stood around a speaker phone as he told us that he was going to have to dissent—that the majority on the court had made a decision to affirm the death sentence. (In his lengthy dissent, Merritt wrote, in part, that the other judges 'make short shrift of O'Neal's mental retardation defense.')

"You could just hear in his voice how disappointed he was," Mohan remembered. "And then he said, 'I'm sorry, Amy, I let you down.' I remember I started to cry, and I didn't want him to know I was crying. And I said, 'No, Judge Merritt. You haven't let me down.' I was obviously disappointed in the panel, but not in him. I still remember that, very well. I knew how hard he had fought to convince that panel and I knew it had affected him also. I think he felt he let me down because I was so convinced that we were right and that the panel was going to agree with us. Of course, I was naïve. This was sort of my first rodeo and Judge Merritt had been through this many times before where he's had to dissent and knows that sometimes you just can't convince your colleagues, but I think he knew how invested I was in the case. And he recognized that and was emotional about it, too. He cared deeply about his cases and his clerks."

• • •

JAY HARBISON HAD a generational pedigree in the law before his clerkship year. His grandfather was the late Tennessee Supreme Court Justice William Harbison, and his father Bill Harbison is a prominent lawyer in Nashville. Jay is in private practice now in Nashville at Neal & Harwell.

"I learned pretty quickly that Judge Merritt is far more collaborative and collegial with his clerks than perhaps most other judges," he told me. "We talked every day. And it's funny, because his offices were in this old and very dated labyrinth, and I had a little office and Jeff Sheehan had a little office next to me and Pam Eddy had an office down the hall, but every office had a couple of chairs, including the judge's chair that was always designated for Judge Merritt. And he'd wander in and come sit down in the chair. And then a co-clerk or two would come wander in and sit down, and then we'd just sit around and talk. And we talked about our cases constantly, every day.

"I've learned now that that was a special thing to do, but that's who he was and that was his process. That's how he reaches decisions: You don't just get the cold briefs and read them and then turn out something—you sit around, and you test ideas, and you debate, you talk."

• • •

Both **Jeff Sheehan** and Harbison have sharp memories of sharing the driving with Merritt on their regular commutes to Cincinnati for court sessions.

"The first time we were heading up to Cincinnati, and I think every time after that, the judge liked to start the driving but did not want to finish the driving, so he would pull out of the parking lot and find his way onto the interstate. That first time, he told us that at some point he would want to stop and maybe let one of us drive, and he did. At some point, he pulled straight over on the side of the interstate, hopped out, switched seats with Jay, and off we went."

These hours on the road were "quality time" with the boss, Sheehan recalled. "In chambers you wouldn't always know when you would catch the judge, or when he would need you. He had a tendency to show up when he needed to be there in the morning, which was usually after we were there, and take care of what he needed to take care of, and then to stroll back to check in with the clerks on whatever was on his mind—whether it was a case, or current events, or a story that occurred to him—but in the car you're right there with him. It was good to know that you'd have some time with him. And we'd talk about the cases and talk about what were the issues that were likely to come up, and he'd listen to what we had to say about it. You'd also get just the war stories of his time as a US Attorney and his time as a baby lawyer doing fender-bender cases and dog bites. The thing that always really struck me was that he was equally animated about the joy of practicing what would be now just General Sessions— the small-dollar negligence cases— as he was about the sort of legal details of the kind of big cases that were coming in front of him, the kind of decisions that were coming down from Supreme Court and from elsewhere. He had that deep joy of the practice of law and loved the things that he had learned from doing that work."

Every one of the former clerks I interviewed spoke to Merritt's way of discussing cases with them in order to flesh out his own understanding of issues and applicable law. There are some judges who work very much on the documents and drafts chiefly. "But that was not Judge Merritt's way of interacting with the clerks," Sheehan explained. "Certainly there was a lot of writing. We prepared memos, to give the judge the first glance at things that would be circulated from his chambers to the other judges. Judge Merritt was one of the first people that I talked with on a regular basis who looked past the papers and thought about, 'What are the motivations of the lawyers in this case?' and 'Why is this case happening, and why is it happening in this way, and how did it come down, and what happens when we decide X, Y, or Z?' A lot of those kinds of what-ifs—discussions that aren't necessarily conducive to 'Sit down and write me a memo on it.'"

• • •

DALTON THOMPSON, THE grandson of US Senator Fred Thompson of Tennessee, was Merritt's last law clerk, serving from 2019 to 2021. In our interview, he spoke of the long talks he would have with the judge while traveling by car to Cincinnati and back.

"I would drive, and Judge Merritt would ride," he told me, "and we had some great conversations—about his upbringing, about Nashville and Tennessee history, the influential figures in his life, politics, why he had been a Kennedy Democrat. And about my future, too, and what I wanted to do—and, sometimes, what he thinks I want to do."

• • •

JOHN J. KULEWICZ is now a partner with a large firm in Columbus, Ohio. He has also been a regular participant in the periodic reunions of all the former Merritt clerks. In 2007, Merritt's official portrait by the artist Michael Shane Neal was unveiled at the Potter Stewart Court House in Cincinnati. The chief judge of the Sixth Circuit, Danny J. Boggs, convened the court and recognized Kulewicz, asking him to bring special remarks on behalf of all of Merritt's clerkship alumni to date.

"I was a member of his third class of clerks," he said. "There are now ninety-two of us who have served in that capacity, and we all had the opportunity last month to join Judge Merritt in Nashville, to celebrate His Honor's thirtieth anniversary on the bench." He went on to summarize the comments of several of the clerks, reflecting on their time in Merritt's chambers over the years, relating them to Shane Neal's fine portrait of the judge that would soon grace the Cincinnati courthouse.

"Like the work that the Court is about to receive, our clerkships have painted in each of our minds a portrait of the penetrating intellect and courage of conviction with which Judge Merritt has served," Kulewicz said. "Because this is a judicial career that one hopes is far from over, those traits continue to evolve."

Part V
Close Calls

CHAPTER 17

THE SPORTSMAN

Gilbert Merritt Sr. once said of his teen-aged son and his youthful athleticism, "He's the most competitive man I've ever known." Young Merritt's early enthusiasm for sports would manifest itself in many ways over the rest of his long life.

One of his earliest memories of his father, in fact, was of the afternoons spent pitching a baseball back-and-forth on the lawn of their home in Hermitage, Tennessee. This doubtless helped to prepare the young man for involvement in multiple sports at Castle Heights Military Academy, where he was a member of the football, basketball, and tennis teams. In his later years, he was a regular tennis player and golfer and an avid skier, as well.

• • •

AT THE MERRITT's family home in Franklin, Gil and Louise had a tennis court installed early in their residence there. This quickly became the scene of many matches, both singles and doubles, with family and close friends.

"We were all big tennis players," son Stroud told me. "Even though I was in a lot of ways better than my dad, because I had started earlier, I hardly ever beat him. And he never let me win. He was very competitive in that way. He would get mad at himself when he hit the ball out or whatever. He would say, 'Gil' or shout 'Gilbert' out loud, at himself. John Seigenthaler would do that, too—kind of, 'Come on, John.' They were interesting to watch. They would maybe make each other feel better about it. Earlier on, they would play singles, but Mr. Seigenthaler's knee, or both knees, got bad and playing tennis was too hard on him."

Stroud described his father, on the court, as a good and focused tennis player who loved to analyze strokes. "He seemed to have a new groundbreaking theory for tennis mechanics-related every couple of weeks or months. He loved to analyze the sport, and we watched McEnroe and

Connors and all of that. We were early adopters of this huge metal satellite dish, on the roof of our house, so we could watch a lot of that stuff."

Very soon, there was a regular group of men friends who would gather for tennis at the Merritt home, usually on Sunday mornings. "Gil and I played a lot of tennis together," John Seigenthaler told me. "In 1970, he built a tennis court at the Franklin house, and we played there many times." Other regulars included Dr. John Sergent, Henry Walker, Herb Shayne, David Pollack, and Judge George Paine. They would sometimes meet at the old Richland Country Club, which was near the Sergent's and Paine's homes in the Whitland Avenue neighborhood, but mostly at Merritt's home court.

"Somewhere around 1980," Sergent told me, "I was invited to play in this tennis game that Gil played in every Sunday morning. It got to be just a really fun thing. We'd play on Sunday morning, usually doubles, then have lunch some place. Gil was a ferocious competitor. He was the only person who would argue the line. If he served and it was called out, he would really get mad and, one time, almost walked off the court. He was ready to just say, 'The hell with it. I'm not playing.' I think I was his partner and I agreed with the call. I said, 'Gil, that serve was out.' Then he got mad at me, sulked around, but he was a good tennis player. All these people were pretty good. Herb was remarkable—he was a big, tall, lanky guy and he had been a goalie for the McGill (University) hockey team. He played the net very well."

• • •

PAINE WAS A judge of the US Bankruptcy Court and a close friend of Merritt's, and he told me how they would often find time at judicial conferences to work in a tennis match after-hours. Paine's fellow Bankruptcy Court judge Keith Lundin would often join them for a foursome when another player could be recruited. Paine especially remembers Merritt's competitiveness on the tennis court in one particular match at Asheville, North Carolina.

At the regional circuit conferences, the Supreme Court justice who is assigned to be a liaison with that circuit usually attends. At this Asheville conference, it was Justice Antonin Scalia who attended. This was during the period when Merritt was the chief judge of the Sixth Circuit.

"I have a picture of Justice Scalia with Keith Lundin and me and Gil, when we played a match at our judicial conference in Asheville,"

Paine told me. "Scalia was a very unorthodox tennis player but aggressive. Keith was a very good tennis player. Gil was a good tennis player, and then I was kind of a journeyman. Scalia was an interesting guy. It was fun to be with him. The match was 2–2, and Gil kind of stopped the game and came over to me and said, 'Do you know what the score is?' I said, 'Yeah, it's 2–2.' And Gil said, 'Let's put him away.' He wanted to beat the crap out of Scalia."

Final score: Merritt-Paine won in two sets, 6–2, 6–1.

• • •

GOLF ALSO BECAME another a steady sports interest for Judge Merritt. According to Stroud, his father "loved analyzing golf in the same way." His father "became very good at golf, very quickly. He had played golf as a younger person, so he had the mechanics."

Judge Merritt, like his father before him, was a member at the Belle Meade Country Club in west Nashville. Years later, he became a member at the Golf Club of Tennessee near Kingston Springs, Tennessee, further west of the capital city. He was also invited, by multiple friends including Seigenthaler as well as Lew Conner, to join in an annual golf weekend each August in Naples, Florida. This was a hybrid group of notable Republicans and a few Democrats who would enjoy a long weekend of golf, good food, and fine wine hosted by the businessman Gordon Inman.

Frank Sutherland, the *Tennessean* journalist who became editor after Seigenthaler retired, told me he found the annual Naples weekend outing to be a political "bridge builder" that enhanced friendships across party lines. Beyond the central core group, participants would vary from summer to summer. Former Governor Don Sundquist and Senator Bob Corker occasionally joined in. Other regulars were Lew Conner, Tom Beasley, Robert Echols, John Stamps, Gary Sisco, Tom Ingram, and Charles Overby. Democrats included Seigenthaler, the Washington consultant Jim Free, the healthcare executive Clayton McWhorter, and a few others.

CHAPTER 18

THE WORDSMITH

Judge Merritt was a craftsman of the written word.

He revealed this talent in a multitude of ways: in letters to friends, essays in the journals of America's law schools, and also in speeches and letters and conversation, as much as in the carefully wrought opinions that he crafted and published from his Nashville chambers.

At Yale he had been an English major, and throughout his career he relished the process of choosing the right word, the building of the artful and communicative sentence, so as to convey the best logic to express himself on the law's meaning.

In this aspect, he had had role models in his life of the first rank: His grandmother Maude Merritt had certainly been a wordsmith and was for a time the Poet Laureate of Tennessee. He was formally exposed to the classics in high school, at Castle Heights Military Academy, where in due course he graduated with honors.

At Yale, one of his classmates was Calvin Trillin from Kansas, who was also called "Buddy" by his own parents. "Bud Trillin," Merritt would write later on, "had more than the normal talent of college students as a writer and potential man of letters." (Trillin, in 2012, would receive the James Thurber Prize for American Humor, recognizing his essays in *The New Yorker* among other work.) On the Yale faculty, Merritt was soon under the considerable influence of two Kentuckians, Cleanth Brooks and Robert Penn Warren, brilliant scholars and authors who had trained early in Merritt's hometown, at Vanderbilt, and who were already known for their towering careers in the history of literature and criticism.

Merritt also became a frequent public speaker. These occasions would often call for his remarks to various community and civic audiences, comments during moot court events (often at Vanderbilt) and in his later years to reunions of his law clerks and peers.

Over his long career, Merritt was a prolific writer, especially for law school journals. In these publications, he wrote often on scholarly topics that interested him and engaged his curiosity. His subjects were often on macro trends in the law, as American jurisprudence evolved (though never on the cases at issue before the Sixth Circuit at the time). He contributed articles to the *Ohio State Law Journal*, the Vanderbilt *Reporter*, *The Journal of Appellate Practice and Process*, *University of Cincinnati Law Review*, and the *Georgia Law Review*.

He took great care with the wording of these messages. He worked hard at perfecting these articles to his satisfaction, and they became models of clarity. Usually, they also made only a sparing use of supplemental notes to the main texts. More than one of Merritt's former law clerks, who regularly assisted him with first drafts for his formal opinions, remember the judge's admonition concerning footnotes: "Use them only if you have no other choice."

• • •

His talents as a writer were demonstrated in many forums, but one singular example was his eulogy in 1999 of a special friend and colleague, Judge Richard Sheppard Arnold of the Eighth Circuit. The two had met as young entering freshmen at Yale, in September of 1953, and would be life-long favorites of each other. Merritt wrote this in 1999:

Tribute to the Honorable Richard S. Arnold
Richard Arnold's playing partners are in for a treat when his golf ball arrives at the green. He pulls out a 100-year-old putter with a worn, but finely polished, antique wood shaft. His grandfather, a lawyer in Texarkana, first putted with it at the turn of the century. Richard's father inherited it and played with it for many years. Now it is Richard's. No telling how many balls it has rolled into the cup. In Richard's steady hands, as another fifteen-footer drops in, the old putter seems like a magic wand with a long memory for how a golf ball will run and break.

But I do not intend to dwell on Richard's golf game. The old putter is not only lovingly connected with Richard's family. It is symbolic of a life and mind rooted in history, with an uncanny memory for people, events and literature, legal and otherwise, and with a sense of balance and moderation based on the Golden Mean and a deep understanding of history. When Richard works, or talks or writes, the ball always seems to drop in the cup.

Richard majored in the classics at Yale and retains to this day his talent for Latin and Greek. A deeply spiritual man, his Biblical learning, like his legal learning and his historical understanding, is a product of a remarkable capacity to combine careful, precise analysis with the ability to synthesize diverse knowledge. It was no accident that in scholarship he ranked first in our class at Yale and at Harvard Law School.

His great love for language (he learned Italian in later life by reading the *Divine Comedy*) has given Richard a poetic writing style-plain, spare, elegant. He recently rebutted the view that Justice Brennan, for whom he clerked in 1960, molded the Warren Court through sheer force of personality and "Irish guile." In five expressive sentences he catches the essence of Justice Brennan's role on the Court:

> Personality, no doubt, is important. Judges are human beings. They live in bodies and react on a personal level. But judges do not cast votes simply because their backs are slapped in a particularly engaging way. What Justice Brennan did, he did as a lawyer and as a judge, and his mastery of the English language, of the history of the Constitution, and of the technical aspects of the law played at least as big a part in his success at constructing majorities as the warmth of his personality and manner.

This simple, clear, concise passage expresses a complex idea with a cadence of iambic pentameter typical of Richard's writing.

I knew that there was something very special about Richard 45 years ago, not long after we sat down next to each other at 8:00 A.M. on September 22, 1953, for our first class as freshmen at Yale College. It was a class in beginning French taught five days a week in a little classroom above Yale's main Gothic gate, looking out over the New Haven green. When we struck up a short conversation before class began that morning, I was relieved. I thought, "This boy from Arkansas is probably just as unsophisticated and unprepared for Yale as am I, a farm boy from Tennessee." That idea did not last long. Within two weeks, he and Monsieur

Tofoya, our teacher, were conversing back and forth in French. Within a month, Monsieur Tafoya had put him up in French 20, which required as preparation two good years of high school French. Before the first semester was out, the French Department put Richard into French 30, an advanced class, where they read Beaudelaire, Stendhal, and other great French writers.

But I do not want to dwell on how smart Richard Arnold is. Articles like this one tend to overemphasize a judge's intelligence and learning to the exclusion of qualities of the heart like a sense of justice, diplomacy, thoughtfulness, humor, loyalty, tolerance, and affection for others. There are many smart people, but only one with the complex mind and spirit of Richard Arnold. It is his heart and character that make all who know him love and admire him.

For his many friends and acquaintances, Richard is a hero and a model-on the one hand, highly competitive, with a great capacity for work and achievement, while at the same time, blessed with an enlarged capacity for sympathy and the ability to put himself into the shoes of another. Even though pressed for time, he cannot pass a beggar by or allow a genuine request for aid to go unanswered. One such time I said, "Richard, the guy is probably an alcoholic or a dope addict."

He responded in good humor, "You never know, he may be an angel." In his mind, the guy is just one of God's children in need.

Richard summons what little anger and hostility his nature owns in the face of the bully who takes advantage of the weakness of others. He is instinctively for the underdog and for the liberty and dignity of the little guy. That sentiment runs subtly throughout his opinions, writings and speeches. His legal and moral philosophy emphasizes the importance of the claims of the less-favored class. Achilles' pitiless enforcers, the myrmidons of the law, are not Richard's friends. He takes basic Christian ethics seriously, reflecting the ancient admonition found in Matthew 25:40: "Inasmuch as ye have done it unto the least of these my brethren, ye have done it unto me." Or as his charming and insightful wife, Kay, said to me once in more modern English: "I was lucky enough to marry the man who is always the last to judge and the first to forgive."

When Merritt delivered that eulogy in 1999, he could not know that ten years later Judge Arnold's daughter Janet, then living in Texarkana, would become his law clerk after receiving her own degree at the Georgetown University law school.

• • •

"MY FATHER RAISED me to admire Judge Merritt," Janet Arnold Hart told me in 2022. She was a Merritt law clerk in 1989–90. "He was close to his clerks. It was the best job of my life. It was a fascinating job, and he was wonderful to work for. When I worked for him, he was chief judge and there were four clerks. The library in his chambers was floor-to-ceiling books, a conference table. We'd come in and the judge would talk about cases. It was a fabulous place to work in, because of the judge's response to the clerks. We'd sit around and he'd talk to us. It was a very congenial atmosphere. He made it interesting because he allowed us to express ourselves; he was comfortable hearing from us. He was incredibly smart, but you didn't feel you were in an ivory tower but thinking how a ruling could apply not just to the litigants but to others.

"Judge Merritt was an intrinsically kind and warm person," she added "He never mistreated anyone but always was kind and generous with others. He was one of my favorite people in the world. I am grateful for his career, and for the chance to have worked for him."

On the day Merritt died, Janet wrote this note of condolence to the judge's children:

> In my experience, it's rare to find a judge who is an intellectual, yet who also cares deeply about the impact his rulings have on litigants. Your father certainly was that type of judge.
>
> One of the first cases I worked on for him was an age-discrimination case. The panel he was on ruled in favor of a woman who was fired for what she alleged was her advanced age. The Supreme Court reversed and remanded the case to the Sixth Circuit. Your father assigned the case to me, and we scoured the relevant statute to see if we could come up with another way to possibly rule in favor of this woman. We did, and he convinced the other members of the panel to go along with this somewhat surprising outcome. The other side was livid, as they assumed the Supreme Court had handed them a victory. We were

relieved when they refused to grant certiorari a second time. I was struck by your father's sense of justice in that case. In his view, just because the Supreme Court reversed did not necessarily mean that she wasn't entitled to a ruling in her favor.

I learned so much from your father: how to be a better writer, a better communicator, and how important it was to understand the human beings behind the litigant names. I will forever be grateful that I had the chance to clerk for him.

• • •

THROUGHOUT HIS CAREER on the Sixth Circuit, Merritt showed appreciation for the handiwork of other wordsmiths, too. He often quoted authors he particularly appreciated to demonstrate a point in his court opinions, whether writing for the majority or the minority view. Outside his chambers, he continued to relish the work of other writers. One of them was John Seigenthaler.

In 1991, during his time as chairman of the First Amendment Center housed at Vanderbilt University, Seigenthaler had composed a one-act play. He titled it *The Greater Truth: The Trial of John Peter Zenger* and it dramatized a central story in the pre-revolutionary history of how press freedom evolved in the American colonies. Zenger had launched a newspaper, *The New York Weekly Journal*, in 1733, in which he published letters, articles, and parodies that were highly critical of Governor William Cosby of New York. Cosby, it was said, had "a low tolerance for criticism." Very soon, in 1734, Zenger was arrested on charges of libel. He was acquitted of this charge, but his trial became an early origin story of freedom of the press in the United States.

Seigenthaler's papers at Vanderbilt University's Heard Library contain his drafts for *The Greater Truth*—and his notes indicate he continued to work on his manuscript as late as December 2000. In the late 1990s, there was one public performance of the play at a local theater in Nashville, in a former church building on Charlotte Avenue in West Nashville that now housed the Darkhorse Theatre.

To this premiere, Seigenthaler invited many Nashville friends, including several current and former colleagues from the *Tennessean* newspaper staff. After the performance, in a room adjacent to the main theater space in the old church sanctuary, he gathered several dozen of his newspaper associates and many other friends, including Judge Merritt.

In the general merriment and congratulations, at a designated moment, Seigenthaler asked the judge to offer a toast.

The room grew silent, and all eyes turned to Merritt. Raising his own glass, he asked the gathering to "repeat with me, as if it were our liturgy, the forty-five words of the First Amendment to the US Constitution." He began, and others in the room joined in...

> Congress shall make no law respecting an establishment of religion or prohibiting the free exercise thereof; or abridging the freedom of speech, or of the press; or the right of the people peaceably to assemble, and to petition the Government for a redress of grievances.

The judge said afterward that he knew of "no better words than those to commemorate such an occasion." It was a liturgy—and a belief—that these two men shared intimately, over many years.

• • •

MERRITT WAS ALSO a lover of poetry. He and his wife Louise, in the early years, had enjoyed reading together in the relaxation of quiet evenings at home, sometimes reclining on the floor, often taking turns reading poetry aloud to each other.

Soon after Louise died, in 1973, Gil composed an elaborate poem to her. It replicated the structure and meter of a favorite by John Donne, published in 1633, that they both had enjoyed. Donne called his 36-line rhyme "A Valediction: Forbidding Mourning" addressing it to his wife Anne before he left on a trip to the European continent. (Louise, in her suicide note, had invoked the title of Donne's work.) Merritt titled his own mournful lines to Louise "Looking at a Stained-Glass Window at St. Paul's Church: A Valediction"—the parish church he knew was her special place—where a remarkable stained-glass window is visible above the sanctuary. It features a Madonna of great beauty, standing alone in a field of lilies.

> In this place you loved:
> Your form encased in glass with leaded iron seam
> Encases not the spirit to escape to ease its spell
> Of love and truth and beauty in my waking dream,
> Nor nighttime in its blackness can its light dispel.

Dear Love, you will never part from me,
For in this special private place for us to dwell,
I hear your voice, and there your beauty see,
Touch your hand and kneel to feel your spell.

The mourning sun to rise, your joys teach;
Your hair and face wash clean the morning rain.
Enduring not our rended hearts or out love's breach,
Your breath on its pane makes whole our souls again.

It's but beveled glass up there, I know,
An old window above an altar in a vaulted nave,
For the laity to observe from the pews below,
Exposed to moving earth and wind's decay.

So let us break the casement and melt its said,
Into air and sunlit rays our love refine,
Obvious to limbs and lips command;
Expand our souls; and sense resign.
Now replaced, its framework spans all space,
Recast and molded from your eternal grace.
Recreated in the likeness of your form and face,
Our tears and fears and hurt to soften and displace.

Our library window is just across the street.
There I can always see you from where I sit.
A few steps bring me over to meet you in retreat,
Where I can touch your beauty and unfading wit.
To watch there with you in the fields down below,
Our children, with your cheer and love made to grow.

Chapter 19

Almost Supreme

In March of 1993, barely two months into the Clinton administration, the new 42nd President was confronted with his first vacancy to fill on the Supreme Court of the United States. With a Democrat now in the White House again, Justice Byron R. White, a Kennedy nominee in 1962, announced he would step down. He had served for thirty-one years, through four Republican administrations.

Clinton had been in office only 60 days at this point. When he spoke briefly to White House reporters on the South Lawn prior to departing for Atlanta, he was immediately asked for his early thoughts on prospective nominees. One reporter mentioned the New York Gov. Mario Cuomo, but the President demurred.

PRESIDENT CLINTON: I don't want to get into personalities now. This is Mr. Justice White's day. And as I said, I never will forget sitting in the Supreme Court as a young attorney general and having had him already tell me that the quality of representation by the States (before the Court) was pretty poor. And then I had worked very hard with a lawyer from my State who was making the argument, and he sent me a note, which I still have in my personal files sixteen years later, saying that we were doing better. So that's what I'm going to try to do every day.

REPORTER: Do you have a long list of possible nominees?

PRESIDENT CLINTON: No. The list may get longer; it may get shorter. I did not anticipate having the opportunity to make an appointment at this early stage, so we don't have a big bank of potential nominees. I'll go to work on it tomorrow. I don't want to discuss any individuals at this point. I will do my best to pick a truly outstanding person just as soon as I can.

Suddenly there was much speculation about whom Clinton might consider. When he was governor of Arkansas in the middle 1980s, President Clinton had worked closely with several Democratic governors as fellow members in the National Governors Association (NGA). Other Democrats who were especially close to Clinton among his generation of NGA leaders were the Governors Bruce Babbitt of Arizona and Richard Riley of South Carolina, both of whom were now in Clinton's young cabinet: Babbitt at the Department of the Interior, and Riley at Education. According to contemporary news reports, these were among as many as forty-two names under consideration by the Clinton White House to succeed Justice White at the Supreme Court. This field narrowed substantially over the summer of 1993.

Presidents hope to minimize the prospects for political opposition in the Senate, which must confirm nominees to the high court. Senate rejections of presidential nominees have been rare over the nation's history. But in 1993 recent exceptions were well known at the White House. In 1969, when Justice Abe Fortas (a Johnson appointee) stepped down, President Nixon lost two of his nominees that same year—Clement F. Haynsworth Jr. of South Carolina, and G. Harrold Carswell of Georgia—for their segregationist views. Haynsworth had served for twenty-two years as a judge for the Fourth US Circuit. Carswell was likewise no stranger to federal judicial service, having been a Judge of both the US District Court in Florida and of the Fifth US Circuit court of appeals, nominated by President Eisenhower in 1958.

• • •

OVER THE ENTIRETY of US history, only four Tennesseans have ever been elevated to the Supreme Court of the United States, and technically none since 1965 when President Johnson nominated Fortas, who hailed from Memphis but later resided in Washington.

Not long after Justice White's resignation was announced, many of Merritt's friends who knew his life story including his unblemished career on the Sixth Circuit went to work in their sundry capacities. Merritt, his supporters agreed, had much to commend him. For important starters, he had several influential friends very near to President Clinton. Clearly, he had been very close politically to Tennessee's Senator Sasser, who was now in his third Senate term and the current chairman of the Senate's Budget Committee. (There was even speculation that if the Senate Majority Leader George Mitchell of Maine were to retire in 1994, and if Sasser as expected would win his own re-election to a fourth term in Tennessee, then he might succeed Mitchell as the next Senate Democratic leader.) Merritt's history with Vice President Gore's family was also well-known among the judge's Tennessee friends.

In fact, in Washington parlance Merritt's name was soon on the "short list" for the appointment. While the early attention had focused on Interior Secretary Babbitt, *The New York Times* reported on June 8 that sources at the White House "emphasized that two Federal appeals judges—Steven G. Breyer of the First Circuit and, to a lesser extent, Gilbert S. Merritt of the Sixth—were still in the running to replace Justice Byron R. White."

· · ·

ALONG THE WAY, there were only a handful of possible issues with Merritt, mostly minor. None of them related to his personal character or conduct in office, but of course any claim or allegation could potentially interfere with a clean vetting by the Senate Judiciary Committee on Capitol Hill. In any case, there was soon a stack of positive letters to the White House from fellow judges across the Sixth Circuit, all testifying to Merritt's probity.

One short-lived episode involved Robin Saxon Merritt, his second wife. She was a legislative lobbyist and was affiliated for a time with the Fulton Governmental Group in Nashville. This was a government relations consulting firm founded by the former Nashville Mayor Richard Fulton after he left office in 1987. Merritt had met Robin Saxon in 1991. She was then working as an attorney and lobbyist in the Nashville law firm of Doramus and Trauger, which leased office space on the same floor as Merritt's chambers in the old Customs House. The story, as both told it, was that they met on an elevator as both were departing the third floor and they struck up a brief conversation. Merritt later asked Saxon out to dinner. (He had been widowed for fifteen years by this time. Robin was twenty-seven years his junior.)

At the Fulton Group, her lobbying work had already become a topic of some controversy in both Nashville and Memphis after she was hired to represent the City of Memphis in its dealings with the Tennessee General Assembly. She was asked whether her husband's position on the Sixth Circuit might pose a conflict of interest for his lobbyist wife.

She had this to say in a long profile by Paula Wade, who was the state capitol correspondent for the Memphis *Commercial Appeal*: "I'm sensitive about it," Robin told the reporter, "because I don't want anyone to attribute where I am in my life to the fact that I'm married to Gil Merritt. I guess I'm sensitive to it because I think it's irrelevant. Who I am and where I am probably has more to do with my upbringing and not my husband? Most of the legislators, except for the lawyers, don't know who Gil Merritt is."

In another local dispute, Robin was named by members of the conservative Eagle Forum who complained that she had represented owners of several nude bars along Nashville's Broadway. The Tennessee legislature had enacted a statute to close the bars, and the bar owners hired George Barrett in hopes he might get a court to nullify the new law as unconstitutional. Barrett recruited the Fulton Group including Robin to his team as lobbyists. Eventually the issue reached the Sixth Circuit appellate court, which upheld the invalidation of the Tennessee law. (Judge Merritt had recused himself from this case.) Barrett and Robin Merritt were named in a formal complaint to the state regulatory board in charge of lobbying oversight, but the Fulton firm was ultimately exonerated.

Robin and Gil had married in 1992, the year before Justice White announced his retirement, and Robin now became actively involved with her husband's effort to advance his prospects, hopefully to the point of nomination by the President. "Gil met with Clinton, and with members of the Senate Judiciary Committee," she recalled in our 2021 interview. "I worked on a lot of the background paperwork that was necessary from the White House."

• • •

BUT IT WAS neither of these local skirmishes that ultimately concerned the Clinton White House about Merritt to the point of passing him over for the highest court—all to the lasting frustration of the judge's closest friends and allies in Tennessee. The disconnect was a case that had begun years earlier and a world away—the matter of Ivan Demjanjuk, an aging Cleveland, Ohio, man accused of being "Ivan the Terrible," a cruel Nazi prison guard at the Treblinka concentration camp in Poland. During World War II, more than 850,000 women, men, and children died there.

Two separate three-judge panels of the Sixth US Circuit—one in 1982, the other in 1985—had thrust Demjanjuk's case back into the public eye. The 1982 case affirmed the District Court's judgment revoking his US citizenship. This prompted authorities in Israel to seek his return, leading to his extradition from his home in Ohio to stand trial in Israel. In 1986, an Israeli court convicted Demjanjuk of having played a sadistic role in the Holocaust. That court heard many witnesses who identified Demjanjuk as their tormentor and rejected his defense of mistaken identity. In 1988, Demjajuk was sentenced to death by hanging.

A capital case verdict in Israel is automatically reviewed by the Israeli Supreme Court. In 1991, after much delay during the appeal process, Demjanjuk's lawyers turned over documents from Russian sources that included dozens of interviews with Russians who had also been at Treblinka. This so-called "Federenko File" was accepted into evidence by the Supreme Court of Israel. In 1992, Demjanjuk's case was before the Sixth US Circuit appealing the earlier federal trial court order that deported him to Israel. At this point, a long article in *Vanity Fair* magazine was brought to Merritt's attention. It summarized Demjanjuk's case and indicated strongly that Demjanjuk, now seventy-two years old, had been framed. The writer, Fredric Dannen, wrote, in part:

> One set of documents indicates that, in their zeal to prove that Demjanjuk was Ivan of Treblinka, US government lawyers used false testimony from an ex-Nazi witness. And as far back as 1978, the Justice Department was aware of a gas-chamber operator at Treblinka named 'Marchenko' who fit the profile of Ivan the Terrible, yet amazingly chose not to pursue this lead.

Merritt, by this time, had become the chief judge of the Sixth Circuit, and he now launched a review of Demjanjuk's case in full. He concluded that attorneys inside the US Justice Department had withheld evidence that might have cleared Demjanjuk. There was no reply from the department, and in due course, the Sixth Circuit court's clerk Leonard Green sent a letter to the US Attorney General, inquiring when the Justice Department might issue a report on this new internal investigation of allegations that evidence had been suppressed. "The court appreciates your immediate attention to this request," Green asked. But there was no reply to that request. On May 4, Merritt sent a second letter, which again was ignored.

As part of the Sixth Circuit's investigation, Merritt now asked the federal District Court Judge Thomas A. Wiseman, Jr. (who had been appointed to the district bench by President Carter in 1978) to serve as Special Master to review the case—to determine the facts of the Justice Department's Office of Special Investigations (OSI)—in the Demjanjuk matter and to report back to the court. Judge Wiseman quickly agreed.

Wiseman, who resided in Nashville, died in 2020. His former law clerk Ben Vernia, now in private practice in Washington, DC, told me how this assignment worked as part of the appellate review in *Demjanjuk v. Petrovsky*. "My understanding," Vernia recalled, "was there was a phone call that Judge Merritt placed to Judge Wiseman, saying 'Could you look into this?' Judge Wiseman said, 'Of course.'

"At the time," Vernia continued, "Demjanjuk was on death row in Israel. His legal team was fighting the extradition and the denaturalization piece in the Sixth Circuit. That's what the courts of appeals are set up to do. Special Masters manage things like discovery. Normally a court of appeals would just remand it (to the trial court) but in this case at the court in Cleveland, I think the trial judge had retired by the time it got to us."

Vernia told me that Wiseman established communications with attorneys for OSI at Justice. "We had an early get-to-know-you kind of hearing, where the judge had summoned the officials to Nashville for an in-person hearing. There was not a lot of dispute among the parties about taking witness testimony. He conducted these things in court, on the bench, wearing his robes, as in a district court proceeding. The factual development started in July or August, maybe a month or so before we got everybody together. There were at least four witnesses, all from the Office of Special Investigations. We went to Boston and borrowed a courtroom. Another time, we went to Los Angeles and took testimony from another lawyer formerly with the Justice Department."

On June 30, 1993, the "Special Master Report" was issued. It was exhaustive, running well over 200 hundred pages. Testimony had been taken from many witnesses and scores of documents analyzed. "For the reasons discussed in this Report," Wiseman wrote, "my recommendation to the Court is that the case of *Demjanjuk v. Petrovsky*, et al., be closed, and that no action be taken against any of the government attorneys who prosecuted Mr. Demjanjuk."

In August, the Sixth Circuit vacated the denaturalization and deportation decisions in a bench ruling telling the parties that a writ of habeas corpus would be issued. In November the Sixth Circuit declared that "government attorneys engaged in prosecutorial misconduct by failing to disclose to courts and to detainee (Demjanjuk) exculpatory information in their possession." Subsequently, the Supreme Court of Israel overturned Demjanjuk's conviction in that country.

• • •

NICK McCALL WAS one of Merritt's law clerks during this period. Reared in Franklin, Tennessee, his legal career would later take him to Knoxville where he became a top staff counsel at the Tennessee Valley Authority. McCall remembers:

"The lack of response—any response—after his first letter was sent to the Department of Justice, inquiring about the new facts arising in the Demjanjuk case, preyed on Judge Merritt. While I do not think any of the four clerks knew about his first letter to DOJ, we certainly came to know his concern as the 'radio silence' continued, and he discussed with us what he thought he needed to do next. That germinated into the second letter that he sent, which several of us did see after he sent it. After this second letter failed to elicit any response, the Judge brought the four of us law clerks—Sue Palmer, Alix Coulter, Dan Abrahamson and me—into his thoughts and concerns.

"The DOJ's continued silence really troubled and perplexed him. If the new facts showed conclusively that Ivan Marchenko was the one-and-only 'Ivan the Terrible of Treblinka,' as the facts clearly seemed to do, then Demjanjuk was perhaps about to be wrongly executed by Israel. That Israel seemingly accepted the evidence amassed in the USA and sent to it by OSI and DOJ—evidence which would not have met American legal standards in a court of law—also bothered him enormously. The fact that he, as the chief judge of a federal court of appeals with powers under the Constitution's Article III, was seemingly being ignored by the DOJ also was highly frustrating to him. This also caused him increasingly to wonder aloud to us if DOJ's issues with the case were not simply ones borne of mistakes but, perhaps, from something worse. Did prosecutorial misconduct occur, and was the DOJ's silence stemming from a desire to hide that misconduct from the court of appeals?"

• • •

IN OTHER WORDS, the Demjanjuk case became one in which Chief Judge Merritt did the right thing for the sake of international justice and due process in the US system—in his insistence on the court's role as a check on the federal executive branch—but it would ultimately derail his chances to join the Supreme Court of the United States.

"When Gil was up for the Supreme court," Aubrey Harwell told me, "I had loved the idea of a guy going to Supreme Court who'd been US Attorney here (in Nashville) and a guy on the Sixth Circuit. Gil is very much an academician. I thought he would make a perfect justice. He was incredibly bright, unbelievably good at researching the law—or telling his law clerks what he wants to see and have them research it—and so I was in touch with (Jim) Neal, and Seigenthaler, and Jack May who wanted him on the court. When he wasn't nominated, I was hurt and disappointed, but the hurt was predicated on the fact the Gil was not named to the court for the wrong reasons? What really happened was that he was torpedoed by some people that had an agenda, and I felt that was incredibly wrong. I thought that he ought to be on the court, and if there was a legitimate reason for his not being named, so be it, but people should not use inappropriate opinions and faults that were not valid to keep him off the bench. And that's what happened."

Harwell continued, "To have a guy who's a great lawyer, who's been in the academic world, Vanderbilt Law School, chief prosecutor for the federal government in one of the major places in Tennessee, and in the Sixth Circuit—Gil had it all together. If you had a checklist and you were checking boxes, you checked every box on Gil: the box on integrity, the box on character, the box on ethics, the box on legal research, the box on analysis, the box on life experiences. And I doubt if there are very many people on the court where you could check the number of boxes that you could check for Gil Merritt. What was so irritating to those of us who supported him was that people didn't worry about checking the boxes, they conjured up comments that were negative and critical of him which were unfair and not well-based in fact."

• • •

MERRITT WAS NOT oblivious to what the political implications of his role in *Demjanjuk v. Petrovsky* might become.

Henry Walker, who had been one of the first Merritt law clerks, remembers working after hours together with Mike Moore, another former Merritt clerk, in the judge's chambers compiling information that might be helpful in the confirmation process. Walker was also privy to other conversations in which Merritt sought advice and counsel from Nashville friends about the conclusions he had come to in the Demjanjuk case.

"Gil polled some of his friends—Herb, Seig, Dave Pollock, me—about the decision he was about to make," Walker told me later. "Every one of them said he shouldn't do it, that it could sink his chances for the Supreme Court. Of course, he went ahead with what he thought was right."

• • •

NONETHELESS MERRITT WAS now criticized publicly by several high-profile voices in the US Jewish community. One was the Harvard law professor Alan Dershowitz, who published an opinion column lambasting the Nashville judge for interfering with the rooting out of Nazi murderers. Another was Abraham H. Foxman, chief executive at the Anti-Defamation League in New York City.

McCall, Merritt's former law clerk, told me years later than any suggestion that Merritt was motivated by personal prejudice and anti-Semitism were ridiculous. "I recall Judge Merritt once speaking vividly of his love of and affection for Judaism—not just as a religion or as a form of spiritual quest, but for its pursuit of justice and its intellectual rigor. He even once told Dan and me that if he could do his spiritual life over again, he might have converted to Judaism." Others also rallied to his cause.

Jack May, seven years older than Merritt, was a close friend and fellow Yale graduate, trained as a lawyer, and from a prominent Jewish family in Nashville, the owners of May Hosiery Mills. May rushed to Merritt's defense, as did several others in the Jewish community of the judge's hometown. In late October 1993, May sent a strongly worded letter to Foxman at the ADL headquarters in Manhattan. It was a powerful clarification of facts about Merritt's judicial role and responsibility, and his duty in the Demanjuk case.

Dear Mr. Foxman,

I am a long-time member of ADL. My family has long been involved in Holocaust mitigation. I will yield to no one in my devotion to saving the memory of the Holocaust for the instruction of mankind.

Nonetheless, your position in the Demanjuk matter strikes me as wrong-headed at the very least and at the worst, disgraceful. That the ADL should be on the wrong side of due process and the protection of the individual, strikes me as bizarre.

We do know that a man has served seven plus years on a discredited charge. We do know that he was trained at Trawniki, but we do not know that he volunteered for this service. We suspect that after his training, he was at Sobibor. However, it is not clear that he was involved as a guard of prisoners. If he were a guard his sentence in Israel likely would have been less than the time he actually served on the erroneous charge.

One suspects that this is a bad man with an evil past, but it needs to be proved. To date it has not been done. That the ADL would take a stand that he should be convicted prior to a level of proof commensurate with our judicial system is shameful.

You have been gentler with the Israeli Supreme Court than you have been with the Sixth Circuit. Why is this? Judge Merritt is a friend of long acquaintance. If there was ever a philo-semite, it is Gil Merritt. Locally, he has served ADL well whenever asked, even as chairman of our ADL fund dinner.

Sincerely,
Joseph L. May

"I simply pointed out to the head of the Anti-Defamation League that Gil's action in the Demjanjuk case was not only correct but honorable," May told me later. "Gil had put principle above politics, but Abe Foxman did not help. But certainly, Gil had plenty of Jewish support. Me, for instance."

• • •

THE SUPPORT FROM back home, and from Merritt's friends elsewhere across the nation, would now be to no avail in Washington, DC.

Some who favored Merritt during this process believed that Vice President Al Gore might have done more on Merritt's behalf. I asked Gore about this in 2022. He insisted that he had been an advocate for Merritt in 1993, and that he had placed his name on the initial "long list" of prospective nominees very early in the process.

"I always had a lot of respect for Gil and considered him a good friend," Gore said. "I was strongly in favor of Gil being nominated, but it wasn't my nomination. It was President Clinton's nomination, and I was one of several people who were vetting candidates in 1993. That would've been during the period when that group (in the White House) was hypersensitive to all the stuff they'd been through with the choices for Attorney General and several other potential nominees. And I think they were just sort of hyper-allergic to any kind of controversy. That's my memory of it."

On June 15, 1993, Clinton announced he was nominating Ruth Bader Ginsburg to the high court. By this time, she had served for thirteen years on the US Court of Appeals for the District of Columbia Circuit. She would be only the second woman to serve on the nation's highest court, following Justice Sandra Day O'Connor. Ginsburg was also the first Jew to serve there since Justice Abe Fortas resigned in 1969.

On the White House lawn that sunny summer day, there was no further mention of Merritt nor of Governor Mario Cuomo, nor of the Cabinet secretaries Babbitt and Riley. Nor was there any utterance from President Clinton, of course, to why any of these had been passed over. And there was only official silence in Washington about the Demjanjuk case, then and ever after, and of Merritt's role that had stirred such outrage—and how he had been right.

Looking back, Gore also told me: "I was a strong supporter of Gil's credentials to be an excellent nominee for the Supreme Court. But if you come in second place to Ruth Bader Ginsburg, there's no shame in that."

Chapter 20

Two Months in Baghdad

In 1900, Judge William Howard Taft resigned his seat on the US Sixth Circuit to accept an assignment to head a federal commission to establish civil rule in the Philippines. In a historical sense, this presaged another international assignment that would come the court's way—this time to Judge Gil Merritt—a full century later.

In 2003, when he was sixty-seven, Merritt had recently taken senior status on the Sixth Circuit when he was called on by the International Judicial Relations Committee (an entity Merritt himself had helped to establish). His assignment was to join a thirteen-member delegation to Iraq. There was not much advance notice: the group would leave in five days. The IJRC was part of the Judicial Conference of the United States.

This special duty originated in a request from the US Department of Defense asking the Justice Department to secure the services of three US judges to act as advisors in Iraq on the restoration of Iraq's judicial system. By this time, the Iraqi dictator Saddam Hussein had been deposed by international coalition forces, led by the United States, and his government routed. In the prior period, Hussein had regarded his nation's courts as his own tools of power, with little pretense at judicial independence.

The Judicial Conference of the United States, the administrative arm of the federal judiciary, identified a group of legal experts that included judges, prosecutors, public defenders, and court administrators. They would study the Iraqi court system and recommend how best to re-constitute it for the future. In a practical sense, this was much in line with Merritt's other leadership roles with the US judiciary. At this point in his active career, the Nashville judge had amassed a good deal of experience with international judicial policy issues.

The group departed on May 4, flying by US military aircraft from Fort Bliss, Texas, to Baghdad. They were told this assignment might keep them in Iraq until July 2.

For his part, while he was in-country Merritt interviewed many members of the Iraqi appellate courts, sought to identify new and improved court facilities, and he discussed with many Iraqi judges and lawyers how a constitution-making process should be designed, including how best to conduct the necessary war crimes trials.

• • •

THROUGHOUT THIS TEMPORARY assignment, Merritt penned a series of guest columns that were published back home in Nashville in the *Tennessean* newspaper. On these dispatches, his byline varied (sometimes with his full name, other times simply "By Gil Merritt" which suggested that his friend Seigenthaler may have personally handled the editing duties). These updates were always accompanied by a half-column photo of the judge.

There were practical difficulties in accomplishing the regular dispatches from the devastated former war zone. Electric power outages were common, and on the dark evenings Merritt read his handwritten notes by flashlight. He used the same flashlight to dictate his finished compositions to the person over a generator-powered satellite phone.

The topics he touched on in these columns varied from day to day. They ranged from his observations on the specific tasks of the study team and the challenges that confronted them, to the competence of the postwar US presence in-country, to descriptions of the religion-based anthropology of Iraqi society. In these published reports, Merritt pulled no punches:

May 18, 2003—I spent the day today talking to Iraqi lawyers. They explained in detail how their court system was designed to operate before Saddam, and how he had made a perfectly reasonable judicial system into an instrument of injustice... The system was totally corrupt, marked by bribes and oppression.

May 22, 2003—The living conditions for the people of Baghdad are terrible in the extreme and do not seem to be getting any better. There is no drinkable water and no natural gas for boiling water. There is no electricity so privately owned generators are necessary, and only a very few have them... Our troops were massed on the borders for weeks before the war started, waiting for the signal. We knew there would be widespread looting without a police force. We knew the electrical system would be badly damaged and that our bombs would destroy the telephone system. Why were there not military police and engineers waiting in readiness to fix what we were about to destroy... The answer is that our postwar planning was bad, and the agency of our government now in charge of civil administration here in Iraq, headed by Paul Bremer, seems incapable of effective action.

June 4, 2003—In Iraq, law is tied very closely to religion, just as would be the case in the United States if 95% of the voters were strong fundamentalist Christians.

June 25, 2003—Through an unusual set of circumstances, I have been given documentary evidence of the names and positions of the 600 closest people in Iraq to Saddam Hussain, as well as his ongoing relationship with Osama bin Laden. I am looking at the document as I write this story from my hotel room overlooking the Tigris River in Baghdad. One of the lawyers with whom I have been working for the past five weeks had come to me and asked me whether a list of the 600 people closest to Saddam Hussein would be of any value now to the Americans. I said, yes, of course...

July 4, 2003—The Muslim faith is clearly a strong element of the nationalistic feeling that will stitch the disparate elements of the country together as a unified democratic country under the rule of law.

That June 25 dispatch, mentioning bin Laden, generated some additional news coverage among other American news media, as well as drawing the immediate attention of the US government.

• • •

THE ASSIGNMENT IN Iraq was to run for only 90 days, but it concluded after a couple of months. On Merritt's return to Nashville, he was interviewed by several US newspapers and law-related publications, including the *Tennessee Bar Journal*, and the *Nashville Bar Journal*. (The judge also returned from his assignment with a personal photo collection from his

Iraqi tour.) In May 2004, Merritt was also on a program at Vanderbilt University titled "Reconstruction and Constitution Building in Iraq," along with Professor A. Kevin Reinhart of Dartmouth College.

In the *Tennessee Bar Journal* interview with Barry Kolar, Merritt spoke of his admiration for the many jurists and others he had met in Iraq. "Iraq has a whole cadre of law professors, judges, and lawyers who have constitutional knowledge," he told Kolar. And the drafting of a new national constitution "needs to be done by people who have the knowledge and background to understand the importance of the rule of law and the actual state of governing and not just the politics of it."

The judge was also candid about his own early personal opposition to the US-led coalition invasion of Iraq. But now, he said, he could see a different dimension of that country and its complexity, and that he had come to believe that the US government was right to lead the campaign to oust Hussein.

CHAPTER 21

"The Long and Troubled History"

Judge Eric Clay, one of Merritt's Sixth Circuit colleagues in Detroit, described for me how appeals are handled in capital punishment cases. In doing so, he spoke with great respect for Merritt's very deliberate approach to considering such appeals where the taking of a defendant's life can be the outcome.

"The death penalty cases are not heard on any kind of regular basis," he said. "Once the lawyers have complied with the briefing schedule, and all the briefs are in, the three judges who are assigned randomly on the death penalty cases confer to sign on to an oral argument date and time. But because of the importance of those cases, they are un-connected to any briefing schedule or any court session. If some of the judges are going to be in Cincinnati at the same time, they may try to schedule the death penalty cases for that time. But, sometimes, some or all of the judges have to make a special trip to Cincinnati for these cases."

Judge Clay continued, "The death penalty cases were especially important to Judge Merritt. They had been a focus of his jurisprudence, and he became sort of known as a death penalty case expert over the years. Those cases were very, very important to him and his career."

• • •

MERRITT BELIEVED THAT capital punishment, where a state government can be cleared to end the life of a convicted person, was both intellectually indefensible and personally appalling. Both those thoughts played a part in his examination of multiple appeals that came for review by the Sixth Circuit during the decades he served there. In the last year of his life, he and I discussed this many times. Over his career on the bench, Merritt also did not limit his judgments to the courtroom and the confines of formal appellate cases only. He frequently spoke out in public and professional forums, registering his personal views in informal, unofficial ways. The consistency of his beliefs on the subject was striking.

In particular, the Reverend Joe B. Ingle, pastor to death row prisoners and a long-time advocate against the death penalty, told me, "Merritt was consistently concerned with whether the accused had had quality representation."

• • •

OVER HIS FORTY-PLUS years on the bench, Merritt was involved with hundreds of death penalty cases. Surveying his work over that time, three particular cases stand out as exemplary of his approach to cases of this magnitude, including two that were ultimately concluded in 2006.

HOUSE V. BELL

Paul G. House was convicted in the 1985 murder of Carolyn Muncey in the Luttrell community near Knoxville. She had been beaten, strangled, and possibly raped. House had lived in this vicinity for only a few months, having moved there after serving five years for aggravated sexual assault in Utah, and very quickly he was a prime suspect in Muncey's death. He was charged with first-degree murder, and at trial the jurors took only four hours to convict and sentence him to death.

While House waited on death row, ever maintaining his innocence, his lawyers kept digging. Lab analysis showed that blood found on his shoes was not Muncey's. This new evidence pointed to Muncey's husband, who was arrested and later convicted. Nevertheless, House was not immediately released but remained behind bars, with state prosecutors insisting that he be remanded for a new trial. Merritt pressed his colleagues to clarify House's status. The lawyers for House ultimately appealed to the US Supreme Court where Justice Anthony Kennedy, writing for the majority, declared:

> I would go further and issue the writ of habeas corpus because the prisoner has affirmatively established a free-standing case of actual innocence. This is that rare and extraordinary case where petitioner has provided 'a truly persuasive demonstration of 'actual innocence' that should free the prisoner immediately.

• • •

STATE OF TENNESSEE V. ALLEY

In July 1985, in a Memphis suburb, Sedley Alley was arrested and charged in the stabbing death of Marine Lance Corporal Suzanne Collins. She had been jogging at night outside Millington Naval Air Station, and her brutalized body was discovered the next morning. Clothing that investigators presumed was worn by her assailant was found nearby. Alley, then twenty-nine, lived on the Millington base with his wife. (He had been discharged from the military years earlier for drug and alcohol abuse.)

At one point during his interrogation, Alley signed a confession statement, though he later insisted it was coerced and false. His attorney noted that it did not match the physical evidence in the case. DNA samples were taken at the time but were not considered by prosecutors. In state criminal court, Alley was convicted of the Collins murder and was sentenced to death.

Officials of the Federal Public Defender's office represented Alley on his appeal, together with the attorney Barry Scheck of the Innocence Project. Their case rested on several factors including inconsistencies with case evidence, circumstances surrounding the signed confession, and also that the state declined to use DNA analysis to confirm whether Alley was the killer. (In more recent years, DNA analysis had become more common in law enforcement and had been used to resolve many cases, including those based on false confessions.) I spoke with Henry Martin, the Federal Public Defender for middle Tennessee, and also with his colleagues Kelley Henry and Paul Bottei.

• • •

HENRY MARTIN, BY this time, had known Judge Merritt for many years. After law school, Martin had worked in Nashville at the Barrett law firm. In 1984, Merritt appointed Martin to his Public Defender position. He had also been to Merritt's home once before, for a lunch meeting. Soon after Merritt became the chief judge of the Sixth Circuit, Martin remembers that they discussed Merritt's "concern with how the court had been dealing with capital cases. I think he felt that some judges saw capital habeas cases as an annoyance," Martin told me, "rather than a last chance to protect a person from a possibly wrongful conviction and sentence."

At the Federal Public Defender's office in Nashville, on Martin's office wall, there are framed photos of the labor leader Eugene V. Debs and of Clarence Darrow.

• • •

BY THIS POINT the date for Alley's execution had been set: June 28, 2006. He was to die by lethal injection at midnight. His legal team was now scrambling to save his life and, they hoped, avert an irreversible miscarriage of justice.

In 2005, when Congress passed the "Antiterrorism and Effective Death Penalty Act" federal courts were stripped of much of their power to grant relief in capital cases. "But," Kelley Henry told me, "they left intact one statute that provides some residual jurisdiction to federal circuit court judges, and a single circuit court judge can grant an original application for a writ of habeas corpus. It's filed originally in the court of appeals, and you can address it to any judge you want. And Judge Merritt was in Nashville."

"We had eight lawsuits pending the day that Sedley was to be executed," Henry noted. "Eight lawsuits specific to Sedley Alley—eight different ways we were trying to stop the execution. And we were just shut down, one right after the other. So, the last 'Hail Mary pass' was to ask Judge Merritt to stay the execution, to give us the opportunity to have this original writ explored by him. It was a novel approach. Nobody had done it before."

The procedure was clear, though untested, Henry said, "We felt Judge Merritt would be open to the argument. We didn't have any guarantee that he would grant it at all. But at that point—I think we filed it maybe at 6:00 that night—we had six hours left before our client was going to be executed, so we had to take our best shot." Merritt's record in death penalty cases was well known.

The public defenders coordinated with Merritt's office, as well as the office of the Tennessee Attorney General. At about 9:00 p.m. they heard from Merritt's chambers that he would grant them a hearing. When this information was relayed to the state lawyers, they declined to participate. In other words, the hearing before Judge Merritt would involve only one side. It would also happen at Merritt's home.

• • •

AFTER THE MERRITT children had departed for college, they were no longer living with him in Franklin. The judge had relocated to a new residence near Kingston Springs, Tennessee, just a half-hour drive west from Nashville, on the grounds of the exclusive Golf Club of Tennessee. The clerk's message to the lawyers gave them the address and gate code for access to his residence.

The clock was ticking. The three public defenders loaded into one car. Henry Martin drove.

At about 11:00 p.m., inside the Golf Club compound, the three public defenders were standing at Merritt's front door. They knocked, and in a moment, Merritt appeared at the door and invited them in. Kelley Henry remembers the judge was wearing shorts (his attire reminded her of her golfer husband) but all knew the meeting's serious purpose. The judge pointed to the sofa and invited them to take a seat. The lawyers had brought copies of the Alley case files, as well as a copy of the rules of federal procedure. Paul Bottei was the senior assistant defender who coordinated the capital habeas unit.

"The three of us were seated on a couch," Kelley Henry remembers, "and Judge Merritt was in his chair. He was not annoyed. He was curious. I would say he was intrigued, and everybody just got right about their business. The state by that time had declined the invitation. And we sat down. He had the paperwork out next to him on a side table.

MERRITT: I understand the state has decided not to come and make argument. Is that correct?"
PAUL BOTTEI: That's correct.
MERRITT: All right, counsel, make your argument.

This discussion took just over an hour. Henry Martin remembers that Bottei kicked off the discussion. "He and Merritt had this high-level conversation about the Eighth Amendment for almost an hour and a half, just back and forth. Gil would ask him a question. Paul would give him an answer, and they'd go on for a while, back and forth and back and forth. And it was probably at 10:30 or 11:00 p.m. or so when Judge Merritt said, 'Okay. I'm going to grant your stay.' Then he asked Paul, 'Have you got it ready?' We handed him the stay-order document—staying the execution—and Judge Merritt signed it."

But the stay would not last.

• • •

WHEN WORD OF Merritt's action reached his colleagues on the Sixth Circuit, two other judges also acted quickly. They vacated the stay order, setting it aside, meaning the execution of Sedley Alley would still go forward on that night.

At the state prison in Nashville, correctional officials and Alley's family had already assembled according to the official execution protocols of the State of Tennessee. Alley himself was not yet in the execution room, but designated observers were beginning to gather under tight security. One of these was Amy Rau Mohan, a television news reporter for the CBS affiliate in Nashville. She was there as an official news media observer; these roles are prescribed in the same protocols. (Mohan changed careers after this and became a lawyer. After finishing law school, in fact, she became a law clerk in the chambers of Judge Merritt, serving in 2012–2013.) Later, she also joined the board of directors of Tennesseans for Alternatives to the Death Penalty. The execution of Sedley Alley indeed went forward that night, at approximatively 2:30 A.M.

The DNA analysis was never performed. Alley's daughter April persisted, filing a separate request for the DNA testing be done post-mortem. She believed that such an analysis would exonerate her father. That request was contested by the state and was ultimately denied by a state court.

• • •

On the 30th of July 2018, Merritt wrote a three-page letter to Tennessee's Governor Bill Haslam, a moderate Republican. Haslam had previously been the mayor of Knoxville, and at this point he was nearing the end of his second and final term in the state capitol. His successor would be chosen in three months.

Merritt's letter has never been publicly released nor published until now. It was unusual in several ways.

First, it was uncommon for a federal judge to engage with a state official, let alone the state's governor, on any policy issue outside of a court proceeding. In his letter, Merritt was careful to make clear he was not addressing Haslam about any particular appeal then pending. (But one that was then pending was the capital case of Billy Ray Irick, convicted in the 1985 rape and murder of seven-year-old Paula Dyer in east Tennessee.) Rather, Merritt said that he was writing to convey the broader context of the death penalty in Tennessee and its applicability in the United States.

> Dear Governor Haslam:
> As you contemplate the decisions you now face about whether to grant clemency or to commute the death sentences of Tennessee death-row inmates, I offer some thoughts on the death penalty in light of over forty years on the bench—including the review of many death-penalty cases. I do not, and cannot, offer any legal advice about specific inmates who might seek clemency from

you. But, as you review the cases that come before you, I hope you will view each case through the lens of the long and troubled history of the death penalty in the United States. As Justice Potter Stewart said many years ago, receiving the death penalty is as random as "being struck by lightning." *Furman v. Georgia,* 408 US 238, 310 (1972) (concurring opinion). I attach his brief opinion, one of many in which individual Justices have said that the death penalty violates the Eighth Amendment to the United States Constitution because it is so irrationally administered.

Your decision should be made with the knowledge that most mainstream Christian religions have called for an end to the death penalty, including the Presbyterian Church in which I grew up, and the Episcopal Church that I now attend. Most recently, in 2008, the General Assembly of the Presbyterian Mission approved "A Social Creed for the 21st Century," which includes the call for Christians to work for "(a) system of criminal rehabilitation, based on restorative justice and an end to the death penalty." Pope Francis said as recently as October 2017 that Catholic doctrine forbids the death penalty because it is a "betrayal of the Gospel." All of the Popes since St. John XXII have appealed to governments to grant clemency. Additionally, all of the Western European nations have abolished the death penalty, as have nineteen states and the District of Columbia.

There is a mountain of information available on this subject, including scientific, legal, and religious writings. As you and your legal team review any requests for clemency, I wish to point out a few of the many problematic issues that I have seen arise repeatedly in the cases before me. These issues may or may not have been presented to the jury that convicted the inmate and sentenced him to death. Many critical issues regarding a person's degree of culpability do not arise or are not thoroughly investigated during the trial process, and they are exposed only on appeal in state court or through the federal habeas process, at which point they become more difficult to address. Death-row inmates often have low IQs, and many suffer from mental illness, both of which may make them less culpable for their crimes. Death-row inmates often experienced deplorable childhoods, surrounded by drug and alcohol abuse in the home, and they often suffered physical abuse. After arrest, DNA evidence is often mishandled, or not used even when available, resulting in the conviction of innocent persons. Finally, the judicial system itself results in the uneven application of the death penalty, as Justice Stewart describes, with racial minorities more apt to receive the death penalty, and local prosecutors in one jurisdiction more likely to seek the death penalty than the prosecutor in a neighboring jurisdiction. Also, as in the cases before you, the executive would be administered twenty-five to thirty-five years after the crime occurred...

Of the many death-penalty opinions I have written from Tennessee over the years, as well as other states, I would point out two as good examples of the gross injustices that can arise. In *House v. Bell*, 386 F.3d 668 (6th Cir. 2004) rev'd and remanded, 547 US 518 (2006), it turned out that Mr. House was innocent, and the state dismissed the case after many years of litigation. In *Owens v. Guida*, 549 F.3d 399 (6th Cir. 2008), I dissented from the majority's affirmance of Ms. Owens' death sentence, setting out the facts about the case. Governor Bredesen commuted the death sentence and Ms. Owens was released from prison shortly thereafter.

I have great confidence in the good judgment and basic Christian ethical principles you bring to these complex issues. Under our state constitution, the governor has just as much of a role in deciding what to do in a death-penalty case as the jury. The state constitution vests in the governor final authority to grant clemency for whatever reason the governor thinks appropriate, including the need for our society to extend mercy instead of demanding the "eye-for-an-eye and tooth-for-a-tooth" philosophy found in some places in the Old Testament—a philosophy that the Gospels reject.

To this letter, Merritt attached a copy of Justice Stewart's concurring opinion in that *Furman v. Georgia* case, in which Stewart had declared, in part, in 1972:

The penalty of death differs from all other forms of criminal punishment, not in degree but in kind. It is unique in its total irrevocability. It is unique in its rejection of rehabilitation of the convict as a basic purpose of criminal justice. And it is unique, finally, in its absolute renunciation of all that is embodied in our concept of humanity.

Merritt's letter did not save Billy Irick. Ten days after it was sent, Irick was executed by lethal injection at Tennessee's Riverbend Maximum Security Institution, on the west side of Nashville.

• • •

JANET ARNOLD HART, who clerked for Merritt in 1989–1990, recalled how death penalty cases would be carefully handled when they arrived at Merritt's desk in Nashville.

"I remember the death penalty cases had kept my father awake at night too," she said of the late Richard S. Arnold of the Eighth US Circuit, Merritt's close friend since college. "When Judge Merritt got death penalty cases, those were some of the cases where he would sit down with us (his law clerks) around the library table. He would give us some instructions on what to research, but he always did his work within the letter of the law. The death penalty cases troubled him greatly."

• • •

THE REVEREND STACY Rector, an ordained Presbyterian minister, is also the executive director of Tennesseans for Alternatives to the Death Penalty. In that capacity she has worked on some of Tennessee's highest-profile cases involving capital punishment. In this capacity, she told me, she developed great respect for Merritt's consistent stance on the subject, ranging over dozens of cases that came to the Sixth Circuit for review. She called Merritt "one of my heroes."

"The rule of law is that principle under which all persons and institutions are accountable to laws that are equally enforced and independently adjudicated," she told me. "For a growing number of attorneys and others like me, who have direct contact with the criminal legal system, the evidence is mounting that the system has lost its way. Of particular concern is that the legal system has become too much about protecting the process and not enough about getting to the truth, about seeking finality to the detriment of fundamental fairness. This distortion of the law is utterly unacceptable, which is why Judge Gilbert Merritt is one of my heroes.

She continued, "Judge Merritt not only has a deep respect for the rule of law, but he also has a deep respect for the principles that are foundational to the law—the pursuit of the truth and the law's equal application. As a truth teller and a justice seeker, Judge Merritt always called it as he saw it, even when doing so was not popular or advantageous for him personally. Judge Merritt's adherence to these principles have led him to call out the death penalty system, which continues to be plagued with racism while also targeting the poor, those with mental illness, brain injury, and intellectual disability. And as the death penalty is used as a political tool to win elections or climb the professional ladder, the system deteriorates even more, becoming a procedural mechanism to maintain convictions and death sentences, even when fairness and the truth get in the way."

"Given these distortions, we need voices, particularly those of the judiciary, to call out the system's failures. Otherwise, the system becomes a prop for those in power, not to respect the law but to use it to their benefit. Judge Merritt was such a voice, who throughout his career, pushed our legal system to become more of what it purports to be, a true justice system."

*Congressman Ross Bass, right, was elected to the US Senate in 1964.
Bass won the Democratic primary, then defeated Howard H. Baker Jr.
in the general election. Merritt was his campaign manager.
Photo courtesy of the* Tennessean.

*Louise Fort Merritt, right, also joined in the Bass campaign for US Senate.
Here, she and her sister Tish Fort Hooker make campaign cookies.
Photo courtesy of the Merritt family.*

Amon Carter Evans (wearing sunglasses), publisher of the Nashville
Tennessean *newspaper, joined his editor John L. Seigenthaler and Merritt at a*
Nashville campaign visit by President Lyndon Johnson on Oct. 9, 1964.
The Tennessean *photo by Jimmy Ellis.*

The Nashville attorney Frank A. Woods stands to the left of the candidate in
this 1966 photo with Hooker and campaign volunteers.
Photo courtesy of Charles W. Bone.

Gil Merritt, John Jay Hooker, and John L. Seigenthaler after a tennis match.
Photo courtesy of Judge Merritt.

Gil and Louise Merritt hold the certificate from President Johnson appointing
him US Attorney for Middle Tennessee in 1966. He was sworn in by
US District Judges William E. Miller, left, and Frank Gray.
The Tennessean *photo by J.T. Phillips.*

John Jay Hooker Jr., left, and Gilbert Merritt, right, seated with their wives, Louise Merritt and Tish Hooker at the Iroquois Steeplechase in 1966. The Tennessean *photo by Jimmy Ellis*

The US Attorney James Neal, Nashville's Vice Mayor Atkinson, and Merritt, attend a Hooker campaign event. Nashville Banner *photo by Bob Ray.* Nashville Banner *Archives, Special Collections Division, Nashville Public Library.*

State Democratic Party Chairman Jim Sasser, second from left, checks off final details of the inaugural gala of Gov.-elect Ray Blanton Jan. 17, 1975. Merritt, at this time, was treasurer of the Tennessee Democratic Party. The Tennessean *Photo by Gerald Holly*

Merritt speaks to reporters covering the 1975 race for Congress from Nashville's 5th District. Seated at the far end of the table are candidates Tom Shriver and Clifford Allen, and on the near right is Mike Murphy. This candidate forum was hosted by the Society of Professional Journalists. Nashville Banner *Archives, Special Collections Division, Nashville Public Library.*

Clifford Allen was the winner of Nashville's special election for Congress in 1975. Democratic leaders joined in this "unity" event with the state party chairman Jim Sasser and Nashville's new Mayor Richard Fulton. From left are State Rep. Mike Murphy, Sasser, Allen, Fulton, Tom Shriver, and Merritt. Jack Gunter photo, in Nashville Banner Archives, Special Collections Division, Nashville Public Library.

Merritt greets presidential candidate Jimmy Carter in Nashville in 1976. The two were introduced by Jim Free of Columbia, Tennessee, who became the coordinator of Carter's Tennessee campaign. Photo courtesy of Jim Free.

*At this 1976 fundraiser in Nashville for Carter's presidential campaign,
the candidate donned the iconic Tennessee coonskin cap, made famous
by the late US Senator Estes Kefauver, presented to him by Merritt.
Photo courtesy of the* Tennessean.

*Merritt, flanked by his daughter Louise and son Stroud, chats with Judge
Harry Phillips at Merritt's swearing in as judge of the Sixth US Circuit,
November 18, 1977. Photo in* Nashville Banner *Archives, Special Collections
Division, Nashville Public Library.*

The new Judge Merritt was honored at a going-away luncheon at his old law firm. Standing is Judge Harry Phillips, chief judge of the Sixth US Circuit. Seated are Chancellor Thomas Wardlaw Steele and B.B. Gullett.
Photo courtesy of Allen Lentz.

After a tennis match after-hours at the 1989 Sixth Circuit Judicial Conference, in Lexington, Kentucky, Merritt cools off with US Bankruptcy Court Judge Keith Lundin, Supreme Court Justice Antonin Scalia, and Bankruptcy Court
Judge George Paine. Photo courtesy of George Paine.

Tennessee Governor Ned McWherter, second from right, talks with Merritt and the attorneys Jonathan Harwell, left, and Bill Willis prior to ceremonies at the US Customs House marking Merritt's elevation to Chief Judge of the Sixth US Circuit. The Tennessean *photo by Ricky Rogers*

This was the Merritt family home for many years on Fair Street in Franklin, Tennessee. Photo courtesy of Rick Warwick, Historical Franklin.

*After the death of Louise Fort Merritt in 1973, the Merritt family eventually
resumed their travels, both in the US and in Europe. In this snapshot on a ski
trip are, from left, son Eli, Merritt's mother Angie, daughter Louise Clark,
Judge Merritt, and son Stroud. Photo courtesy of Judge Merritt.*

*Merritt attended the 50th anniversary celebration of the Willis & Knight law
firm in 1996. From left are US District Court Judge Tom Higgins, Bill Willis,
Merritt, Russell Willis, George Barrett, and John Seigenthaler. Photo courtesy
of Seigenthaler Collection, Vanderbilt University Library.*

Merritt in Baghdad, during his assignment by the Judicial Conference of the United States. He was in country for two months, advising on the restructuring the Iraq's judicial system following the ouster of Saddam Hussein.
Photo courtesy of Judge Merritt.

Henry A. Martin, the Federal Public Defender in Nashville, discussing Merritt's career on the appellate bench. On Martin's office wall are vintage photos of Clarence Darrow and Eugene V. Debs. Photo by Keel Hunt.

Justice Steven Breyer delivered the "Cecil Sims Lecture" at Vanderbilt Law School in 2010. From left, Judges Jane Branstetter Stranch, Martha Craig (Cissy) Daughtrey, Breyer, and Merritt. Photo by Rusty Russell, Courtesy of Vanderbilt Law School

Sara Pettit, the judge's long-time administrative manager, joined him at this re-union of law clerks in Nashville. Photo courtesy of Sara Pettit.

The larger group of attendees at a reunion of Merritt law clerks in Nashville. After 44 years on the bench, Merritt employed more than a hundred young men and women in his office. Photo courtesy of Sara Pettit.

Long-time close friends included Delores and John L. Seigenthaler, left. Jane and Dick Eskind were close family friends of Merritt's dating back to the early 1960s. They would travel together and frequently dine out in Nashville. Photo courtesy of Lynn and Jack May.

Other close friends included Herb Shayne and Lynn May, seen here in 1991 at the 60th birthday party for Nashville attorney Harris A. Gilbert. Photo courtesy of Lynn and Jack May.

*Merritt often traveled with Herb and May Shayne together
with Jack and Lynn May. Here, visiting the Russborough House in Ireland in
1995 are May Shayne, Jack May, Merritt, Lynn May and Herb Shayne.
Photo courtesy of Robin Saxon.*

Martha Ingram and Judge Merritt at the 2007 Symphony Ball in Nashville.
Photo courtesy of the Tennessean.

Martha and Gil, at the 2014 Iroquois Steeplechase in Nashville.
Photo courtesy of Martha R. Ingram.

Merritt and his children Eli, Louise and Stroud.
Photo courtesy of Judge Merritt.

Part VI
And the Road Went Ever On

CHAPTER 22

A PROUD DAD

In Judge Merritt's chambers on the third floor of the old Customs House, on a wall above his own desk, hung a large photographic portrait of his three children. The frame occupied a place of honor in a space he revered for many years.

In his retirement, at Merritt's home on the west side of Nashville, the judge kept many bookshelves heavy with photo albums and other personal mementos of his long life and distinguished career. Among these keepsakes were countless snapshots of family trips and celebrations, organized into binders of many types: photos of Louise and the children on Fair Street, of his parents Angie and Gilbert Senior at Stone Hall, and dozens of newspaper clippings, Christmas cards received, and notes and letters from political campaigns and elections over the years.

By far the largest number of these treasures were photos showing the children in the many joyful scenes from their wide-ranging travel with their father: the Merritts in Paris and Jamaica and St. Moritz, Merritts in Aspen and Sun Valley and Delray Beach, and the Merritts together in the Alps. Gil and Louise had enjoyed many travels together as young marrieds. After her death in 1973, these travels also became an essential part of the healing for the four surviving members of the family she had left behind.

Each of the Merritt children—Stroud, Louise, and Eli—was much beloved by their father, especially through his later years. The judge was proud of them and their accomplishments, and grateful for their love and attention. In adulthood, they each came to reside in different parts of the United States. Their careers took Stroud and Eli to opposite coasts, while Louise settled with her own family and career in Nashville.

Stroud graduated at Vanderbilt, then studied law as his father had, and eventually settled near the eastern shore of North Carolina, in the tiny town of Bath on the Pamlico River. On behalf of his family, Stroud took a special interest in the preservation of Stone Hall, which now sits on a hilly segment of the Metro Nashville Greenways above the Stones River. He helped arrange through the Land Trust of Tennessee for the house and grounds to be protected in perpetuity.

In my first meeting with Judge Merritt on this project, sitting in his chambers at the old Customs House, he called Louise "my angel" in deep gratitude for her assistance in his later years. After college at Vanderbilt, Louise received her medical training and the M.D. degree at the Quillen College of Medicine of East Tennessee State University. Her psychiatry training was at The Menninger Clinic for its emphasis on psychoanalysis and pharmacology. Dr. Merritt began her private practice in Nashville, and thus she lived the closest geographically to their father over the following years.

Eli followed in his father's college-bound footsteps to Yale, where he received his B.A. in history and his masters in ethics. He earned his medical degree at Case Western Reserve. Dr. Merritt settled with his family in San Francisco. He has served on the Clinical Faculty in the Stanford University Department of Psychiatry & Behavioral Sciences. He has been president of the San Francisco Psychiatric Society and founded a mental health consulting practice. He is also on the faculty at Vanderbilt where he researches the interface of demagogues and democracy. He is writing a political history of the American Revolution, to be published this year.

• • •

"The Christmas after my mom died," Louise told me, "was when we started going to Aspen. We went every Christmas for three or four years. That's where we learned to ski—the three of us and Dad. Dad was a brave soul. It was just pretty much him, on occasion someone else, but it would pretty much be him taking us on these trips."

She recalled it was at St. Moritz, in Switzerland, where their father became a serious skier. "He and my mother went to St. Moritz just for a trip, and that's really where Dad learned how to ski. Mom had just had her third baby in essentially two and a half years, so she didn't ski, but they had a great time together. Dad had this Swiss ski instructor. He said, 'the only English he knew was, "Get up, get up!"—which I think is a funny story."

Stroud recalled years later how skiing helped introduce him to what might be his life's work. "I developed a love for skiing when I was eight, right after my mom died. We went skiing in Colorado, and I just loved it—took to it. Skiing ended up playing a role in my life because by the time I got to be fourteen, I started to get in trouble—not major trouble, but just be a little wild. We were in Colorado, my dad and I, going up a chairlift when I was maybe sixteen and I told him, 'You know, I wouldn't mind going to school out here in a place like this.' Dad loved to recall that was the first positive thing about school that he had heard me say in a long time. We looked at a couple of schools. We flew out to the Colorado Rocky Mountain School in Carbondale, Colorado, and met the headmaster and admissions person. That was very formative for me… that was a very unique school. Anyway, Dad has always been sort of 'Do what you want, Stroud.' He'd let us have a lot of independence early on—that was a little dangerous, but we made it through."

Stroud and Eli even attended a year of high school abroad, at the American School of Paris. It was Stroud's senior year and Eli's junior. They shared an apartment in the 18th Arrondissement, near Sacre Coeur. The apartment was owned by a friend of Judge Merritt's who was in the US diplomatic service. The boys cooked their own meals and commuted by bus or train to the school campus.

"Dad was thrilled with our excitement, with learning new things and being excited about life, you know? He gave us a lot of freedom. A lot of freedom. And we put it to good use and didn't get into too much trouble or turn out too bad. Lots of museums in Europe, lots of Michelin guides and other books. Dad loves history. He majored in history at Yale, and he loved history and he loved to underline, he would underline the Michelin guides. We would all talk about it and we learned a lot of history. He was an intellectual and he had that intellectual curiosity. That he passed on to me, which is just a love of thinking. I'll sometimes spread myself a little too thin, but I love to learn. I got it from him."

Stroud recalled another trip, in France and Switzerland, when their father and sister Louise (Gil called her "Clark") joined them. Merritt had rented a plane, and Stroud remembers them flying through threatening weather conditions that the French air traffic controllers might have helped them avoid.

"Flying in Switzerland one day, in the Alps, the weather changed pretty rapidly, as it can do in the mountains," he told me. "We were flying in the Alps with a very low ceiling, under the cloud layer—in other words, a ceiling below the mountaintops—so we couldn't go higher. We were 'underwater' so to speak, and we had to fly for quite a way. We were okay, but we could tell Dad was very nervous and he was a fantastic pilot. He never took risks, as in flying a stunt plane. He was meticulous in going through all the protocols, checking everything, going through a checklist, and he was a very good pilot in terms of being very cautious. I always thought he was a really good pilot, and of course he was carrying his children. Later, when we were on the ground, I remember him saying, 'Wow, that was dicey.' But it was the air traffic controllers who got us into that situation—not my dad. We did not have a lot of experiences like that."

• • •

ELI ALSO REMEMBERS his father was "a careful pilot." He noted that his father had stopped flying for several years after his own father had died in the accident at Murfreesboro. "My father's father had died of a plane crash, and my father felt guilty about it." Eli associates that tragedy with his father's choice to transfer from Harvard Law School to the Vanderbilt Law School early in his life. "If his father hadn't died, he almost certainly would have stayed at Harvard, he wouldn't have been in this grief. He also broke up with a girlfriend, another source of grief. He came back to Vanderbilt, and I think in some ways he found some very remarkable surrogate fathers there."

Of the year abroad with his brother, attending high school in Paris, Eli commented: "My father has always been strongly on the side of supporting our autonomy... the parent that supports autonomy and trusts you. I wouldn't, for my life, take anything for that year in Paris. It was the greatest thing in the world. Obviously when you're thrust out in the world like that, you do a lot of growing and you develop a lot of confidence. We did do that. We had an incredible time."

CHAPTER 23

ADVICE TO A NEW DEAN

Kent D. Syverud is the chancellor/president of Syracuse University. Earlier in his distinguished academic career, in 1997, he became the dean of Vanderbilt's law school in Nashville. Over the time of his VU deanship, Syverud recalls how both the VU law school and the university more broadly would shed much of their southern "old ivy" public image while he was there. Vanderbilt emerged from this period with an institutional determination to integrate more fully—socially and programmatically—with the Nashville community. Syverud credits both Judge Merritt and the publisher John Seigenthaler for advice he received from them early on in his deanship to take the Nashville law school forward externally.

Syverud's career and Merritt's had intersected in two ways in the 1990s. Aside from their scores of mutual colleagues in academia and the judiciary, one significant case—*Grutter v. Bollinger*, in which they performed different roles—would come to affect virtually all of American higher education.

He had first joined the VU Law faculty in 1987, teaching courses in complex litigation, insurance law, and civil procedure. Syverud's own law degree was from the University of Michigan, and afterward he clerked for two federal judges: US District Judge Louis F. Oberdorfer and later the Supreme Court Justice Sandra Day O'Conner. Through all this he developed a respect for these wise judges and their young law clerks.

"I first knew of Gil Merritt because one of my classmates in law school had clerked for him," Syverud told me by phone from his chancellor's office at Syracuse. "But those were the only two people I knew in Nashville. So, you know how much Nashville has changed and how breathtaking the change has been since that time. The most breathtaking decade of change in Nashville, really, was 1997 to 2007 and that was my decade there. "When I came, there was still a chewing tobacco factory right near the state capitol. Downtown was a mess. All the talk was about the governor (Ray Blanton, 1975–1979) and how he had gone on the Phil Donahue show. So, when I said, 'I'm leaving Ann Arbor for Nashville,' everybody I knew from anywhere in the country basically said, 'Nashville?' So, it was a leap of faith, and it changed so much in a decade that it was breathtaking. All the planets aligned, Mayor Bill Purcell and Governor Phil Bredesen and business, and everything happened. But Gil was my guide in the first years, in connection to the unique network and the old values Nashville was about but also this progressive vision of what it could be."

He spoke to me frankly about the public posture of Vanderbilt, both the university and its law school, when he first arrived in Nashville. "The law school at Vanderbilt at the time when I arrived was not in great shape. They'd had an unhappy dean, and a chancellor who didn't like the law school and didn't like the dean and the dean didn't like the chancellor. So, it was a pretty dysfunctional place. And Gil played a fairly major role in turning that around and saying how important Vanderbilt Law School was to Vanderbilt University."

"Gil was in many ways as close to the 'establishment' in Nashville as you can imagine, with a long family history and position. He was able to be a unique idiosyncratic person, but everybody viewed him as one of the insiders. And yet, even in my first conversation with him when I got there, he had this vision for what Nashville could be that was both progressive and thriving—and 'not Atlanta.' He wanted it to be Nashville, and uniquely Nashville, but he thought Vanderbilt could be so much more than what it was. It was a sleepy Southern school that seemed to turn its back on a lot of people. He didn't say the 'Harvard of the South', but he thought it could be one of the best institutions in the world. And he thought the law school could be a key part of that and something that the rest of the university was proud to have, rather than an appendix. And, of course, he was right—both about Nashville and about the law school and about Vanderbilt. It's breathtaking to me also how far Vanderbilt has come as a university, and I do think that a significant part of that vision was Gil's. Now, he would advance that vision in the most humorous, polite way at dinner parties, on the golf course, in adopting whoever came to town, including a New York lawyer. That would be me, right? But he advanced it, and it was deeply engaging, and it just had a lot of effect on a lot of people."

Part of this, Syverud remembers, was Merritt's insistence on the need to build institutional bridges locally with two historically Black universities in town: Fisk University and Tennessee State University. "One of the things Gil pushed heavily on me and us was, he said, 'Nobody from

Vanderbilt has set foot on the Fisk campus in thirty years, or on the TSU campus. Get out of your damned office. Go over there and introduce yourself to people.' And it was a whole bunch of very concrete steps he recommended. Another, he told me I had to become a member of the Tennessee Bar, and I said, 'I'd be glad to do that, it takes a really long time to transfer your law license, and you have to document every place you've ever lived, and you have to get these references from fourteen people. I'm sure I'll be able to become a member of the bar of Tennessee next year.' A week later, he had me standing in front of the Tennessee Supreme Court, being sworn in."

He continued, "So I sat around occasionally with John Seigenthaler and Gil and, mostly, they told me how Nashville worked. What they said was that they love Vanderbilt Law School, that it should be a gem of the university and the university should be a gem of the rebirth of Nashville, and that they would like to see that happen. And they thought it was possible given that the planets were coming into alignment in terms of governance in Davidson County, in the university leadership, in the local Bar, and in the press. They wanted Vanderbilt to aim to be more than a strong regional private school for the south. They wanted it to be a national leader and they thought the law school could play a significant role in helping that happen. And that would require a major enrollment challenge in Vanderbilt, at the time it was losing many undergraduate students after the first year, and they were mostly women who didn't get pledged to the sorority of their choice. There were almost no Jewish students at Vanderbilt, and there were relatively few black students except in the law school. They were suggesting that the leadership in the region could be very helpful to the law school in recruiting great faculty and students, but the law school could be really helpful to making the university one of the great privates.

"I recall John saying, 'How come Atlanta has Emory University, and Vanderbilt doesn't play that role in Nashville.' Today in 2021, Vanderbilt has, in my humble opinion, blown past Emory in almost every respect. And that's despite Emory being in Atlanta, in such a bigger community and a media market and everything else. That's what they said."

• • •

THE *GRUTTER* CASE, which originated in a college admissions case at the University of Michigan, became a landmark for the concept of giving racial preferences in university admissions decisions. Syverud presented expert testimony during his time at Vanderbilt, through the years the case was appealed to the Sixth Circuit, and finally to the Supreme Court which ruled in 2003.

The trial court had rejected the Michigan law school's consideration of race and ethnicity in admissions decisions, saying they violated the Equal Protection Clause of the Fourteenth Amendment and Title VI of the federal Civil Rights Act. The circuit court reversed, though the judges divided sharply, the majority saying the school's policy served a compelling interest in achieving a diverse student body. The Supreme Court, with strong opinions registered in both concurrences and dissenting opinions, affirmed the Sixth Circuit ruling 5–4.

"I worked on the *Grutter* case from the time when the student applied to law school at Michigan to when Justice O'Connor handed down the opinion for the Supreme Court. I knew everybody at every level. I testified in the trial, filed reports on appeal. I was an *amicus* in the Supreme Court opinion. Justice O'Connor and I talked about it along the way. I can't believe the Supreme Court isn't going to go in a fairly different direction in the next five to six years." In his "expert opinion" statement, Syverud had asserted this:

> I have come to believe that all law students receive an immeasurably better legal education, and become immeasurably better lawyers, in law schools and law school classes where the student body is racially heterogeneous. It has been my experience from many conversations over the years that the vast majority of committed law teachers agree. When my students reflect on their law school experience, whether Black or White, Asian or Hispanic, conservative or liberal, they also often volunteer this conclusion. I now view this agreement as indicating that those people most directly involved in the law school classroom can see the difference that racial heterogeneity makes in legal education. I have many reasons for now believing that considerations of race in law school admissions are particularly vital to providing the best possible legal education to training the best possible lawyers.

"The Sixth Circuit had fractured very severely," Syverud remembers. "It was the most challenging circuit in terms of polarization at the time. It seemed to most of us in law, that it was the worst polarization that you could imagine in a court. It was uncivil. It was due to some recent appointees. I won't say any more than that, but it wasn't pleasant. And ultimately the Supreme court took the case without the Sixth Circuit issuing an opinion. Which is very unusual, the Supreme Court took the case before the Sixth Circuit decided it. And that was because the opinion was delayed so long by the battles among the judges in the Sixth Circuit. Judge Cissy Daughtrey (a Clinton appointee) played a fairly significant role on one side, and Judge Danny Boggs (a Reagan appointee) was on the other. I can't say more than that, other than nevertheless, the record was preserved well, and it was teed up well to the Supreme Court and unexpectedly Justice O'Conner wrote the majority opinion, affirming the law school's holistic approach."

"And that's why we have consideration of race in college admissions today, as controversial as it still is," Syverud observed in our 2021 interview. "It ended with a famous sentence that said this was important to rectify previous wrongs, but that it should be over within twenty-five years. Since that was 2003, twenty-five years would be 2028, or seven years from now. And so now there are multiple cases pending around the country, most notably against Harvard, by various Asian American groups, challenging affirmative action. So, it will probably be back up before the Supreme Court in the next year or two."

CHAPTER 24

MARTHA AND GIL

Travel has always been a part of the Merritt family story. All the generations, from the judge's early forebears who came by flatboat to the unsettled Nashville region in the eighteenth century, have had an essential measure of adventure and wanderlust. It was much a part of Judge Merritt's story from childhood on through his adult years, and in turn it has figured prominently in the lives of his children and grandchildren to the present day.

In his own generation, Merritt liked to take his own family with him on vacation trips, and they traveled together to far-flung destinations both domestic and overseas. Sometimes these excursions were to places in Ireland and Scotland, and many trips to Aspen in Colorado and Delray Beach in Florida. Merritt also enjoyed traveling with close couple friends, most often Jack and Lynn May, Herb and May Shayne, and John and Delores Seigenthaler. And this fondness for travel eventually extended to a special friend, one who came into his life much later: Martha Rivers Ingram.

Martha told me that she and Gil met after his marriage to Robin Saxon had ended, in 2006. It is possible Martha and Merritt had been acquainted earlier, though distantly, through the sundry business and social connections of the Hooker and Ingram families. Henry Hooker (brother of John Jay and Teenie) was the husband of Alice Ingram, sister of Martha's husband Bronson. Those two families supported some of the same charitable causes, and Bronson also became one of the early investors in the Hooker brothers' short-lived "Minnie Pearl's Fried Chicken" franchising venture. Bronson (who died in 1995) had taken his profit early, before the company collapsed in 1970, and with the proceeds built the new swimming pool Martha had wanted at their fashionable Hillwood area home on the west side of Nashville. Ever after, Martha called it "our Minnie Pearl pool."

Martha meanwhile had long been deeply involved with her personal advocacy and philanthropy for the performing arts in Nashville. Born and reared in Charleston, South Carolina, she regularly vacationed there, but she and Bronson had lived in Nashville since 1961 when the Ingram family businesses began to grow, and she soon became the city's preeminent patron of the performing arts. Between 1972 and 1980, she was the leading promoter of a new Tennessee Performing Arts Center in downtown Nashville. In 2002, she spearheaded the drive to build a new concert hall home for the Nashville Symphony Orchestra that opened with a gala event in September 2006. It was to that festive event, that Martha invited Gil to be her solo guest at one of the Ingram banquet tables.

• • •

MARTHA AND GIL actually had much in common.

Each of their childhoods respectively had unfolded in circumstances of family wealth. In Charleston, Martha's parents—John M. Rivers Jr. and Martha Robinson Rivers—were the owners of WCSC, Inc., which operated AM and FM radio stations there, as well as the city's first television station. One manifestation of their family wealth was that Martha and Gil both matriculated at elite private colleges in the northeast, Martha at Vassar, Gil at Yale. They also were contemporaries; their birthdates just six months apart.

She told me about their first proper date.

"Our first date was really quite amazing," she said. "It was in January by the time Gil was fully divorced, and he asked me if I'd have dinner with him. I said, 'Well, why don't we just have dinner at my house? We've never been out together—let's just do it quietly in the kitchen? I have a big fireplace there, and I'll have dinner left for us, and we'll just have a nice chat there.'

"So, he arrived, as planned, and I sort of put out my hand to shake his hand. Instead, I found myself in a big embrace and big kiss I was not expecting. So, I was a bit flustered, but I said, 'All right, now let's go to the kitchen.' The kitchen of the Ingram home had a large fireplace that Martha was accustomed to using. "We go light the fire. What I didn't know was while I'd been out of town, my helpers had closed the flue on the big fireplace. So, you can imagine, the fire started, and all of a sudden, the room was filled with smoke, and the smoke alarm went off. And the amazing thing to me was, as I started opening doors and the windows to let the smoke out, Gil meanwhile reached into the fire and just pushed the vents open. But by then the fire truck was in the driveway. And that was our first date."

She says the judge made a good impression that evening. She continued, "We got acquainted, all right. But I must tell you, I was quite impressed at his cool—putting his hands into the flames like that. Fortunately, he didn't catch on fire, but anyhow it was a memorable moment, shall we say. Fortunately, things calmed down after that. Our dates were more normal after that one."

In the months that followed the "fire in the kitchen," Gil and Martha became a regular item, dating often, and appearing more and more in her social circles both in Nashville and out-of-town. Newspaper photos showed them attending some of Nashville's highest-profile charitable functions, including the Symphony Ball, the Iroquois Steeplechase benefiting the Monroe Carell Children's Hospital, and the Swan Ball that supports the Cheekwood Estate and Gardens. The two made a glamorous couple in these venues, as their photos in the society pages revealed to a broader hometown public. Gil also accompanied Martha on visits to her own hometown, where she introduced him to friends at the Spoleto Festival USA, a long-running cultural interest of hers in Charleston.

They enjoyed tennis and golf together. It was also during this period that Merritt relocated from his residence on Fair Street in Franklin to a home near Kingston Springs, at The Golf Club of Tennessee. In the 1980s, Martha's late husband Bronson had been one of the co-founders and the first board chairman of this private club. Martha helped Merritt find his new home here, a house overlooking the fourth green with a vista of the rolling Tennessee hills.

• • •

MARTHA RECALLED ONE evening in Washington DC when the philanthropist Catherine B. Reynolds, a Vanderbilt grad, hosted a private dinner for some two dozen guests at the John F. Kennedy Center for the Performing Arts.

Martha had been an early member of the Kennedy Center's national advisory board, where she and Catherine had developed a friendship around philanthropic support for the arts. (In 2002, the Virginia-based Catherine B. Reynolds Foundation made a $100 million gift for a new building to house the Center's programs and exhibitions. At that time, Reynolds' gift was the largest donation to date in the Kennedy Center's thirty-year history.)

Gil was Martha's date to that private dinner. While it was not a court-related function, the guest list included two sitting justices of the Supreme Court. Martha remembers she was seated next to Justice Antonin Scalia. Across the table, Gil was seated beside Justice Ruth Bader Ginsburg.

• • •

BY THIS TIME Merritt, now in his middle 70s, was no longer piloting his own plane. Instead, he would take commercial flights to his court duties in Cincinnati but more frequently would travel there by car, usually accompanied by one or more of his law clerks who would share in the driving. Professor Glenn Reynolds, who had clerked for Merritt in 1985–1986, remembers the judge telling him that he was now happy to let someone else do the flying and just enjoy the ride himself.

"I hadn't seen Judge Merritt in ten or fifteen years," Reynolds told me. "This was probably around his 70th birthday. And I asked him if he still flew, and he said, 'Well, no, Martha has 'the Ingram Air Force' now, so I can just whistle up a jet when I want.' I asked him, 'Do you miss flying?' And he said, 'Well, it's nice to fly your own plane, but it's nice to sit in the back with a bourbon while somebody else flies the plane.'"

Reynolds also told me he had been happy to learn of Merritt's new-found relationship with Martha Ingram. "I know of her, and I've met her. She seems like a magnificent woman," he said. "I've never had that much close contact with her, but she seems swell—and if he likes her that much, she has to be. I'm just happy because he deserves it. When I first started in clerking, I didn't really realize quite how tragic his back-story was. That's not the sort of thing you talk about at a clerkship interview, but I sort of absorbed it over time and I kind of edited my respect for all the stuff that he had done and handled."

• • •

THEIR TRAVELS TOGETHER took them far and wide, literally around the world. "We traveled all over Europe," Martha recalled. "We went on many Yale trips. We went on a Vanderbilt-organized trip to China, then Russia, ending up with the three weeks on a train. Fortunately, we took his family, Louise Clark and her daughter, and Eli and his wife and their two sons. That was Gil's idea, because he wanted to take his children on an exotic trip.

"We started in Beijing, and then we went up through Mongolia, and then Siberia, all of this on the train. We flew to Beijing. So, we took first the Chinese train and had to change because the width on the rails, the gauge of the Chinese train did not match up with the *Czar's Express* that we were on. It's like the Orient Express but, curiously enough, it's owned by the Germans, although it functions all over Russia. Every day the train stopped somewhere, and we had a tour of the town, wherever we stopped. We ended up in Moscow. And when we were there, we went to the opera, and the ballet, and all those things. It was a Vanderbilt-organized trip, and we had with us Vanderbilt professor Frank Wislo, a historian of modern Russia, his wife, Jane, and a Russian interpreter who spoke pretty good English. It was wonderful."

Gil's health was worsening now. In particular, his legs were failing him, and he needed a wheelchair in the airports. "I just told him after-wards, 'Gil, we can't do this anymore. It's too hard. We've had many wonderful trips, but I'm not putting you through this anymore. It's just too hard for you.'" Alan Valentine, the chief executive of the Nashville Symphony Association, was in this final traveling party for that last ex-cursion. He remembers how he and others in the group would take turns pushing Merritt's wheelchair.

• • •

YES, GIL AND Martha discussed marriage—and they decided against it.

Both had found joy and fulfillment in first marriages, Martha's to Bronson, Gil's to Louise. Children came into each of those unions—four to Martha, and three to Gil—and in time they both experienced great sadness. (Bronson, at sixty-three, died of cancer in 1995.) They had also been in other relationships over the years, notably Martha's with Kenneth Schermerhorn, music director of the Nashville Symphony and Gil's second marriage to Robin Saxon that ended in divorce after four-teen years. Martha described one of these conversations with Gil, about the possibility of marriage, and how it advanced to a mutual decision to just remain good friends. The best of friends.

"Everything was going so well in our relationship," she told me, "and our main thought was, why change it? I liked Gil's children, of course, but I just thought, why change this? He was thinking I would be expect-ing him to sign some sort of legal settlement, in case things didn't work out between us. At the time I was still involved with Ingram Industries, our family businesses, and my piece that I was in charge of. Bronson had given me more than the 'widow's mite' so that I would never be challenged by anyone. I said to him, 'Bronson, that's simply not necessary.' He said, 'It's what I want to do.' It became a lovely gesture, and generous beyond words. So, why get involved with that?"

She continued, "Gil and I traveled all over the world. We could spend as much time together as we wanted to, and we did. I led my life, and so did he, without complicating either of our lives. I've had several serious relationships. After Bronson died, my children always said, 'Mom, we're behind you, whatever you want to do.' After Bronson became so ill, he had said, 'You will re-marry.' I said, 'No, I don't think I'll marry anyone else. I just want our family to be a family.' Then I had grandchildren coming along—now there are thirty-four people related to Bronson and me. I'm a great grandmother now.

"Gil was my special friend, my special partner, but my family was my family. I want my family to feel they were family. So, we did the next best thing. I never went out with anyone else while Gil was alive.

"Bronson had encouraged me to re-marry. I said 'Bronson, I don't think I'll ever remarry.' It was my own sense of purpose, I guess you would say, to carry on his family. I didn't want to do anything to break the sense of our family. Certainly, I would say I had a lovely relationship with Kenneth, then with Gil that was really quite singular. Other than not being married, we were as close as two people could be. Gil was understanding of it. He very much wanted to be my special partner, and he thought we didn't really need to call it anything. We didn't need to be married. It worked so smoothly.

After Merritt's death, in January 2022, Martha told me: "One thing I really miss now: I often think I'd like to pick up the phone and ask Gil 'What do you think?' about this or that. We talked every day, sometimes more than once. I asked him once, 'How would you like me to refer to you?' He said, 'Call me your partner.'"

• • •

IN MY INTERVIEW with her in September of 2021, just four months before Merritt died, she told me their relationship had been a splendid adventure.

"Gil and I have had a nice history together, which I'm proud of and pleased to have shared with him. Fourteen of these past fifteen years have really been very, very nice and a great adventure."

Chapter 25

The Last Reunion

On Monday, January 17, 2022, the morning air in Nashville was cold and bitter. Snow had fallen overnight, and the winter skies over the city would be gray and drear all day.

It was MLK Day, and in Tennessee's capital city Nashvillians gathered for scores of programs, parades, and prayer recalling the life and legacy of Dr. Martin Luther King, Jr. This was also the 86th birthday of Gil Merritt, and it was on this same morning that the long-serving judge of the US Sixth Circuit passed away.

In the days preceding this, Merritt's immediate family had gathered in Nashville to be near him at the end. Stroud had arrived from coastal Carolina, Eli from southern California, joining with their sister Louise. By this time, the judge had been in hospice care at his Richland Place apartment since the week before Christmas. His prostate cancer had returned in the fall. All now understood that, in the words of Merritt's oncologist, his time remaining would most likely be measured in months, at most, not years.

On the following Saturday, January 22, scores of friends and former colleagues gathered with the extended Merritt family for the morning service at Christ Episcopal Cathedral. More than 60 others joined in via an internet link that carried the proceedings electronically far and wide. The Reverend Gordon Peerman, the Episcopal priest and psychotherapist in private practice in Nashville, brought the eulogy.

Afterward, in a reception at a downtown hotel, there was further remembering—with shared tales, some laughter, as well as tears. Where the church service had been sober and fitting, the reception was a time for bittersweet remembering among old friends and colleagues. The mood in that reception, in fact, was almost festive in a gentle way, a way that Merritt himself would have enjoyed.

John Michael Seigenthaler, son of the late editor and a long-time friend of the Merritt children, served as the emcee. He called on nine speakers. Eli went first, and the others were Nancy-Ann Min DeParle, Ralph Davis, Henry Walker, Sara Pettit, Jim Free, George Paine, Judge Jeff Sutton, Judge Amul Thapar, and Martha Ingram.

• • •

JIM FREE BROUGHT a personal message from President Carter, the 39th President, who was now ninety-seven years old. But before he read Carter's letter, Free spoke from his own heart.

"Back in 1976," Free recalled, "as a young fella I became Jimmy Carter's Tennessee campaign manager and Gil became the treasurer. Gil brought wise counsel and became my safety blanket and was immeasurable on his guidance and contribution to the campaign. Gil was part of a posse—a group of accomplished, fun-loving tennis playing, socializing guys—Seig, John Jay, Jim Neal, and others. In the language of that time, they were the coolest... and I must say all these years later in my memory they still are. These men all came out of Jack Kennedy's New Frontier of public service and helping government help those who needed assistance. And that group with Gil at the forefront left their mark on this city and state.

"President Carter appointed Gil Merritt to the Sixth Circuit federal court and was forever proud of that appointment... let me close with a quote from a new friend of Gil and Martha's, Senator Sheldon Whitehouse of Rhode Island. When hearing of Gil's passing, Sheldon texted me the following: 'Gil was a sweet and very distinguished man—not a common combination.'" Free then read the letter from President Carter.

January 19, 2022
To the family of Judge Gil Merritt:

Rosalynn and I were saddened to learn of the passing of our friend Gil Merritt. He was our campaign treasurer for the 1976 presidential campaign in Tennessee and later served with honor and distinction in the United States Court of Appeals for the Sixth Circuit. Please know you all are in our hearts and prayers during this difficult time. We hope that your warm memories and the support of Gil's loving family and the many people whose lives he has touched will be a comfort to you in the days ahead.
Sincerely,
Jimmy Carter

• • •

NOT ALL WHO wanted to be there were able to travel to Nashville, some of them kept home by Covid-19. One of these was Judge Gibbons of Memphis.

She had been a member of Governor Lamar Alexander's policy staff from 1979 to 1983. By Alexander's appointment, she became the first woman (and youngest person ever) to be a judge of a Tennessee trial court of record. In 1983, President Reagan nominated her to a US District Court judgeship in Memphis. President George W. Bush elevated her to the Sixth Circuit in 2001, when Merritt took senior status. On the day of his funeral, Gibbons penned this note to Merritt's children from her home in midtown Memphis, recalling some of the ways her career and Merritt's had intersected:

> I clerked on our court for Judge William Miller from Tennessee. After Judge Miller's death, during a conference in Cincinnati after an en banc hearing, Judge Merritt succeeded him. Then I succeeded Judge Merritt when he took senior status. Judge Merritt (and Sara) thought that was an appropriate succession. The historical circumstances of my appointment to this court are interesting (at least to me). I was nominated for the court in 2001, at a time when the Democrats controlled the Senate, and no Sixth Circuit nominees were receiving confirmation hearings. But Senator Fred Thompson, then our senior senator, in the tradition of Tennessee Republicans who thought it important to work with their Democratic counterparts, went to work to get me a hearing, a task in which he succeeded. And he had some help from Tennessee Democrats. Prominent among those was John Seigenthaler, the former publisher of the *Tennessean*, a founder of *USA Today*, and founder of the First Amendment Center at Vanderbilt. Seigenthaler knew me slightly, but he was one of Judge Merritt's closest friends. And Seigenthaler sent a beautiful letter to Senator Patrick Leahy, who at that time chaired the Senate Judiciary Committee. Judge Merritt's hand was surely in that as well as some other acts of kindness during the process.

One other aspect of Gil's service to the judiciary deserves particular mention. He was an excellent leader. Back in the 1990s, I chaired the Judicial Resources Committee of the Judicial Conference at the same time Gil chaired the Conference's Executive Committee. We were both appointed by Chief Justice Rehnquist. And when Gil was chief judge of our court, I was chief judge of the district court. He was a natural in both of those roles and did much to promote good will as we went about the business of the judiciary.

Of course, there were times when Gil and I disagreed, a natural thing on an appellate court. But I am extraordinarily grateful for his friendship and his service.

• • •

AL GORE, THE former Vice President, recalled in a statement to news media how close Merritt had been to the generations of the Gore family.

Judge Merritt was a cherished friend of my entire family. A deeply intelligent and deliberative legal thinker, he was an ardent defender of the liberties that form the foundations of our Constitution. He understood the power of his position and sought to use it to advance justice for the Americans he served and to help build democracies abroad.

He was a man of great integrity, and I am lucky to have benefited from his mentorship, wisdom, and friendship. Judge Merritt believed in the power of the legal system to advance civil rights and provide equal opportunity under the law. So, on what would have been his 86th birthday and on the day of our annual celebration of the life of Dr. Martin Luther King Jr., may we all recommit ourselves to the pursuit of justice for all.

• • •

THE WEEKS THAT followed were a time full of sadness for the Merritt family and for many friends who had been closest to the judge. Sara Pettit coordinated the final closing of his office in the Old Customs House on Broadway.

The Merritt children, especially Louise and Eli, worked closely with Sara on sorting out the personal mementos of his storied career. Stroud, three months after his father's death, told me in mid-April, "My world has changed so much since my father died. I continue to try to send him love, thanks, and apology. I think about him so much now."

WHAT THE LAW MEANS

Among his many other credentials, Merritt was a scholar in the law and legal philosophy, in addition to his work as a practitioner at the bar in his early post-graduate years, and as jurist on the bench thereafter. His preparation was assiduous and he demonstrated his grasp of law and legal processes in many ways.

Merritt was knowledgeable and eagerly conversant in the current legal philosophy of his time. Of all the most prominent legal philosophers in his day, none was more respected by Merritt than John B. Rawls, the Princeton and Harvard professor of towering influence on social and legal thought in the latter half of the 20th Century. Rawls's seminal first book, titled *A Theory of Justice*, was published in 1971. Rawls's memorable contribution was to formulate "justice as fairness" not merely as a competition between cultural and legal notions of justice and equality. Merritt frequently cited Rawls in articles and lectures ever after.

Merritt was 35 years old when he read *A Theory of Justice*, just past his service as the US Attorney for the Middle District of Tennessee. He was now back in private law practice in Nashville, and he found Rawls's new book riveting—in how it supplied a philosophical framework for reconciling the liberal tradition with decisions about what justice truly requires in society. Out of his own reflections on all this came a long but spirited book review of *A Theory of Justice* that covered 21 pages of *the Vanderbilt Law Review*. Merritt noted that his review was "intended to introduce Rawls's thought to the broad legal community."

John Rawls's new book on social and legal philosophy, Merritt writes, "appears likely to become a monument of systematic thought comparable to Locke's Second *Treatise of Government* and Mill's *Utilitarianism*. It provides answers systematically to the most difficult questions of our time and promises to shape the thought and action of men for many years. Daniel Bell, a noted social scientist, has said that in Rawls 'we can observe the development of a political philosophy which will go far to shape the last part of the 20th Century, as the doctrines of Locke and Smith molded the 19th.'"

• • •

Apart from his written commentaries, Merritt seemed always to enjoy public speaking. Over the years, his was a familiar voice in various legal forums, from his law school lectures and panel discussions to moot court sessions and on the pages of various law reviews. More than one of his former clerks told me that the daily work in Merritt's chambers often struck them as "Judge Merritt thinking out loud."

One exemplary occasion was in the spring of 2008, when Merritt was guest speaker at the annual "Law Day" observance of the Nashville Bar Association. Merritt used this opportunity to deliver his own definition of what the term "Rule of Law" meant to him—what it was all about and why it was so important in American society. His comments echoed the lessons he had learned and embraced from John Rawls.

"The Rule of Law is an uncertain, multi-dimensional phrase that comes from many different strains of philosophy and history—from ancient natural law theories to the fight of Lord Coke and other 17th and 18th century lawyers to establish judicial independence and the liberties incorporated in our constitution. The concept is at odds with the modern pragmatic view of legal realists that law is simply the command of the sovereign or what the judge had for breakfast...

"The Rule of Law that we revere combines five basic thoughts.

First—It is not the rule of monetary public clamor or the rule of money and status and not just a collection of orders primarily to benefit the interests of a particular class, religiou, race, political party or military-industrial party. It includes but is much more than the protection of property rights and freedom of contract. It is an ordinance of reason for solving the public problems and the private disputes of our time.

Second—It holds to the idea that using precedent widely we can achieve an equal, impartial, and consistent administration of rules.

Third—It tries to create the maximum libery compatible with an equal liberty for all.

Fourth—It has a strong element taken from the gospels and other religions—a system of equality that counteracts and softens established rules when they work an unexpected hardship, especially on the poor and disadvantaged or, as the King James Version of the Book of Matthew says, on "the least of these, my brethren."

Fifth—It is an ideal for the creation of a well-ordered society that fosters mutual trust and the more gentle treatment of each other."

• • •

Over several days in 2018 and 2019, as Gil Merritt approached the time of his full retirement from the US Sixth Circuit in 2021, he sat at home with the members of his extended family to record a series of intimate interviews. By turns, his children and grandchildren posed questions about his childhood and career, the lessons he had learned, and even what legacy he hoped to leave them.

This was a time of controversy and division within the US government and, more broadly, across the nation. Importantly it was the courts—at many levels, and in many jurisdictions that were seen as upholding the rule of law and the US Constitution as in other critical times in American history.

In the final interview session, joined by his younger son Eli, who produced this priceless family video, Merritt reflected on his life and work.

ELI MERRITT: Let's talk about your work as a judge and starting with, what is your sense of the top two or three experiences you've had as a judge that were important?

GIL MERRITT: Well, one of the most important things is to develop a philosophy of justice that you can be comfortable with. And of course, justice, in the sense of the legal system, it is a product of a moral philosophy or in the sense that we are turning principles of moral philosophy into laws. And it's hard to express that in a one sentence or in an easy way. But the idea that I would think comes close to expressing the development of a legal philosophy, a sense of justice comes from a case that Chief Justice Warren wrote many years ago, in which he said that the system should be based on evolving standards of decency that mark the progress of a maturing society. Now that is a particular idea that comes from the enlightenment clearly, that is that we can do better.

In our system, law and the rule of law means what is above the Supreme Court building frieze: 'Equal Justice Under Law.' And you have to impose on the system of law, a principle of equality. It's important I think, to realize that in this, putting a just system together or trying to improve it and maintain the rule of law, much of it comes from our heritage. And I like to think of the two most important elements of it as the 'Golden Mean' and the 'Golden Rule'. The 'Golden Mean' is Aristotle, who says that before you get too far away from moderation, you better think hard. And that the 'Golden Mean' is that way of thinking, that way of acting that is between the extremes.

So, it's a principle of moderation, which itself is a principle that you better look carefully because you may be wrong. The other, the 'Golden Rule' is from our basic Judeo-Christian heritage of doing to others as you would have them do onto you. And it seems to me, those two principles one from the Greeks and the other from Roman times and our Christian heritage, form the basis of the rule of law, of course, in our country and in Western civilization.

ELI MERRITT: Are there cases that you think of in particular that exemplify any of these or that sort of stand out as most important experiences or most important cases?

GIL MERRITT: There have been lots of interesting cases. It depends because the cases are interesting for a whole lot of different reasons. I've had a lot of death penalty cases and I'm opposed to the death penalty.

And we in this country do recognize the death penalty although not quite half of the states have abolished it. All of the European countries have abolished the death penalty. Now, if you're going to belong to the European Union, you can't have the death penalty. And that's for a whole lot of different reasons. One of which is we make a lot of mistakes. People have been executed who are innocent. I've had a couple of cases in which we set aside the death penalty because it turned out after we looked into the case that the person who's about to be executed was totally innocent. Didn't do it. Just flat out. And also, a reason for ameliorating the death penalty is so much of nowadays at least, used to be that we had the death penalty for all kinds of things, stealing, whatever.

Now it's almost down to homicide, killing another person, but that is problematical because there are so many mental health problems out there. People who are responsible for what they do, but who have an aspect of insanity let's say, or an aspect of very bad mental health. That's another reason why I am opposed to the death penalty. One of the things that judges and lawyers should be aware of is that the system is always one of trial and error and the idea that standards of decency evolve, and that justice evolves over time to hopefully get better, is a very important thing for us to understand, rather than a system that is static.

ELI MERRITT: Let me ask this: So, what do you think are the major problems we have in federal government and just to make it a little more dramatic, if you had fiat power, what would you change in federal government to make it either a more efficient government or a more just government?

GIL MERRITT: Well, quite a few. Within the last week former justice, John Paul Stevens, wrote an op-ed piece for *The New York Times* saying something that I think he'd long felt, that we just ought to repeal the Second Amendment. The Second Amendment is now said to be about guns and it's been interpreted oh, fifteen or so years ago to guarantee that people could have guns. And it's been used as a propaganda device, Second Amendment for the National Rifle Association, which is financed at least in part, by the people selling guns. The Democrats and Republicans have a hard time talking to each other and reconciling their views. And we built up systems of communication through television, where one channel is at the other channel's throat. I mean, Fox News and CNN or whatever. They hardly agree on anything. And I noticed now that they're at each other's throats criticizing each other.

And so, I think the problem is, if democracy and the rule of law are going to survive, we've got to do something to have the electorate, which is the source of our democracy. I mean, the Preamble to the constitution, in order to form a more perfect union. We, the people, we are the people. We do that to form this more perfect union. Well, I think the union has been more perfect in times past than it is right now. And we're losing balance and the ability to reconcile different ideas because our electorate is in great need of further education in civics and in the way government works.

ELI MERRITT: If you had fiat powers, you would abolish the death penalty and repeal or revoke the second amendment. And then as you were talking, I was also reminded sort of you talked about the political system. You've talked a lot about money in politics.

GIL MERRITT: Yes. We really need to take seriously "Equal Justice Under Law." And we need to have a theory of justice that says, basically we're not going to allow laws that harm the least favorite class. That is to say, a law that hurts the poor and designates the poor for harm should be outlawed under the equal protection clause. So, we need to enhance equal justice under law and underline "equal." Again, that goes back to the idea of evolving standards of decency that mark the progress of a maturing society. And I think that the problem is that money talks and we know that, and that's always been true. Now, the system has gotten itself set up in a way that allows money to talk too loud. And we're the only nation in a civilized world who allows assault weapons for example. I mean, you can practically go buy a tank. You can go buy assault weapons and have them at home, which is a weapon that is for war time.

And at certain times in the past, we have been, we may not be too lucky right now, but we have been lucky. In times of trouble, we elected George Washington, we elected Abraham Lincoln, and we elected Franklin Roosevelt. By virtue of their leadership and other factors, we've come through difficult times. And it seems to be kind of a difficult time right now, whether society is polarized and where we have leadership, particularly in the executive branch that is not up to this task at hand. Well, I think the founding fathers were right in the sense that there is only one way to have a competent electorate. And that is through education. People coming through the educational system who learn not only what they should be doing in order to get a job, but what they should understand in order to perform what I would say is their obligatory role as a citizen.

We can lose our democracy. I don't think people understand. You can lose a democracy yesterday, tomorrow, either through the outside where somebody conquers us. Or we just don't keep up the government. So internally, we can lose the quality of the government we've got now. I think nothing's inevitable about democracy. I think that's one of the problems that our

electorate does not understand. I think they think
that we've got this democracy and that it's permanent, always going to be there, which in my view,
is wrong. Because the Greeks lost their democracy in classical times, the kind of democracy that
Pericles had. And we're going to lose ours, too.

• • •

It was a sobering note on which to end the day's interview session, but a
fitting one. He had summed up, in a few words, his years of scholarship
and jurisprudence and expressed what he regarded as the central imperative of life and politics in the United States. After a lifetime of studying
and adjudicating the American society and government, Merritt well
understood the complicated times in which the nation had now found
itself at the end of his life.

Gilbert S. Merritt, Jr.
January 17, 1936–January 17, 2022

A Note on Sources

My direct access to Judge Merritt—to learn his own memories of a storied life and brilliant career—was unfortunately limited by his own declining health to a period of less than twelve months. During that time, he was nevertheless an eager interviewee. Not once did he deflect or avoid any question that I put to him, either about his personal life or his jurisprudence. On each visit he answered me fully and lucidly and, in fact, gave every indication that he enjoyed the process. Sometimes he would yield to his physical fatigue and we would adjourn after an hour or so. But not once did I sense that he regretted getting himself into what can be an exhaustive interview process. Our last interview was in early December of 2021 by phone.

His health status, in turn, placed great value on the other 145 individuals who shared with me their valuable time and invaluable recollections. Many of these were surviving spouses and adult children who helped me on this journey by locating friends of Merritt's and former colleagues and knowledge about how to reach them. This enabled me to schedule phone calls or in-person visits with many of the judges, lawyers, other knowledgeable people, and guiding me to relevant records and other source materials for telling the Merritt story. In some cases, they were helpful in locating photographs, letters, memoranda, newspaper clippings, and other historical items that became essential to understanding Merritt and his times. Some lent me books, letters, journals, and other priceless artifacts. The author owes a particular debt to Pam Eddy, Merritt's career law clerk for twenty-seven years, for identifying his most significant court decisions.

A special acknowledgment is owed here to Judge Merritt's daughter, Louise Clark Merritt, who shared precious notes, letters, and journals left behind by her late mother in 1973. There have been many other acts of kindness and assistance: Nashville Metro Councilmember Kathleen Murphy, hosted me in her own home for my interview with her father, the former State Representative Mike Murphy, about his memories from the 1975 congressional race. Gray Sasser helped me with scheduling phone interviews with his father, the former Senator and Ambassador Jim Sasser. Four other men—Lieutenant General John Bradley (retired), Sam Hatcher, and alumni director Rob Hosier and the Nashville lawyer Jack Robinson—gave me an appreciation for the demanding life of a young cadet at Castle Heights Military Academy in its heyday.

The 145 interviewees are listed separately in this appendix, but the author gratefully acknowledges here all the individuals who helped me in my research, including connecting me to documents and associates who helped to amplify aspects of this story.

Alexandra Burlason	Keith Miles
Joe Cain	Kathleen Murphy
J. Greer Cummings	Jim O'Hara
Pamela Eddy	Lisa Presley
Gary Everton	Terry Reuther Quillen
Deb Faulkner	Grace R. Renshaw
Beth Prichard Geer	Ricky Rogers
Barb Glover	Gray Sasser
James Gooch	Robin A. Saxon
Sam Hatcher	Mark Sturtevant
Kem Hinton	Susan Pearlman
Rob Hosier	Robert P. Thomas
Virginia Banks Lazenby	Katy Varney
Allen D. Lentz	Hedy Weinberg
Monica W. Mackie	Anna Durham Windrow
Henry A. Martin	Cathy Young Thomas
Louise Clark Merritt	

Finally, several of the interviewees also assisted me by reviewing portions of the manuscript for accuracy: Charles W. Bone, Lee Breckenridge, Jim Free, Hal Hardin, Henry Martin, George Paine, Sarah Pettit, Ben Vernia, and Henry Walker. Any errors of fact or interpretation that might remain are, of course, not theirs but mine alone.

THE INTERVIEWS

Any biography is a compilation of memories, and that is always subject to the passage of time. Merritt was 84 when he and I began this project together, and he did not live past his 86th birthday. I was therefore especially eager to talk with his closest friends and professional colleagues, but of course many of these were also gone by this time.

All of this put a special emphasis on the importance on reaching out to family, friends, and other associates who knew Merritt best. Essential to my research were personal interviews with 144 of his family members, friends, journalists, and other significant associates over his long career. Some of these I interviewed multiple times. With much gratitude, I name them here.

Judge Gilbert S. Merritt Jr.
Stroud Merritt
Dr. Louise Clark Merritt
Dr. Eli Merritt
Rachel Merritt McAllister

• • •

Victor Ashe
Paul R. Bottei
Charles W. Bone
John A. Bradley
C. Dewey Branstetter, Jr.
Robert S. Brandt
Lee P. Breckenridge
Mary Barrett Brewer
Judge Joe B. Brown
Carole Bucy

Andrew W. Byrd
Marianne Menefee Byrd
Chris Cabot
Judith Kinnard Cabot
Judge Eric Clay
Steve Cobb
Chief Judge Guy Cole
Lew Conner
Judge Waverly Crenshaw
J. Greer Cummings

Judge Martha Craig Daughtrey

Ralph Davis

Nancy-Ann Min DeParle

Bruce Dobie

James C. Duff

Vince Durnan

Natilee Duning

Pamela L. Eddy

Gary Everton

David S. Ewing

William H. Farmer

Deb Faulkner

Chloe Fort

Tish Fort

Jim Free

Michael J. Gerhardt

Judge Julia Smith Gibbons

Harris A. Gilbert

Vince Gill

Tam Gordon

Al Gore

Frank Grace

Leonard Green

Judge J. Ronnie Greer

L. John Haile

Jay Harbison

Hal Hardin

Judge Marian F. Harrison

Janet Arnold Hart

Robb Harvey

Aubrey Harwell

Harris Haston

Sam Hatcher

John Hehman

Kelley J. Henry

Kem Hinton

Ryan T. Holt

Rob Hosier

Joseph B. Ingle

David B. Ingram

Martha Rivers Ingram

Tom Ingram

Victor S. (Torry) Johnson III

Doug Johnston

Kenneth W. Jost

Judge Ray Kethledge

William C. Koch

John J. Kulewicz

Theodore H. Lavit

Ted Lazenby

Virginia Banks Lazenby

Allen D. Lentz

Carlton Lewis

Dwight Lewis

Jack Lowery

Randy Lowry

Judge Keith Lundin

Henry A. Martin

Joseph L. (Jack) May

Lynn Hewes Lance May

Jack H. (Nick) McCall

Mark McNeely

Bradley A. MacLean

Sam McPherson

Amy Rao Mohan

Bill Morelli

Judge Karen Nelson Moore

Mike Murphy

Roy M. Neel

Jeanie Nelson

Maria O'Brien

Jim O'Hara

Judge George Paine

Ophelia Paine

Sara L. Pettit

Wendell Rawls

Randy Rayburn

Stacy Rector

Robert L. Reeves
Glenn Reynolds
Rich Riebeling
Ann Roberts
Kenneth L. Roberts
Sandra Roberts
Jack Robinson, Sr.
James F. Sanders
Senator Jim Sasser
Robin A. Saxon
Walter T. Searcy III
John Michael Seigenthaler
Dr. John Sergent
Jeff Sheehan
Susan Simons
Luke Simons
Charles E. Smith
Jim Squires
Judge Jane B. Stranch
Mark Sturtevant
Frank Sutherland
Kent D. Syverud

Vijay S. Tata
Raymond Thomasson
F. Dalton Thompson
Judge Aleta A. Trauger
Byron Trauger
Steve Turner
Alan D. Valentine
Marsha Vande Berg
Cecil VanDevender
Ben Vernia
Paula C. Wade
Henry Walker
Rick Warwick
Hedy Weinberg
Russell Willis
Anna Durham Windrow
Larry Woods
Linda T. Wynn
Jeff Yarbro
Edward M. Yarbrough
Cathy Young Thomas

Judge Merritt's Address to the Yale Class of 1956

March 13, 2003

It's only been fifty short years since as freshman first we walked through Phelps Gateway to begin Yale College—1953 to 2003. But that was another era, not only sexually but demographically, culturally, technologically, scientifically. The population of the country was 150 million vs. 290 million today. Only 35 percent lived in urban areas larger than 25,000. Now it is more than 90 percent—most in areas more than one million.

For me, coming east for the first time from a dairy farm in middle Tennessee, Yale was a different culture, more diversity than I had ever experienced. The lens of my mental life all of a sudden at age seventeen zoomed out from the security of life on the farm to an expansive cultural horizon. Cows, milking machines, and silos were replaced by tea at the Elizabethan Club and an all morning long nude physical exam in the grandeur of the Payne-Whitney gym. But, of course, by today's standards, we were a homogeneous lot of white males—no women, few African Americans, Asians, or Hispanics.

Not many of you had milked a cow or fertilized a field with manure before coming to Yale. I found you deficient in the arts of agriculture. But certainly not in the art of bull.

I was, and still remain, impressed by your brilliance. I will never forget my first two weeks in beginning, intensive French. I sat down next to a young man at 8:00 a.m. on September 22, 1953, for our first class in one of the small classrooms over Phelps Gateway looking out over the New Haven green. When we struck up a short conversation before class began that morning, I was relieved. I thought, "This boy from Texarkana, Arkansas, is just as unsophisticated and unprepared as I am." That idea did not last long. Within two weeks, he and our teacher, M'sieur Tofoya had put him up in French 20 requiring two good years of high school French. And before semester was out, the French Department put Richard Arnold into French 30, an advanced class where they read Beaudelaire, Stendahl and other great French writers.

A few semesters later in daily themes it became clear that a boy from Kansas, Bud Trillin, had more than the normal talent of college students as a writer and potential man of letters. His life as a writer, like the lives of many others of our class, present company included, has given us a degree of immortality.

Our twelve hundred strong were called the so-called "silent generation" of the "Gray Flannel Suit." The country was looking forward to a quieter life after twelve years of exertion and hardship leading to a momentous victory in Europe and a stalemate in Korea. The parents of the silent generation wanted a restoration of normal life in America and Europe. But it turned out that we were coming of age at the dawn of the H Bomb and the Cold War and the age of television. The space race and the multiple revolutions in computer science, biology and DNA, pharmacology, medicine, agriculture, plate tectonics, and literary criticisms were still ahead.

• • •

How much of human ethical and legal behavior is a direct product of biology and how much is cultural only? The abstract question is now what got me interested in law and biology. My interest was much more mundane, specific and self-serving. How do old federal judges, appointed for life, stay alive, relatively sane, and healthy after sixty or seventy or eighty or ninety? So that they can continue to decide the great issues of the day and sup at the public trough. That is a question worthy of analysis.

• • •

Shakespeare describes my motive better in Sonnet 73, when he says, "I am like the twilight." His words are:
    In me, Thou seest the twilight of such day,
    As after sunset fadeth in the West,
    Which, by and by, black night doth take away,
    Death's second self, that seals up all the rest.

After the body of the Sonnet about growing old, he ends it with a couplet, as though speaking to his wife:
    This thou perceivest, which should make thy
    Love more strong,
    To love that well which thou must leave ere long.

• • •

OUR CLASSMATE, Don Maffly's wife, Valerie, a Jungian psychologist, reminded me what Karl Jung has to say about aging:

> In the morning, the ego rises up from the nocturnal sea of unconsciousness and looks upon the wide, bright world...steadily widens the higher it climbs in the firmament... We cannot live the afternoon of life according to...life's morning. What was great in the morning will be little at evening, and what in the morning was true will at evening become false.

Jung may have captured the twilight years better than Shakespeare. The modern wife does not seem to think that old age should make love more strong ere we leave.

• • •

I WAS PROMPTED to intellectualize on old judges and biology also because of a letter I recently received from a club I belong to, made up of mostly old golfers. The letter says, "Dear Member...

2003 is the 50th Anniversary of another event—the amazing discovery of DNA. After millions of years in the dark, we discovered the engine of life in 1953. It was 50 years ago almost to the day that Watson and Crick discovered what a gene is—the chemical structure of the gene, the double helix of DNA—the two carbon and phosphate chains connected by four chemical bases. Their findings, the most important in biology since Darwin discovered evolution as the explanation for our existence, were then published in Nature magazine on April 25, 1953.

As a Tennessean, I am especially interested in law and biology because Tennessee is where the first law and biology case in American history was tried. I will read you the transcript of some testimony from that remarkable trial:

> Q: Do you claim that everything in the Bible should be literally interpreted?
> A: I believe that everything in the Bible should be accepted as it is given there.
> Q: But when you read that Jonah swallowed the whale—or that

the whale swallowed Jonah—excuse me, please, how do you literally interpret it? You believe that God made such a fish, and that it was big enough to swallow Jonah?

A: Yes, Sir.

Q: Perfectly easy to believe that Jonah swallowed the whale?

A: If the Bible said so. One miracle is just as easy to believe as another.

This testimony was given in July 1925, in Dayton, Tennessee, in the criminal case of *Tennessee v. John Scopes*, in which John Scopes, a high school teacher, was charged and then convicted of teaching Darwin's theory of evolution in violation of Tennessee law. The prosecuting attorney was the three times Democratic nominee for President (and self-proclaimed Biblical scholar), Willian Jennings Bryan. The defense lawyer was Clarence Darrow, the most famous defense lawyer of the twentieth century. It was a sensational case—covered by reporters from around the world. In defending Scopes, in an unheard-of move, Darrow called Bryan, his opposing counsel, to the stand, qualified him as an expert on the Bible, and proceeded to cross-examine him at length along the lines just recited.

Biology had virtually no impact on the law until after World War II. But since the 1950s, the Darwinization of the law has proceeded quickly. In many post-1950s cases arising under the First Amendment, the courts, including the Supreme Court, have struck down *Scopes*-type laws. Other biology cases have become hot topics—*Roe v. Wade* and the question of a woman's right to choose an abortion are still heatedly debated, along with right-to-die cases, surrogate mother cases, and birth defect cases of all types, from the Rubella cases of the 1960s to the Benedectin cases of the 1980s and 1990s. Biology has led us to the smoking cases, the radiation and toxic tort cases, the complex, perplexing patent cases concerning the ownership and commercial exploitation of genetically engineered plants and animal tissue, and the environmental cases concerning the effects of the dirty air and water and hazardous waste, wetlands, endangered species, and so on.

• • •

EVEN MORE CONTROVERSIAL, now our legal system faces two new problems arising from major advances in genetics following the discovery of DNA. First, are we acquiring too much new genetic information about our biological inheritance before we know what to do with it? Second, are we fast becoming capable of changing human nature through gene therapy and genetic enhancement? We may be able to correct myriad disorders ranging from arthritis to obesity and change personal attributes like intelligence and skin color. All the characteristics that are controlled or influenced by the 3.6 billion base pairs of DNA that make up the human genome presumably can be reengineered.

. . .

WITHIN THE LAST six months, I wrote an opinion in a death penalty case that turns on DNA testing. The man was on death row for twelve years before DNA testing showed that he did not rape the woman he was convicted of murdering. The theory of the prosecution at the trial was that he raped her immediately before he murdered her. Now it is clear that the semen was her husband's, and it was not the semen of the man on death row. His motive could not have been to cover up a rape.

On the subject of homicide and the death penalty, did you know that 98 percent of three thousand death row inmates in the USA are male and over 90 percent of homicides worldwide, according to empirical studies, are committed by males under 35? Homicide, like pregnancy, is age and gender specific.

. . .

WITHOUT MUCH TECHNICAL expertise in genetics, I should know better than to talk about the relationship between the new biology and law and morals. I am probably like Voltaire's famous character, Old Dr. Pangloss, from the novel *Candide*. He was asked how it came about that we developed oblong, straight noses that come to a point. He considered for a long moment, removed his glasses and announced solemnly that, "Noses evolved for the purpose of holding up spectacles."

. . .

THE HUMAN GENOME Project that the Government funded to the tune of $2 billion is for biology what the Manhattan Project was for physics.

Imagine the following type of problems that society and the law are going to have to confront, as a result.

First, through devious means, a newspaper finds out that the genetic structure of the President of the United States contains the gene with the highest risk for Alzheimer's disease. The President, a Ronald Reagan type, is now seventy and up for re-election. Should the newspaper be allowed to publish the President's genome? What about employment or college admission discrimination based on the applicant's genes, or genetic discrimination by institutions that provide health care, insurance, education, adoption services, or marriage licenses? Once such genetic information is available, it seems obvious that it will be used to make distinctions among people, just as credit history and education are used now.

Second, what is the judicial system of the twenty-first century going to do with information that particular genes "wire" individuals with a propensity for certain types of criminal behavior? What do we do should it become clear that the conduct of an individual criminal defendant was the product of an unfortunate set of genes that control the person's biochemical makeup? What will happen in criminal law if the presumption of free will must be seriously modified? And what of the fundamental legal distinction between act and status? While the government may pass laws classifying conduct—if a person commits Act A, she will suffer consequence B—it decidedly may not create classes among citizens on the basis of who they are rather than what they do. Any society that classifies its citizens on the basis of who they are—that is, on status alone—takes a large step toward creating a highly ordered caste society.

Third, when we move from genetic testing and diagnosis to genetic enhancement, an even greater series of moral and legal questions arises for society. By legislation, will we try to fix some of the bad genes of the criminal or prevent them from being passed on to succeeding generations. How much of such genetic modification and retooling will we permit? Should we try to increase memory and intelligence or a runners' endurance? Will we want to try to fix people so that they will live to an average age of one hundred and twenty years?

• • •

THESE ARE MIND boggling questions. They remind me that years ago my youngest son, Eli Merritt, came home from school in his first year in high school. His grades were down a bit, particularly in biology. As I frowned in reading his report card, he said with his winning smile, "What do you think the trouble with me is, Dad, heredity or environment?" Eli has recovered well and I am proud of him. He graduated from Yale in 1989 and is now a practicing psychiatrist in San Francisco after doing his residency at Stanford.

• • •

FIGURING OUT THE relationship between genes and human behavior is what the new biology is all about. And it is already having a major impact on the law. Who knows what its impact will be in the next several decades? But our own experience over the last fifty years—from watching our own children grow up, to reading the daily newspaper—teaches us that the *Law of Biology—the Law of Life—Is Change*. Let us hope that we can steer it along in a path of growth and improvement and maintain a system of justice that encourages liberty, due process, and the equal protection of the law.

How to Sustain a Constitutional Democracy: The Legacy of Judge Gilbert S. Merritt

By Eli Merritt

On January 21, 2022, four mornings after Judge Merritt died, this essay by his son Eli was published in Nashville. It is reprinted here by permission of the *Tennessean*, a part of the USA TODAY Network.

My father, Gil Merritt, passed away Monday at a moment in our history when wise democratic thinkers like him are needed most.

A judge on the Sixth Circuit Court of Appeals for 44 years, he believed that the success of American democracy is rooted not only in an intelligent Constitution and sound institutions but in an active citizenry imbued with a spirit of justice, truth, and self-sacrifice for the greater good.

"Liberty and democratic spirit," he often said, "must exist within the hearts of the people."

To him, democracy was a paradox. It mandates a system of government based on the rule of law, not the rule of men and women.

But this free form of government can only be sustained by fiercely determined citizens—most importantly, leaders—who are willing to stand up as courageous guardians of our freedoms against the forces of corruption and tyranny.

How to fight against the forces that threaten democracy

Throughout his life, he was most inspired by Winston Churchill, defender-in-chief of liberal democracy during World War II. Even on his deathbed, the judge continued to remind others that adults and children alike must study historical figures like Churchill—and draw courage from them—if we wish to preserve democracy.

One speech by Churchill, more than any other, inspired his own daily work on behalf of democracy and equal justice for all. It is the British prime minister's "We Shall Fight on the Beaches" address, delivered to the House of Commons soon after Hitler's conquest of France, Luxembourg, the Netherlands, and Belgium.

Against the onslaught of Nazi rule, the prime minister said on June 4, 1940, "we shall not flag or fail. We shall go on to the end, we shall fight in France, we shall fight on the seas and oceans, we shall fight with growing confidence and growing strength in the air... we shall fight on the beaches, we shall fight on the landing grounds, we shall fight in the fields and in the streets, we shall fight in the hills; we shall never surrender."

My father did not consider that these words applied only to the defense of democracy from foreign threats but also from internal subversion.

The way to fight the forces of internal corruption and lawlessness, he clarified, was not resort to arms but the relentless deployment of the Constitution, the courts, the rule of law, and the spirit of liberty to thwart every danger.

"You can lose a democracy yesterday"
In an interview in 2018, he had much to say about the fragility of democracy and the necessity of constantly refreshing the democratic spirit. Foremost, he called upon us not to be naive about the inherent strength or durability of our constitutional government.

"We can lose our democracy," he said, alluding to the collapse of the Athenian democracy the 4th century BC. "You can lose a democracy yesterday— tomorrow. There is nothing inevitable about democracy. We can lose ours too."

On the question of how to sustain a constitutional democracy, my father counseled others to rouse the spirit of Washington, Madison, Churchill, FDR, Lincoln, and MLK, among other historical figures who were willing to give their lives and fortunes for our liberties.

In this vein, he frequently made reference to a speech by a federal judge he admired greatly, Billings Learned Hand, appointed to the US Court of Appeals for the Second Circuit in the 1920s.

In the speech, entitled, "The Spirit of Liberty," Judge Hand described American democracy in 1944 as "a faith in a common purpose, a common conviction, a common devotion." It was, Hand said, a shared responsibility grounded in "the conscience and courage of Americans."

"I often wonder," Hand continued, "whether we do not rest our hopes too much upon constitutions, upon laws and upon courts. These are false hopes. Liberty lies in the hearts of men and women; when it dies there, no constitution, no law, no court can even do much to help it."

Democracy must exist in our minds and our hearts.
That is why Judge Hand and Judge Merritt believed until their dying days that the last best hope for democracy resides in education.

In this shared belief, the two jurists were not merely pointing to classroom learning about civics and constitutional structures.

More fundamentally, they meant that we, each of us, must hand down the love of liberty and democracy to the next generation—and they to the next generation after them.

As my father said in the 2018 interview, democracy is a conviction that must exist not only in our minds but in our hearts. "If you have never had it, you do not know how to have it. It's got to be bred."

LAW CLERKS BY YEAR

In the Chambers of Judge Gilbert S. Merritt
1977–2021

1977–78   Henry Walker
            Lee Breckenridge

1978–79   Chris Cabot
            Mike Moore
            Mary Schaffner

1979–80   Betty Fowlkes Boner
            John Kulewicz
            Gary Tepper

1980–81   Neil Ellis
            Peter Lancaster
            Judith McMorrow
            Ellen Pollack

1981–82   Irene Keyse-Walker
            Vijay Tata
            Robert Lough

1982–83   Jane Harbaugh Graham
            Elaine Galler Levine
            Dieter Snell

1983–84   Mike Gerhardt
            Nancy-Ann Min DeParle
            Jay St. Clair

1984–85   Jason Johnston
            Bob Lipkin
            Jane North

1985–86   Steve Chidester
            Maria O'Brien Hylton
            Glenn Reynolds

1986–87   Ralph Davis
            Steve Kargman
            Kathleen Paisley
            Betsy Turner

1987–88	Ted Carey Neal Roach Jackie Wood Welch
1988–89	Angela Cox Janet Halley Jayne Workman
1989–90	Peter Appel Janet Arnold Hart Linda Rippey Moore Dan Yeager
1990–91	Kathy Ayres-Lundin Eric Klopfer Barr Linton Sue Palmer
1991–92	Dan Abrahamson Alix Coulter Cross Nick McCall Sue Palmer
1992–93	Karen Eisenhauer J.D. Fugate Steve Knight Jim Ward
1993–94	Dale Bryk Duke Eggleston Bill Kunze Michelle Leslie Jacobs
1994–95	Howard Brodie Henry Fincher Alex Mishkin
1995–96	Lydia Arnold Alyse Graham Catherine Sheehan Bruno Stewart Moritz Pamela Eddy

1996–97   David Flickinger
           Carl Riehl
           Eric Rogers
           Pamela Eddy*
           Gittel Hilibrand

1997–98   Steve Lane
           Scott Smith
           Gittel Hilibrand
           Pamela Eddy

1998–99   Loring Justice
           Ben Kerschberg
           Mike McCabe
           Pamela Eddy

1999–2000 Sara Fowler Getsay
           Sal Hernandez
           Brian Michael
           Pamela Eddy

2000–01   Adam Feibelman
           Adam Newton
           Sam Williamson
           Pamela Eddy

2001–02   Will Berry
           Harwell Wells
           Pamela Eddy

2002–03   John Bradford
           Jennifer Coffin
           Pamela Eddy

2003–04   Curtis Bridgeman
           Jennifer Coffin
           Pamela Eddy

2004–05   Rob Stone
           Jeff Yarbro
           Pamela Eddy

2005–06   Lauren Spitz
           Russell Taber
           Pamela Eddy

2006–07	Chris Champion Samar Ali Pamela Eddy
2007–08	Lori Gutzman Addison Thompson Pamela Eddy
2008–09	Cecil VanDevender Alex Morgan Pamela Eddy
2009–00	Allison Holt Ryan Harvey Pamela Eddy
2010–11	Ryan Holt Deke Sharon Pamela Eddy
2011–12	Elizabeth Cadot James Clayton Pamela Eddy
2012–13	Ben Raybin Amy Mohan John Williams Pamela Eddy
2013–14	Wyatt Sassman Emma Soichet Pamela Eddy
2014–15	Jay Harbison Jeff Sheehan Pamela Eddy
2015–16	Rascoe Dean David Watnick Pamela Eddy
2016–17	Chris Climo James Balser Pamela Eddy

2017–18	Ashley Robinson
	Eric Lyons
	Pamela Eddy
2018–19	Michael Tackeff
	Pamela Eddy
2019–10	Dalton Thompson
	Pamela Eddy

• • •

*Pamela Eddy was the "Career Law Clerk" on Merritt's staff. She served in that capacity for 27 years.

MEMORIAL RESOLUTION OF
NASHVILLE BAR ASSOCIATION

GILBERT STROUD MERRITT, JR.

Gilbert Stroud Merritt, Jr., a distinguished member of the Nashville Bar, died on January 17, 2022—his eighty-sixth birthday. A longtime fixture of both the federal judiciary and Tennessee politics, Judge Merritt will be deeply missed by many. He is survived by his three children (Stroud, Louise Clark, and Eli), three grandchildren, and longtime partner Martha Rivers Ingram.

Gil was born in Nashville, attending public elementary school and Castle Heights Military Academy. He graduated from Yale University in 1957 and Vanderbilt Law School in 1960, where he was a member of *Order of the Coif* and managing editor of the Vanderbilt Law Review. He also earned a Master of Laws from Harvard Law School in 1962.

Gil began private practice at the Nashville firm of Boult, Hunt, Cummins and Connors where he tried numerous cases, often interviewing witnesses in the morning for afternoon trials. He then served as an associate attorney for the City of Nashville and was instrumental in the approval of the Metropolitan Government. In 1966—at just 29 years old—he was appointed U.S. Attorney for the Middle District of Tennessee. In that role he appointed both the first woman, Martha Craig Daughtrey, and the first Black person, Carlton Petway, to serve as assistant U.S. Attorneys for the district.

Gil returned to private practice in 1970 as a partner at Gullett, Steele, Sanford, Robinson, and Merritt. On August 25, 1977, President Jimmy Carter appointed him to a vacancy on the United States Court of Appeals for the Sixth Circuit, a seat he would hold for the next 44 years (making him the longest-serving judge in our circuit). In the 1990s, he was twice considered for nomination to the U.S. Supreme Court. He was also one of three American jurists selected to travel to Iraq after the fall of Saddam Hussein to help rebuild the country's shattered judicial system.

In addition to his decades on the federal bench, Judge Merritt taught on Vanderbilt's adjunct faculty for many years—including a seminar on the death penalty (because according to him, the best way to become an expert at something is to teach it). He staunchly opposed the death penalty both publicly and privately, denouncing what he called a "Middle Ages practice" and highlighting its disproportionate use against Black defendants.

Judge Merritt's devotion to the rule of law cannot be overstated. A deeply intelligent and deliberative thinker, he was an ardent defender of the liberties that form the foundations of our Constitution. He believed in duty to three causes: (1) his family; (2) the U.S. Constitution; and (3) "to the pursuit of equal justice under the law for all Americans, regardless of race, religion, ethnicity, gender, sexual orientation, or incarceration status." He understood the power of his position and sought to use it to advance justice at all costs, calling cases as he saw them—even when doing so was unpopular or not personally advantageous. He pushed our judicial system to become more of what it purports to be; a true justice system. His ceaseless devotion to doing justice above all else left our world a better place.

THEREFORE, BE IT RESOLVED, by the Nashville Bar Association that we honor the life and work of Gilbert Stroud Merritt, Jr. and mourn in his passing the loss of a brilliant legal mind.

BE IT FURTHER RESOLVED that this Memorial Resolution be placed in the permanent records of the association and stored in the "In Memoriam" minute book of the Chancery Court of Davidson County, Tennessee and that copies thereof be furnished to members of his family.

Respectfully submitted this ⟨26⟩ day of May, 2022.

_____
CHANCELLOR

APPROVED FOR ENTRY:

_____
Aubrey B. Harwell, Jr.

_____
Hal Hardin

_____
William J. Harbison, II

Presentation of the Portrait of Judge Gilbert S. Merritt

United States Court of Appeals for The Sixth Circuit
December 5, 2007

Remarks of John J. Kulewicz
Vorys, Sater, Seymour and Pease LLP
Columbus, Ohio

Thank you, Your Honor. May it please the Court:

In August 1979, exactly four score and seven law clerks ago, it was my privilege to become a law clerk to Judge Merritt. I was a member of the third class of clerks. There are now ninety-two of us who have served in that capacity, and we all had the opportunity last month to join Judge Merritt in Nashville, to celebrate His Honor's thirtieth anniversary on the bench. Especially in view of the caliber of the other members of the group who I have gotten to know, it is a special honor to be asked to speak today on behalf of all of Judge Merritt's law clerks.

When each of us sees this fine portrait in the years ahead, I am confident that it will evoke the gratitude and pride with which we all look back on our service to the Court and Judge Merritt. Characteristic of our feelings are the reminiscences of eight of the law clerks in support of his successful nomination for the 2003 American Inns of Court Sixth Circuit Professionalism Award.

One of the first clerks wrote that Judge Merritt "was an inspiring mentor and guide. I look back with great fondness to that year, when every day brought new intellectual challenges and discussions energized by a search for fairness and a sense of public service. We were swept up in a time of intensive collaborative work with a strong sense of joint purpose." She remembers fondly Judge Merritt's "good humor in times of controversy" and "down-to-earth approach to problems."

From a different perspective, perhaps because the Judge has also been a pilot, comes the recollection of her successor that "I felt that I could see the law from 30,000 feet, and from that height perceive the true shape of it. I have tried to keep this lofty perspective and will never forget that it was Judge Merritt who first took me up to altitude." She added that, "of the many contributions Judge Merritt has made to my legal career, none has been more important than his belief that 'the law should make sense.' It was a wonderful, heady experience, sitting around the library table piled high with books, arguing cases with a judge on the US Court of Appeals! But it was also an incredible education."

Another clerk, reflecting perhaps more on the law court than the tennis court, recalled that Judge Merritt's actions "were always tempered by humility."

One clerk remembered how Judge Merritt "would call us in to discuss every angle of the case and the strengths and weaknesses of the arguments. They were lively and spirited discussions." He also recalled that Judge Merritt "was always available to give his law clerks invaluable advice about their career objectives and choices."

What struck another of my fellow clerks was Judge Merritt's "intelligence, judgment, wit and good humor" as he "walked through the fires of public policy debate."

One especially grateful clerk wrote that he often referred to his clerkship "as my fourth year of law school. My clerkship with Judge Merritt pulled all of the pieces together." ("Pulling the pieces together" was a matter of the utmost practical importance for all of us who faced the bar exam after having followed a more esoteric path to the law at Yale, one of the predominant sources of law clerks for Judge Merritt.) The same clerk also noted that the Judge "taught me how one can treat an adversary with respect without compromising the client's case and how important it is for a lawyer to be honest and forthright with the court and others."

Another clerk recalled that "during my clerkship, Judge Merritt taught me how to focus on the central issue," and "gave me the most important professional advice I have ever received: 'from your very first day on the job, focus on the type of work you enjoy and try to maximize that aspect of your practice.'"

Finally, and probably characteristic of the job interviews that all of us went through, one clerk remembered that "Most of the interview involved discussion of John Rawls's *A Theory of Justice* (a well-thumbed copy of which lay on the end table next to the judge's chair)." The late John Rawls was indeed a central figure in each of our experiences with Judge Merritt.

Sharing center stage with John Rawls, of course, has been the extraordinary Sara Pettit, herself a fine lawyer, who has always been a model of efficient administration and dedication to this Court in the way that she has managed the chambers.

For the benefit of these experiences, each of us is grateful to Judge Gilbert Merritt.

Like the work that the Court is about to receive, our clerkships have painted in each of our minds a portrait of the penetrating intellect and courage of conviction with which he has served. Because this is a judicial career that one hopes is far from over, those portraits continue to evolve.

On the Sunday afternoon last month when we gathered at Judge Merritt's home, atop a hill that overlooks a beautiful part of Middle Tennessee, several of us engaged your colleague in a discussion about his experiences in Iraq, as a representative of the American judiciary, shortly after the conflict had begun. It was a spellbinding moment.

My family and I reflected as we left shortly afterward that visitors to the hilltop of Monticello two hundred years ago must have felt the same way as they listened to the sage words of an earlier American statesman, rendered in the same melodious Southern accent, on matters of equally great national importance.

I share this with you not to extol Judge Merritt, because he would certainly balk at that, but to thank him for reminding us, through the distinguished contribution that he continues to make, that we are creating the history of our nation as much today as in the beginning, and, especially upon the presentation of this portrait, to thank him for giving each of my fellow law clerks and me the opportunity to learn from him and serve with him, even if only for a year, in the painting of that great work-in-progress that we call the United States of America.

Thank you very much.

Bibliography
& Other Recommended Reading

Ansolabehere, Stephen, and James M. Snyder Jr. *The End of Inequality: One Person, One Vote, and the Transformation of American Politics.* W. W. Norton, 2008. (History of the Baker v. Carr decision.)

Associated Press, via NBC News. "Judge: Retry death row inmate or free him," May 28, 2008.

"Did Tennessee Execute an Innocent Man?" *The New York Times,* February 9, 2021.

Badger, Anthony J. Albert Gore, Sr.: *A Political Life.* University of Pennsylvania Press, 2018.

Berke, Richard L. "2 Republicans Oppose Naming Babbitt to Court," *The New York Times,* June 9, 1993.

Boggs, Squire Patton. "Interview with Sixth Circuit Clerk Leonard Green," *Sixth Circuit Appellate Blog,* July 1, 2011.

Bone, Charles W. "We need to remember Robert Kennedy's words of hope," The *Tennessean,* April 2, 1968.

Bravin, Jess. "Team to Rebuild Iraq's Courts Includes Three Federal Judges," *The Wall Street Journal,* April 29, 2003.

Cabot, Judith Kinnard. Remembering Ruthie: *The Life of Ruth McDowell Kinnard.* Cold Tree Press, 2006.

Carnevale, Mary Lu. "Obama Announces Sebelius and DeParle for Health Posts, *The Wall Street Journal,* March 2, 2009.

Cass, Michael. "Civil rights attorney George Barrett dies at 86," The *Tennessean,* August 26, 2014.

Cochrane, Emily. "Who Is Michael J. Gerhardt? Professor Made Impeachment His Specialty," *The New York Times,* December 4, 2019.

Collins, Michael. "Soldier has eye for justice, Merritt finds," Scripps Howard News Service, July 31, 2003.

Congressional Record, Confirmation of Gilbert S. Merritt of Tennessee to be US Circuit Judge for the Sixth Circuit, October 29, 1977, pp. S18149–50.

Crutchfield, James A. Hail, *Castle Heights! An Illustrated History of Castle Heights School and Castle Heights Military Academy.* Castle Heights Alumni Association, 2003.

————. *A Heritage of Grandeur.* (Historic homes of Williamson County, Tennessee.) Carnton Association, 1981.

Dannen, Fredric. "How Terrible is Ivan?" *Vanity Fair*, June 1992.

DemCastUSA.com. "Judge Merritt: The Colin Kaepernick of the Criminal Justice System. Should He Have Been the Next US Supreme Court Judge?" October 28, 2020.

Devitt, Edward J. "Ten Commandments for the New Judge," *American Bar Association Journal*, Vol. 47, No. 12 (December 1961), pp. 1175-1177).

Donelson, Angie Fields Cantrell Merritt. "My Life and Times," as recounted to Eli Merritt. December 1993.

Douglas, Lawrence. *The Right Wrong Man: John Demjanjuk and the Last Great Nazi War Crimes Trial.* Princeton University Press, 2016.

Durham, Walter T. "James Ralph Sasser," *Tennessee Encyclopedia of History and Culture*, Tennessee Historical Society, 2018.

Dwyer, Jim. "Her Father Was Executed for Murder: She Still Wants to Know if He Did It." *The New York Times.* May 1, 2019.

Eddy, Pamela. Memorandum to Author, detailing Merritt's "Notable Opinions." June 21, 2021.

Elliott, Sam. Review of *Rush to Justice? Tennessee's Forgotten Trial of the Century: Schoolfield* 1958. TBA Law Blog, Vol. 52, No. 8 (August 2016), Tennessee Bar Association.

Friedman, Thomas L. "The Supreme Court: Clinton Expected to Pick Moderate for High Court," *The New York Times*, March 20, 1993.

————. "Latest Version of Supreme Court List: Babbitt in Lead, 2 Judges Close Behind," *The New York Times*, June 8, 1993.

Garrigan, Liz. "Paul House Case Gets National Attention,' *Nashville Scene*, May 28, 2008.

Gerhardt, Michael J. "The Democratic Judge," Vanderbilt Law Review, Vol. 50 Issue 2 (March 1997).

Hale, Steven. "Memphis Judge Dismisses Petition for DNA Testing in Sedley Alley Case," *Nashville Scene*, November 18, 2019.

Hatcher, Sam. Notes from Lebanon's First 200 Years: *Tennessee's City of Cedars*. Grassleaf Publishing, 2019.

Haven, Hank. Three video compilations produced in conjunction with Haven's book *The Copilot*, Semmes Media, 2003.

Hemphill, John. "People Around Hooker: All Ages, Fresh Ideas," The *Nashville Tennessean*, July 31, 1966.

Hersch, Joni. "Affirmative Action and the Leadership Pipeline," *Tulane Law Review*, May 20, 2021. Forthcoming, Vanderbilt Law Research Paper No. 21–23, Available at SSRN: https://ssrn.com/abstract=3850294

Horn, Dan. "6th Circuit on losing streak in high court cases," *The Cincinnati Enquirer*, February 20, 2011.

Hudson, David L., Jr. "Alfred H. Knight, Lading Libel Lawyer, Dies," Freedom Forum Institute, October 13, 2011.

Hunt, Keel. *Coup: The Day the Democrats Ousted Their Governor*, Vanderbilt University Press, 2013.

Ingle, Joseph B. Last Rights: *Thirteen Fatal Encounters with State's Justice*. Union Square Press (2008).

———. *The Inferno: A Southern Morality Tale*, Westview Publishing, Inc. (2012).

———. *Slouching Toward Tyranny: Mass Incarceration*, Death Sentences and Racism. Algora Publishing (2015).

Johnson, Rob. "Iraq's struggle to lift justice from desolation harder now, judge says," The *Tennessean*, July 3, 2004.

———. "Justices hampered in Baghdad; Merritt irked by US clamp on information," The *Tennessean*, July 17, 2003.

Jones, Yolanda. "Appeals court denies DNA testing in Sedley Alley case," *Daily Memphian*, May 12, 2021.

Kolar, Barry. "Out of the Iraqi Rubble," *Tennessee Bar Journal*, Vol. 39, No. 10, October 2003.

Lane, Charles. "Two 6th Circuit judges clash over affirmative action case," The *Washington Post* (as published in The *Tennessean*), June 8, 2003.

Leftwich, J.B. *View From the Hill*, JB Leftwich Family, 2014.

Loggins, Kirk. "Civic leader Judge Kinnard dies," The *Tennessean*, May 18, 2001.

Martin, Douglas. "George Barrett, Tennessee Lawyer Who Fought for Desegregation, Dies at 86," *The New York Times,* August 30, 2014.

Martin, Jane. "Going on 100, She's a Woman with a Mission," The *Tennessean*, January 20, 1980.

May, Joseph L. (Jack). *A Confetti of Papers*, 2008.

———. *The (& I) Rest*, 2013.

McNutt, Ron. "Reflecting on Local Law Firm Racial Integration," *Nashville Bar Journal*, August-September 2020.

Merritt, Eli, et al. "Gilbert S. Merritt Family & Career," video compilation dated Feb. 28, 2019. Available at https://youtu.be/U4Xbr3wpwDE

Merritt, Eli. "When a Loved One Commits Suicide," Michael Krasny's Forum, KQED/National Public Radio, San Francisco, May 17, 2016. Audio available at https://www.kqed.org/forum/2010101854643/when-a-loved-one-commits-suicide

———. "Gilbert Merritt's legacy: How to sustain a constitutional democracy," The *Tennessean*, a part of the USA TODAY Network, January 21, 2022.

Merritt, Gilbert S. Jr. "The Decision-Making Process in Federal Courts of Appeals," *Ohio State Law Journal*, Vol 51 Number 5 (1990).

———. "Lowered Expectations and the Law," *The Reporter*: *The Vanderbilt School of Law,* Vol. 11, No. 1 (Summer 1980).

———. "Remarks Before US. Sentencing Commission," October 29, 1986.

———. "Government Has Not Ended Efforts to Control Free Speech," Presstime, February 1991, page 37.

———. "Justice as Fairness: A Commentary on Rawls's New Theory of Justice," *Vanderbilt Law Review*, Vol. 26 Number 4 (May 1973).

———. "Dean John W. Wade," *Vanderbilt Law Review*, Vol. 48 Issue 3 (April 1995).

———. "Judge-bashing only undermines public confidence in judiciary" (editorial guest column), *Nashville Banner*, July 3, 1996.

———. "Tribute to the Honorable Richard S. Arnold," *The Journal of Appellate Practice and Process.* Volume 1 Issue 1 (1999). Available at: https://lawrepository.ualr.edu/appellatepracticeprocess/vol1/iss1/13

———. "From the Scopes Trial to the Human Genome Project: Where is Biology Taking the Law," William Howard Taft Lecture, *University of Cincinnati Law Review*, Volume 67, Number 2 (Winter 1999).

———. "Why Does a Hearse Horse Snicker Hauling a Lawyer Away?" *George Law Review,* Volume 36, Number 4 (Summer 2002).

———. "Gag order contradicts US value Iraqis like," The *Tennessean*, March 6, 2003.

———. "Why such a slow road to a self-ruled Iraq?" The *Tennessean*, January 19, 2004.

———. "A Letter About Ruth Kinnard," April 25, 2005, correspondence of Gilbert S. Merritt.

———. "Excerpts from Judge Gilbert Merritt's Law Day Speech," *Nashville Bar Journal*, May 2008.

———. Letter to Bill Haslam, Governor of Tennessee, July 30, 2018.

———. "Democracy and Distrust," *Dayton Law Review*, 1981.

———. "Courts, Media and the Press," *St. Louis University Law Journal*, Spring 1997.

———. "Owen Fiss on *Paradise Lost*: The Judicial Bureaucracy in the Administrative State," *Yale Law Journal*, 1983.

Moss, Michael. "Iraq's Legal System Staggers Beneath the Weight of War," *The New York Times*, December 17, 2006.

Nakashima, Ellen, and David Maraniss. "Big Sister" (newspaper profile of Nancy Gore), *The Washington Post*, July 29, 2000.

Nashville Bar Association. Historical NBA CLE Videos, *Baker v. Carr, Chapter 7, Harris Gilbert, John Jay Hooker, Gilbert Merritt*. September 21, 2017. https://www.youtube.com/watch?v=7SROVuNX-4I8&list=PLY41A-hkTv39ZpnAYwG-jZ4RBUtzFUn_4&index=7

Phillips, Harry, et al. *History of the Sixth Circuit*, A Bicentennial Project. Published under the auspices of the Bicentennial Committee of the Judicial Conference of the United States, 1976.

Price, Polly J. *Judge Richard S. Arnold*: A Legacy of Justice on the Federal Bench. Prometheus Books, 2009.

Pulle, Matt. "They Might Be Giants: How the Vanderbilt Law School class of '57 shaped a city," *Nashville Scene*, February 14, 2002.

Rawls, John. *A Theory of Justice*. Belknap Press (Imprint of Harvard University Press), 2nd Edition (September 1999).

Rector, Reverend Stacy. "Comments about Judge Merritt," Note to Author on August 17, 2021.

Reed, M. Neil; Tom Vanderloo, and Stephanie Woebkenberg. "A History of the United States Court of Appeals for the Sixth Circuit: Ohio, Kentucky, Michigan, and Tennessee," *The Federal Lawyer*, August 2016, pp. 34–38.

Reinhart, A. Kevin, and Gilbert S. Merritt. "Reconstruction and Constitution Building in Iraq," *Vanderbilt Journal of Transnational Law*, Vol. 37 Number 3 (May 2004).

Renshaw, Grace. "All in the Family: Judge Jane Stranch '78, the newest member of the Sixth Circuit Court of Appeals, brings 30 years of complex litigation experience to the bench," *Vanderbilt Lawyer*, Vol. 39, Number 1, Vanderbilt University Law School.

Ritter, Frank. "Issue: Admission of Negro Lawyers," The *Nashville Tennessean*, October 4, 1965.

Roberts, Kenneth L. Nashville Public Library's "Nashville Business

Leaders Oral History Project: The Turner Interviews." (Interview with Cabot Pollard Pyle, July 27, 2006).

Roberts, Sam. "Boyce F. Martin Jr., Liberal US Judge in Seminal Cases, Dies at 80," *The New York Times*, June 7, 2016.

Robinson Sr., Jack W. "NBA Oral History Interview," Nashville Bar Association, March 16, 2011.

Round, Ian. "Destroyed evidence offers little chance of redemption for convicted," *Daily Memphian*, March 7, 2022.

Simbeck, Rob. *Daughter of the Air: The Brief Soaring Life of Cornelia Fort*. Grove Press, 2001.

Skorneck, Carolyn. "How to Anger a Court: Ignore Its Letters," The Associated Press, August 22, 1993.

Solomon, Linda. "Centenarian, Fulton Share Celebration," The *Tennessean*, January 20, 1980.

Squires, James D. *The Secrets of the Hopewell Box: Stolen Elections, Southern Politics, and a City's Coming of Age*. Crown Publishing Group, 1996, 2d edition Vanderbilt University Press, 2013.

Stinnett, Joel. "Hal Hardin's Lifetime of Achievement Winner," *Nashville Business Journal*, June 26, 2020.

Summers, Jerry H. Rush to Justice? *Tennessee's Forgotten Trial of the Century*: Schoolfield 1958. Waldenhouse, 2016.

Sutton, Jeffrey S. 51 Imperfect Solutions: *States and the Making of America Constitutional Law*. Oxford University Press, 2018.

Syverud, Kent D. "Expert Report of Kent D. Syverud in Grutter v. Bollinger," *Peabody Journal of Education*, 2004, (Vol. 79, No. 2), Commemorating the 50th Anniversary of Brown v. Board of Education: Reconsidering the Effects of the Landmark Decision (2004), pp. 136–140. Published by: Taylor & Francis, Ltd.

Talbot, Margaret. "Supreme Confidence: The jurisprudence of Justice Antonin Scalia, *The New Yorker*, March 28, 2005

Thomas, Evan W. First: *Sandra Day O'Connor*. Random House, 2019.

Thornton, Lee Ann. *Victorian Memories*, Historic Nashville Inc., 1970.

Wade, Paula. "Lobbyist offers no apologies for who she is; Controversy follows brassy former Memphian," *The Commercial Appeal*, January 21, 1996.

Walker, Henry. "Interview with Judge Gilbert Merritt," *Nashville Bar Journal*, October 2003.

Ward, Getahn. "Nashville risks losing historic US Customs House," The *Tennessean*, April 21, 2016.

Weinberg, Hedy. "George Barrett, 'the Citizen,'" *Nashville Scene*, December 23, 2014.

Wissner, Sheila. "Daughtrey sworn in, credits others," The *Tennessean*, December 7, 1993.

Zepp, George. "Southside home offers a glimpse of yesteryear," *The Tennessean*, September 4, 2002.

INDEX

Page locators in *italics* indicate photographs.

SPECIAL ACKNOWLEDGMENTS

Merritt's career touched many people, and evidence of his long service and associations survives him in many places. I am grateful to the many individuals who kindly assisted me in locating such artifacts and other people. I list them here, with much gratitude.

Charles W. Bone
John A. Bradley
Alexandra Burlason
Beverly Burnett
Joe Cain
Lew Conner
J. Greer Cummings
Deb Daugherty
Madeleine Donovan
Maria De Varenne
Pamela Eddy
Gary Everton
Deb Faulkner
Ken Fieth
Beth Prichard Geer
Barb Glover
James Gooch
Hal Hardin
Harris Haston
Sam Hatcher
Kem Hinton
Rob Hosier

Virginia Banks Lazenby
Allen D. Lentz
Henry A. Martin
Kathleen Murphy
Jim O'Hara
Sara L. Pettit
Lisa Presley
Terry Reuther Quillen
Stacy Rector
Grace R. Renshaw
Ricky Rogers
Gray Sasser
Robin A. Saxon
John Michael Seigenthaler
Mark Sturtevant
Susan Pearlman
Frank Sutherland
Robert P. Thomas
Alan D. Valentine
Katy Varney
Rick Warwick

Thanks to Thom Donovan for his immeasurable help proofreading and editing this book.

SOURCES OF PHOTO COLLECTIONS

For permission to use the photographs that appear in this volume, I gratefully acknowledge the following:

Cover Photo: Merritt Portrait by Michael Shane Neal

Merritt Family Collections: Gil Merritt, Rachel Merritt McAllister

Charles W. Bone

John A. Bradley

Gary Everton

Jim Free

Hal Hardin

Rob Hosier, Castle Heights Alumni Association

Martha R. Ingram

Allen D. Lentz, Gullett Sanford Robinson & Martin PLLC

Jack & Lynn May

Judge George Paine

Robin A. Saxon

The *Tennessean*: Maria De Varenne, Ricky Rogers, Beverly Burnett

Nashville Public Library, Special Collections Division: Kathleen Feduccia

Vanderbilt University Special Collections: Zach Johnson, Philip Nagy, Molly Dohrmann

Rick Warwick, Historical Franklin

Author Photo: Olivia F. Hunt
Other photos by Keel Hunt

Madeleine Donovan, as always, was critical to assembling and organizing the photographs that appear on these pages.

ABOUT THE AUTHOR

KEEL HUNT is the author of two books on Tennessee political history: *Coup: The Day the Democrats Ousted Their Governor* (2017) and *Crossing the Aisle: How Bipartisanship Brought Tennessee to the Twenty-First Century and Could Save America* (2018), both published by Vanderbilt University Press. He has been a columnist for the *USA Today* Tennessee network since 2013. In his early career, he was a journalist and Washington correspondent. Read more about him at www.KeelHunt.com.

Photo credit: Olivia F. Hunt

Printed in the USA
CPSIA information can be obtained
at www.ICGtesting.com
JSHW081909091023
49910JS00002B/5